APPLIED RESEARCH
IN GERONTOLOGY

Applied Research in Gerontology

WILLIAM J. MCAULEY
Virginia Polytechnic Institute and State University

with contributions by

ROSEMARY BLIESZNER
Virginia Polytechnic Institute and State University

CYNTHIA A. BOWLING
Virginia Department of Medical Assistance Services

JAY A. MANCINI
Virginia Polytechnic Institute and State University

JEAN G. ROMANIUK
Virginia Commonwealth University

LAURIE SHEA
Virginia Polytechnic Institute and State University

 VAN NOSTRAND REINHOLD COMPANY
———————————————————————— *New York*

Manufactured in the United States of America.

Published by Van Nostrand Reinhold Company Inc.
115 Fifth Avenue
New York, New York 10003

Van Nostrand Reinhold Company Limited
Molly Millars Lane
Wokingham, Berkshire RG11 2PY, England

Van Nostrand Reinhold
480 La Trobe Street
Melbourne, Victoria 3000, Australia

Macmillan of Canada
Division of Canada Publishing Corporation
164 Commander Boulevard
Agincourt, Ontario MIS 3C7, Canada

15   14   13   12   11   10   9   8   7   6   5   4   3   2   1

Library of Congress Cataloging in Publication Data
McAuley, William J., 1946-
    Applied research in gerontology.
    Includes bibliographies and index.
    1. Gerontology—Research.   I. Blieszner, Rosemary.
II. Title.
HQ1061.M375   1987   305.2′6′072   86-18994
ISBN 0-442-26468-2

DEDICATION

*This book is dedicated to the memory of Donald P. Kent
(1916–1972) and S. Elizabeth Thompson McAuley
(1888–1967). Don Kent was an outstanding role model for
all gerontologists who seek effective ways of combining
research and practice. Bess McAuley probably never heard
the word gerontology, but her life was a perfect illustration
of how to grow old successfully.*

Contents

Foreword / *xi*
Preface / *xiii*

PART I: INTRODUCTION TO APPLIED RESEARCH AND
PROBLEM SOLVING IN GERONTOLOGY / 1

Introduction / **3**

Purpose of This Book / 4
Applied Versus Basic Research / 7
A Problem-Solving Approach to Research / 10
How to Get the Most from This Book / 11
Summary / 12
Suggested Readings / 12
References / 12

1: Problem Solving and Decision Making in Applied Research / **14**

Overview of the APS Model / 15
Importance of Attitude / 17
Role of Evaluation / 18
A Closer Look at the Steps in the APS Model / 19
Summary / 29
Suggested Readings / 30
References / 31

PART II: PLANNING AND DOING RESEARCH / 33

2: Choosing and Stating a Research Problem / **35**

Sources of Applied Research Problems in Aging / 36
Searching for More Information on the Problem / 44
Evaluating Potential Research Problems / 46

Writing the Problem Statement   /   49
Summary   /   55
Appendix 2-1: Selected Research and Policy Issues from the 1986
Fiscal Year Office of Human Development Services Discretionary
Funds Program   /   56
Appendix 2-2: People to Contact for Applied Research Topics   /   57
Suggested Readings   /   57
References   /   58

3: Designing a Research Project   /   59

Description Versus Explanation   /   61
Cross-Sectional Versus Longitudinal Research   /   62
Nonexperimental Versus Experimental Techniques   /   65
Nonexperimental Designs   /   66
Experimental Designs   /   70
Designing Needs Assessments and Program Evaluations   /   73
Summary   /   74
Suggested Readings   /   75
References   /   76

4: Selecting Measurement Strategies   /   77

Introduction to Measurement   /   77
Importance of Measurement   /   78
Variables and the Measurement Process   /   79
Operationalization of Variables   /   83
Levels of Measurement   /   85
Desirable Qualities in Measures   /   89
Decisions Regarding the Selection or Construction of
Instruments   /   94
Summary   /   101
Suggested Readings   /   102
References   /   102

5: Deciding How to Collect the Information   /   104

The Use of Existing Information   /   105
Methods of Collecting New Information   /   111
Things to Consider When Selecting Methods   /   117

Summary / 118
Suggested Readings / 119
References / 119

6: Selecting People to Study / 121

Why Sample? / 121
Steps in Selecting a Sample / 123
Special Problems in Sampling Older Community Residents / 141
Summary / 143
Suggested Readings / 144
References / 144

7: Planning and Preparing for the Research / 145

Planning a Timetable / 145
Pretesting and Revising / 151
Selecting and Training Interviewers / 154
Addressing Ethical Issues / 162
Summary / 168
Suggested Readings / 169
References / 169

8: Gathering the Information / 171

Locating Respondents and Obtaining Permission to
Interview / 172
Conducting and Ending the Interview / 177
Problems That May Arise When Interviewing Older
Respondents / 181
Monitoring and Recordkeeping / 184
Maximizing Participation in Telephone and Mail Surveys / 186
Summary / 188
Suggested Readings / 189
References / 189

9: Making Sense of the Information / 191

Getting the Information Ready / 192
Analyzing the Information / 196

Summary / 211
Suggested Readings / 212
References / 212

10: Presenting the Information to Others / 214

Assumptions about Research and Researchers / 215
Focus on the Original Problem / 215
Focus on the Audience / 216
Communicating Effectively / 218
Written Communication / 218
Oral Communication / 223
News Media / 226
Summary / 226
Suggested Readings / 227
References / 227

PART III: CONCLUSIONS AND PERSPECTIVES / 229

11: Putting it All Together / 231

A Real-World Example of Applied Gerontological Research: The
Statewide Survey of Older Virginians / 231
Conclusions / 238

APPENDIX: A Brief Guide to Proposals and Funding / 240

Grants Versus Contracts / 240
Purposes of Proposals / 241
Development Process of Proposals / 241
Seeking Sources of Funding / 241
Characteristics of Successful Proposals / 243
Summary / 246
Suggested Readings / 246
References /. 246

Author Citation Index / 249

Subject Index / 252

Foreword

In this book Jim McAuley and his colleagues have made an important and welcome contribution to the field of academic gerontology. For too long we have had to try to adopt an introductory research course for gerontology students using texts from other fields. These texts were inadequate on two counts: the interdisciplinary field of gerontology uses methods from several disciplines and few texts address this problem; and second, the illustrations are foreign to the subject matter of gerontology students. This text fills a long-felt void and will be greeted by both students and teachers with enthusiasm. Its clearly presented material should take the fear that has inhibited generations of students out of research.

The appearance of a text for gerontology research is an important milestone in the development of this still new discipline.

CORA A. MARTIN

Preface

The idea for this book arose from a sense of frustration some of my colleagues and I have experienced while teaching introductory applied research methods to graduate students in gerontology. No available text covered the major issues in applied research from a gerontological perspective, and the readings that had to be pulled together never seemed to fit adequately the requirements of the course. This text was designed to meet the need for an introductory applied research text that presents examples drawn for gerontological problems and emphasizes the special problems encountered in research with older populations.

The book is also meant to allay some of the fears and frustrations that students frequently experience as they begin a course on research methods. A full chapter is devoted to the topic of problem solving so that students will have a set of strategies for creatively dealing with the challenges and problems of planning and conducting research. An attempt has also been made to limit the research jargon and to define terms that may be unfamiliar. I hope these strategies give students a feeling of confidence about their ability to carry out applied gerontological research.

While students are the main audience, the book should also be of benefit to planners, practitioners, and administrators in the field of gerontology. Most of these individuals find they have to deal with applied research, in some form, on a regular basis. This text emphasizes the practical aspects of applied research in the hope that it will help people in applied settings negotiate effectively with researchers, and evaluate the value of research carried out by others, as well as plan and conduct their own research projects.

I want to acknowledge the valuable contributions of the colleagues who wrote some sections of the text: Rosemary Blieszner, Cindi Bowling, Jay Mancini, Jean Romaniuk, and Laurie Shea. The book certainly benefits from their involvement. I also wish to thank the many students who pretested earlier versions of some of the chapters as part of their coursework. Their comments and suggestions were invaluable in preparing the final manuscript. My sincere appreciation also goes to Connie Babcock, Gloria Bensen, and especially Emily Wikstrom who were responsible for typing the manuscript. The many individuals who reviewed parts of the manuscript also deserve special credit—particularly Shirley Travis who put other work aside to review and edit the final draft. Will McAuley deserves special recognition for deftly managing his father's increasing irritability and crankiness as the manuscript deadline approached.

WILLIAM J. MCAULEY

Part I

INTRODUCTION TO APPLIED RESEARCH AND PROBLEM SOLVING IN GERONTOLOGY

Introduction

Expansion and *experimentation*—Such terms would have to be included in any description of recent trends in services to the elderly. Since the passage of the Older Americans Act in 1965, the number and types of services directed toward older people has increased phenomenally. Funds appropriated for implementation of the Older Americans Act increased from less than 8 million dollars in 1966 to over 824 million dollars in 1984, and total federal expenditures for the elderly were estimated to be more than 263 billion dollars in 1985 (Special Committee on Aging, 1985). A recent study of the federal initiative in aging turned up eighty programs addressing such divergent issues as income maintenance, employment, volunteer services, housing, health care, social services, transportation, training, and research (Lee and Estes, 1979).

Because they are relatively new and have grown so rapidly, aging services are still very much in a period of experimentation. Laws and regulations are being revised, model programs are being funded, and new approaches and techniques are being tried. Workers agree very little on even the most basic policy issues, such as the types of services to be offered, who should receive services, and the most effective organizational structures and funding mechanisms. The recent emphasis on fiscal austerity has increased the significance of applied research in aging (Estes et al., 1983). As public funds are more tightly controlled, there will be greater emphasis on assuring that services are appropriately targeted and cost effective.

A great deal is still to be learned. As Robert Atchley (1977, p. 327) has noted, "There is not a single area of social gerontology that does not need more answers to crucial questions." This statement is especially true of applied gerontological research. Well-designed, creative research can have an important role in structuring the kinds of policies and types of services

3

that will most benefit the elderly. This text is not only an introduction to the methods and procedures of applied research in aging, but is also an invitation. We hope this book will encourage you to join the growing cadre of applied researchers in gerontology.

PURPOSE OF THIS BOOK

This text is designed as an introduction to the methods of applied gerontological research. Because it is an introductory text, many of its objectives are shared with standard introductions to social science research. For example, its primary purpose is to acquaint you with some of the typical techniques and procedures used in carrying out research. They are described in sufficient detail so that you can evaluate their relative value in addressing a specific research problem. Additionally, the book is intended to improve your ability to carry out successful research projects. We expect that after reading it you will be more proficient at developing meaningful statements of research problems, designing research that can adequately address a problem, and carrying out research and analysis in an efficient manner.

Another common objective of this and other research methods texts is to improve your effectiveness as consumers of research. One important component of effective consumption is the ability to judge the value of a particular research project and to determine whether its findings are applicable to your own situation. When you read a journal article or the results of a political poll in a news magazine, you have no control over the way the study was carried out, but you are able to decide whether to use the findings and, if so, how. Another important aspect of effective consumption is the ability to talk to and negotiate with researchers whose studies may affect your work. From time to time you may need to contract with outside investigators for a research project or cooperate with researchers in your own organization. When such occasions arise we hope you will view them as opportunities rather than inconveniences, because we believe that the active involvement of potential users greatly increases the value of applied research. Whether your consumption of research consists solely of the evaluation and use of finished products or includes active participation in the design and execution of a study, your understanding of the basic research methods and terminology will make you a more discriminating consumer.

Because this text shares the preceding objectives with more traditional introductions to research methods, you will find that much of the content is also similar. All good researchers or consumers of research should have at their disposal an extensive common core of information. A large portion of this book is devoted to the presentation of these core materials.

Despite sharing some common objectives, this book is not at all a typical social science methods book. We have designed the text especially for persons who are preparing to work with older people or who are already involved with services to the aged. People who work with the elderly come from a variety of professional and technical backgrounds and include nurses and other medical personnel, sociologists, social workers, planners, library scientists, architects, administrators, and psychologists, to name only a few. Many work in settings that draw upon knowledge from several traditional disciplines. Throughout the book, we use examples from real or hypothetical applied gerontological research projects. These examples cover a wide variety of topics because the research problems encountered by practitioners in aging services are as varied as their professional backgrounds and work settings.

Although applied gerontological research covers many different issues, two general forms of research are most common. One type is concerned with understanding the characteristics and conditions of the target group in order to establish or revise program objectives or to improve services. Research projects designed for such purposes are often called *needs assessments,* although there is much disagreement about the use of this term. The other general form of research, *evaluation studies,* is concerned with the extent to which programs are meeting their established goals and objectives. This text will describe these two basic types of applied research as you will no doubt encounter them in your own work.

The book also addresses the special methodological problems that arise in gerontological research. Robert Atchley (1977) has described five such issues: (1) definitions of older people, (2) heterogeneity of the older population, (3) sampling, (4) research design, and (5) measurement.

In terms of defining older people, there is little consensus on how old age should be measured for research purposes. In some cases, an arbitrary index of chronological age is used, while in others, a functional definition is attempted. Although it may be analytically more appropriate in many instances to use a functional definition of old age rather than number of years since birth, developing a functional definition that is both conceptually meaningful and readily measurable is often very difficult. In applied research, the definitional problem is often further complicated by the need to study the "impaired elderly" or the "vulnerable elderly". We will describe how to define elements of research so they are both measurable and meaningful.

One of the most striking features of the older population is its great diversity. No other group is so wide-ranging in its characteristics. This great heterogeneity of the older population can lead to some special methodological problems. For example, careful attention should be given to whether questions have the same meaning across different subgroups. Additionally, certain ways of gathering information may be more useful when focusing on a particular segment of the older population. The issue of heterogeneity among the elderly and ways of dealing effectively with it will be addressed throughout the text.

In carrying out research, we do not usually obtain measures from everyone in the group of interest. We instead select a few people who can represent all others. This process of selection is known as *sampling*. Some special problems are encountered when obtaining a representative sample of relatively rare populations, such as the elderly or a particular subgroup of older people. For example, there are no really good, accessible lists of older people from which a representative sample can be chosen, although, of course, the elderly are readily accessible in some special settings (e.g., nursing homes or senior centers). But persons selected from such settings are not at all like the general population of older people. We will discuss ways of drawing samples that are appropriate for meeting the goals of a given research project yet do not unduly tax available resources.

The issue of research design is important no matter what the topic or the population of interest. However, sometimes gerontological research problems can lead to very special design issues. For example, longitudinal designs (studying the same individuals over a period of time) are often required. All of the major types of designs will be discussed in this text, along with examples of their use in applied settings.

All research is based upon the measurement of some phenomena. Measurement can be carried out in many different ways, including asking questions and recording responses, observing and recording behavior in natural settings, counting the number of times a word or phrase appears in a book, and so forth. Many measures used with the elderly were actually designed for use with younger people. While they may be just as useful with older individuals, their value and utility are often undetermined. Therefore, the text will describe the problems of measurement and present ways of assuring the validity and reliability of measurement techniques with older people.

Besides the methodological issues addressed by Atchley, still others may arise during research with the elderly.* We will discuss these issues at appropriate points throughout the text as well. Our goal is to introduce these special issues of aging research in the context of a thorough presentation of basic methods and procedures, because good researchers must have a broad

---

*See Committee on Research and Development Goals in Social Gerontology (1969, 1971*a*, 1971*b*) for descriptions of some important methodological issues in policy research with the elderly.

methodological background as well as an understanding of the unique problems that arise in their specific areas of study.

APPLIED VERSUS BASIC RESEARCH

The emphasis on applied research is another important distinction between this and standard methods texts. What is applied research? Consider for a moment the following questions.

Is the reality orientation program for patients of our nursing home meeting its objectives?

What is the demand for adult day care services in my area?

Are older outpatients at my clinic taking their prescription drugs appropriately?

Why are so few older people in my region making use of property tax relief benefits?

What is the demand for library services to homebound older people in my city?

Are the adult nutrition projects in my district serving the persons in greatest need?

If eligibility requirements for home health services were reduced, how many additional older people might use them?

What happens to older people who have been receiving companion services when these services are suddenly withdrawn?

All of the preceding topics are examples of applied research. When a study is designed chiefly to answer program or policy questions or address social issues (Finsterbusch and Motz, 1980), we call it *applied* research to differentiate it from studies whose goals are to develop theories and learn about the underlying mechanisms that give order to the world. Of course, in many instances, this distinction between applied and basic ("pure") research is blurred. The findings of an applied research project can be very helpful in theory development, for example, and the results of basic research can often have important policy ramifications. All research may have value for policy in the long run. Thus, another important distinction between applied and basic research is based upon the immediacy of intended impact on policy. As you can see in Figure 1 applied research is designed to have direct and immediate impact on policy and program issues.

These differences in kinds of goals and intended immediacy of use are contributing factors to the frequent gap between research and policy. Few basic research projects can be expected to have any practical impact on policy in the short run, because they were not designed for this purpose. Quite a long time may pass before the results of such studies reach the service provider or policy maker in a useful form. Unfortunately, many studies that are called applied research because they are concerned with policy-related topics suffer the same fate because of flaws in the design that make the findings highly questionable or of little immediate use. Additionally, no established mechanism may be available to ensure that the findings of applied research are translated into action (Lebowitz, 1981). Furthermore, as Estes and Freeman (1976) have pointed out, many so-called applied projects fail to deal with issues that can be effectively manipulated through political or administrative processes. This text deals with ways of choosing and stating research problems and designing studies to ensure their effectiveness as policy tools.

Applied and basic research are also differentiated by the context within which each occurs. Applied research, by definition, takes place in a political context. In many instances, the goals are to decide what kinds of changes are needed in programs or policies or to determine whether a particular program is meeting its goals. In this environment, maintaining one's objectivity is

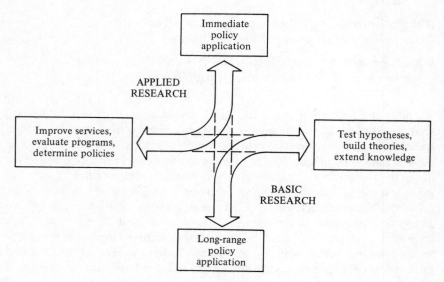

Figure 1.   Goals of applied and basic research.

especially difficult. The importance of a balanced study design carried out by a responsible researcher is never greater than in applied research. Therefore, a major objective of this book is to help you make decisions that will lead to useful research designs, taking into account the special problems brought about by research in a politically charged environment.

While these differences between applied and basic research exist, some similarities are also important. These points of common ground have to do with the methods and procedures used and the importance of approaching the problem from a rigorous scientific perspective.

Both basic and applied researchers can draw from the same storehouse of methods and procedures. Applied researchers may depend more often upon certain methods because they have been found useful for dealing with past research issues or were emphasized in earlier training, or because available resources limit possible choices, or because of force of habit. But all methods are at least potentially available. Good research designs are the result of creative combinations of methods and procedures. One objective of this book is to provide you with the tools that will help you to design creative but practical projects.

All researchers, whether they are engaged in basic or applied studies, have a responsibility to carry out their work in a rigorous, scientifically acceptable manner. Babbie (1973, pp. 12-19) has set forth eight characteristics of science that should serve as goals of all researchers.

Science is *logical.* It is a rational activity based on logical reasoning.

Science is *deterministic.* An important philosophical foundation of science is that "all events have antecedent causes that are subject to identification and logical understanding."

Science is *general.* Scientists must be concerned with the generalizability of their findings to other situations and other populations.

Science is *parsimonious.* "(T)he scientist attempts to understand the reasons for . . . events using as few explanatory factors as possible." The effective scientist learns to disregard irrelevant factors.

Science is *specific.* In designing and carrying out research, it is always necessary to clearly specify both the research problem and the methods and procedures used to measure the concepts under study.

Science is *empirically verifiable.* The results of scientific inquiry must be open to evaluation and verification through additional empirical research.

Science is *intersubjective.* While no researcher may be completely objective, "two scientists with different subjective orientations would arrive at the same conclusion if each conducted the same experiment." This quote points to the importance of careful regard for and documentation of methods and procedures.

Science is *open to modification.* Science is characterized by revision and change. It is unlikely that truth will be discovered in any area. "In an important sense, science does not even seek Truth, but rather utility." Scientific research is a process of trial and error. No single research design will provide the ultimate answer, although some will be far more useful than others.

These ideal characteristics of science are no less important for applied researchers than they are for basic researchers. The commitment to scientific rigor should not be diminished by the immediacy of need for information or by the political context in which much applied research takes place. Applied researchers have a special responsibility to the ideals of science because their results are often translated into policy before they can be verified through additional research. Therefore, while we make it a point throughout the text to describe the necessity for compromise and for a realistic assessment of what is possible, we strongly believe that applied research is indeed scientific research, not some "poor relation."

A PROBLEM-SOLVING APPROACH TO RESEARCH

Another feature of this text that sets it apart from standard methods textbooks is its emphasis on problem solving as a technique for helping you design research. We have included a problem-solving model for two reasons.

First, research is problem solving, typically carried out to ameliorate some kind of problem. In basic research, the problem might be how to test a hypothesis; in applied research, the problem may be how to evaluate the success of a program or to determine the demand for a new service. The example questions referred to earlier may all be viewed as problems that require the gathering and analysis of information to resolve.

Second, our own experience tells us that one of the chief stumbling blocks for students in introductory research courses is the transition from learning about different techniques of research to the application of these techniques for a specific project. Frustration begins with selection and statement of the research problem, but even after a researchable problem is selected, many students feel they are powerless to deal with what appears to be a very ambiguous situation. Problem-solving techniques are tools that will help to reduce this ambiguity and thereby increase your confidence.

The problem-solving model introduced in the next chapter is designed to help newcomers to research make the decisions necessary to design a useful research project. We do not want to mislead you about its objective. It is not meant to be a generic formula for research. Each research project and its setting must be carefully evaluated to design a study that will work, and many different designs may be equally good. The researcher must carry the major responsibility for putting together an effective project. Hopefully, the problem-solving framework will reduce the ambivalence associated with starting out and help you to answer for yourselves the two questions we hear most often from students undertaking their first research project—"How do I get started?" and "Where do I go from here?"

HOW TO GET THE MOST FROM THIS BOOK

We strongly urge you to plan and execute a small research project as you work your way through the text. There is a natural resistance to beginning an actual research project until you have a sense of closure on the methods and procedures. But you probably already have many of the skills necessary to do research, and the contents of each chapter are designed to help you make the decisions needed to carry out a project. Your first project may not be perfect in all details; but no research ever is perfect, and by carefully analyzing your own mistakes, you will become better-prepared for the next project.

If you work in an agency, you should have no difficulty finding a problem that can be resolved, or at least better understood, through research. Usually the more difficult decision is which problem to tackle first! If you are a full-time student, you may want to talk to your instructor or visit local agencies that work with older clients. Additional sources of research topics are described in chapter 2.

To actually begin working is important because you will have an opportunity to actively apply the information presented in the text to your specific area of interest. Doing your own project will also help you view research as a unified process and will make you more aware of how the many steps in the process interrelate. Finally, and perhaps most importantly, once you have begun a project and worked through those self-doubts that often arise at the outset, you will have an opportunity to experience for yourself the challenge, the sense of discovery, and the opportunity for meaningful contribution that pervade applied gerontological research. This enthusiasm is far more easily experienced than described or taught. We are confident that once you get going, you will be pleasantly surprised at how exciting and rewarding applied gerontological research can be.

SUMMARY

The expansion and experimentation taking place in services to the older population make applied gerontological research a fruitful and exciting undertaking. This text is designed as an introduction to the methods of applied gerontological research. Its principal objectives are to develop your ability to plan and conduct successful applied research in aging and to help you to become better consumers of research. In order to meet these objectives, major methodological issues in gerontology are addressed and special problems in applied research are discussed as basic research methods are presented.

The book emphasizes problem solving as a strategy that can facilitate the research process. Problem solving is a useful technique not only because applied research is oriented toward solving problems, but also because knowledge of this strategy should make you feel more comfortable about becoming involved in research. Your understanding of the materials will be enhanced if you begin work on an applied research project as you read through the text. Your involvement will also help you experience the excitement and rewards of applied gerontological research.

SUGGESTED READINGS

The following special issues of *The Gerontologist* give valuable descriptions of the variety of research problems and methodological issues that exist in applied gerontology.

Committee on Research and Development Goals in Social Gerontology. (1969). The status of research in applied gerontology. *The Gerontologist,* **9,** (4:2).

Committee on Research and Development Goals in Social Gerontology. (1971). Research designs and proposals in applied social gerontology: Third report. *The Gerontologist,* **11,** (4:2).

REFERENCES

Atchley, R. C. (1977). *The social forces in later life: An introduction to social gerontology* (2nd ed.). Belmont, Calif: Wadsworth.

Babbie, E. R. (1973). *Survey research methods.* Belmont, Calif.: Wadsworth.

Committee on Research and Development Goals in Social Gerontology. (1969). The status of research in applied social gerontology. *The Gerontologist,* **9,** (4:2).

Committee on Research and Development Goals in Social Gerontology. (1971*a*). Research proposals in applied social gerontology: Second report. *The Gerontologist,* **11** (1:2).

Committee on Research and Development Goals in Social Gerontology. (1971*b*). Research designs and proposals in applied social gerontology: Third report. *The Gerontologist,* **11** (4:2).

Estes, C. L., and Freeman, H. E. (1976). Strategies of design and research for inter-vention. In R. H. Binstock and E. Shanas (Eds.), *Handbook of aging and the social sciences.* New York: Van Nostrand Reinhold.

Estes, C. L., Newcomer, R. J. Benjamin, A. E., Gerard, L., Harrington, C., Lee, P. R., Lindeman, D. A., Pardini, A., Swan, J. H., and Wood, J. B. (1983). *Fiscal austerity and aging: Shifting government responsibility for the elderly.* Beverly Hills: Sage.

Finsterbusch, K., and Motz, A. B. (1980). *Social research for policy decisions.* Belmont, Calif.: Wadsworth.

Lebowitz, B. D. (1981). Funding agencies and the research community. *The Geron-tologist,* **21,** 382-387.

Lee, P. R., and Estes, C. L. (1979). Eighty federal programs for the elderly. In C. L. Estes (Ed.), *The aging enterprise.* San Francisco: Jossey-Bass.

Special Committee on Aging. (1985). *America in transition: An aging society* (1984-1985 edition). Washington, D.C.: U.S. Government Printing Office.

1

Problem Solving and Decision Making in Applied Research

Jean G. Romaniuk and William J. McAuley

A Problem: 1. A question or situation that presents uncertainty, perplexity or difficulty
2. A person who is difficult to deal with
3. A question put forward for consideration, discussion or solution

(from *American Heritage Dictionary*)

Where do problems come from? And how can they ever be solved? Problems can spring up anywhere, anytime, and almost always when they are not needed. It is not difficult to know when a problem occurs; usually, we perceive that something isn't going quite as it should, and no readily available action can be taken to solve the mess. Examples abound in real life.

Problem: How will I ever be able to go to school, work, and manage a household at the same time?

Problem: How can I locate a good dentist in my area?

Problem: Why are my utility bills getting larger and larger while my wallet is getting thinner and thinner?

Problem: How can I get my children to get ready for school on time?

Examples of the many problems in the work setting that can occupy our time in dealing with the needs of and services to older clients can include the following.

Problem: What barriers are preventing older people from pursuing additional education at my institution?

Problem: What method of counseling works best to help older clients cope with chronic health problems, such as arthritis?

Problem: Is the friendly visitor (or meals-on-wheels) program for older persons in my community meeting its intended goals?

Problem: How can I increase appropriate referrals (or minimize inappropriate referrals) to nursing homes in the state?

Problem: How many older people in the district are at risk of institutionalization?

Problem: Which type of energy assistance program would best meet the needs of clients in my area of the county (or city)?

Problem: Where should the new nutrition site be located?

Problem: How can I use existing local census information to help plan for services with older clients?

Problem: Is there a sufficient demand for another subsidized housing complex for the elderly in the community?

In other words, in all facets of our lives, we are faced with dilemmas or problems which have no easy answers. Usually, we must act on these problems, and to do so requires a substantial effort on our part. This chapter is designed to help you think about the approaches to solving problems and how they can be used to assist you in understanding and managing the research process. Although these ideas are not new, it is sad to say that many of us were never sufficiently trained in how to solve problems creatively and apply these methods to the realities of our everyday work and personal life. An Applied Problem Solving model (APS model) is proposed in Figure 1-1. It is simple and direct and forms the basis for much of the discussion in the following chapters.

OVERVIEW OF THE APS MODEL

As you can see from Figure 1-1, there are five basic steps in the Applied Problem Solving model. Steps in the problem-solving process have been proposed by many others in several different frameworks (Davis, 1973; Eden, Jones, and Sims, 1983; Koberg and Bagnall, 1981; Parnes, Noller, and Biondi, 1977). However, all the different problem-solving models seem to have the same basic components that are included in Figure 1-1. In fact, we use many of these steps every day without consciously thinking about them when we are faced with a problem. For example, when buying a gift for a friend, probably we would consider many different alternative gift ideas (step 3) and evaluate which one would be most suited to the individual's needs and tastes (step 4) before actually deciding on a single choice (step 5). In this example, step 2 (specifying the problem/challenge) is already fairly well defined (purchasing a birthday gift) so a great deal of effort was not required to reach this step.

In applied research, however, often the most difficult step is the development of a concise statement of the problem. In the previous problem example "How many older people are at risk of institutionalization?" the problem is very nebulous because terms such as *at risk* could be defined as an inability to get needed medical care, an inability to maintain activities of

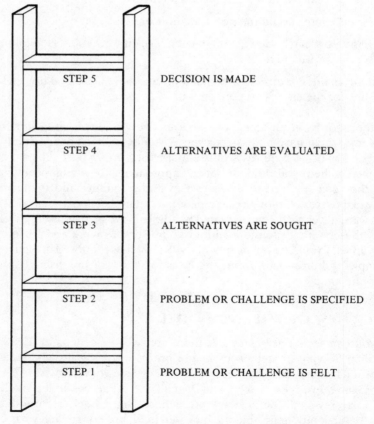

STEP 5	DECISION IS MADE
STEP 4	ALTERNATIVES ARE EVALUATED
STEP 3	ALTERNATIVES ARE SOUGHT
STEP 2	PROBLEM OR CHALLENGE IS SPECIFIED
STEP 1	PROBLEM OR CHALLENGE IS FELT

Figure 1-1. Steps in the Applied Problem Solving (APS) model.

daily living as defined by a trained interviewer, or the older person's personal perception of his or her likelihood of becoming institutionalized. Similarly, *institutionalization* could mean admission to a mental institution or a variety of other care settings such as a skilled nursing facility, intermediate care facility, adult home, and so forth. Thus, a solution to the problem is not readily apparent, or researchable, until the problem has been defined clearly.

It is important to recognize that the steps in this model represent a simplified version of how we actually go about the problem-solving process. At each major step along the way, we must tackle many small steps or "ministeps." The ministeps are rarely broken down or identified in problem-solving models and in these areas additional information would be most useful. For example, in the applied research problem just mentioned, how do you get from the initial statement of the problem to a more precise researchable statement of how to assess who is at risk of institutionalization? Or, once you have specified some alternatives for investigating the problem, how do you go about deciding how to evaluate the different alternatives? These nuts and bolts of problem solving usually need further elaboration for many beginning researchers and will be the focus of further discussion in this text.

It should also be noted that there is not just one method for solving a problem. Each person will have a slightly different approach to the solution, and many different approaches may be just as useful in solving the problem. Also, the sequence of solving a problem may sometimes vary from the unidirectional approach outlined in the APS model (i.e., step 1-5 in order). For example, if you were seeking alternatives to solve the problem "How can the privacy of each nursing home resident be maintained?" it might become clear that the crucial issues center on maintaining the morale of each resident. This focus, in turn, would lead you back to step 2 to a redefinition of the problem—"How can the morale of each nursing home resident be maintained?"

IMPORTANCE OF ATTITUDE

One of the most important elements in approaching any problem-solving situation is our own attitude in tackling the problem. Researchers in the field of creative problem solving have recognized that certain attitudes towards problem solving (such as curiosity, willingness to try new approaches to problems, willingness to take risks, perseverence, and self-confidence) are highly related to our effectiveness in solving problems. That is, when problems are viewed as challenges, our attitudes toward them may also change.

If we restated the problem mentioned earlier "Problem: What barriers are preventing older people from pursuing additional education at my institution?" as "Challenge: How many different methods could I develop to increase older adult participation at my institution?" the whole nature of the problem and approaches to solving the problem might change.

In fact, when problems are viewed as challenges, they can even take on the aura of a gamelike adventure. Therefore, each of us must approach problems as challenges and be willing to be flexible in stretching our imaginations while we tackle each step in the problem-solving process.

ROLE OF EVALUATION

A second important factor to keep in mind when approaching applied problem solving is the role of evaluation. Without evaluation in the weighing of our ideas, decision making would be very difficult and less effective. However, the evaluation of ideas must be suspended at key points in the problem-solving process, ensuring an uninhibited flow of creative ideas and alternatives. When ideas are evaluated too abruptly (e.g., when each idea is presented and immediately assessed), the net effect is often a dampening of enthusiasm and idea production. Sometimes this evaluation takes place in a group setting ("That idea could never work here," "It's too expensive," "That would take forever," etc.), but often we do it individually when we are merely thinking to ourselves ("Everyone would think I was crazy, or stupid, or both," "I couldn't do that even if I tried," etc.). Clark (1958) has compiled a list of idea squelchers that probably sound quite familiar. Here are just a few examples.

"We've never done it that way before."

"It's not in the budget."

"You don't understand the problem."

"What idiot thought that up?"

"Sounds good, but don't think it will work."

"They'll think we're crazy."

"Somebody would have suggested it before if it were any good."

"Let's discuss it at some other time."

"It will offend others."

"It's not our responsibility."

In addition to these "killer phrases," Clark also identifies the "apologetic phrase" as another guaranteed way to squelch new ideas. These phrases occur most often when new ideas are presented to others without confidence. We have all probably caught ourselves prefacing our ideas with some of the following phrases.

"This may not work, but . . . ."

"This may sound crazy, but . . . ."

"You aren't going to like this, but . . . ."

"You can probably do better, but . . . ."

"I'm not too familiar with this, but . . . ."

"You'll probably laugh, but . . . ."

"I realize this doesn't solve the problem, but . . . ."

As you can see, it is easy to identify evaluative statements that have the effect of squelching our ideas. Such statements often are made without thinking, and practice and effort are required to effectively suspend evaluation while ideas are being generated.

In the APS model depicted in Figure 1-1 the suspension of evaluation in many places is crucial to the process. Step 3 (seeking alternatives), for example, is one of the most obvious places. More generally, evaluation and idea production can be thought of as "alternating currents": first ideas are generated, then they are evaluated at each step and especially in the ministeps.

In summary, the APS model is only a simple approximation of the problem-solving process you will likely follow. The importance of certain attitudes, such as the willingness to try new approaches to problems and see problems as challenges, as well as the ability to practice suspending idea evaluation, can only increase creative solutions. We hope that this APS model will provide a framework for thinking systematically about the decisions that have to be made in conducting applied research. We also hope that it will become a tool for you to improve your decision-making skills in general.

A CLOSER LOOK AT THE STEPS IN THE APS MODEL

Problem or Challenge Is Felt

A problem becomes a problem when we are unable to solve it to our satisfaction. This common-sense approach to the definition of a problem certainly has some merit. Also, what is a problem for you may not be a problem for me. However, if you believe or perceive it as a problem, then you should not invalidate your perceptions by denying its existence. In the *All New Universal Traveler,* Koberg and Bagnall (1981) claim that the first real step in the problem-solving process is to accept the situation by assuming responsibility for the problem and agreeing to make the adaptions necessary to deal with it. Thus a problem becomes crystallized when we acknowledge that it is something to be reckoned with. Of course, this step is not always easy but is the first and necessary step in the problem-solving process.

Problem or Challenge Is Specified

As was stated before, developing a concise definition of a problem is both very difficult and crucial to the problem-solving process. Often when a problem is clearly defined, the solution also becomes obvious. Thus, stating the problem can often be half of the battle. Stating the problem requires at least two ministeps. First, an approach that encourages us to stretch our imaginations to think about all the possible ways the problem can be specified is usually helpful in the initial stages of defining the problem. Second, once the key problem seems to emerge, the problem must be worded in such a way as will enable us to research the idea. Unfortunately, this choice of wording requires some understanding of what research entails—precisely what students in beginning research classes usually do not have. However, with some information on how to state a research problem, combined with some general, nontechnical information on the various kinds of research that are possible, this task is not as difficult as it would first appear to be. This text, designed to provide you with a broad knowledge of research methods that might be used to address problems in aging, should give you the foundation necessary to specify the problem so it can be researched.

In stating a research problem, you should assess the assumptions and biases in your approach to the situation. Two exercises that can assist you in exploring your assumptions about the problem and defining your initial problem statements more clearly are the *why* and *restatement* exercises. The *why* exercise allows you to test assumptions about the problem that you might not have been aware of previously by forcing yourself to question all parts of the problem. The *why* exercise consists of listing as many explanations or justifications for the problem or its components as possible. In the *restatement* exercise, you are trying to explore as many different ways of stating the problem as possible to encourage a broader array of potential directions for further study. These two exercises may be carried out either independently or in combination with one another. Table 1-1 illustrates how these two exercises can assist you in the initial stages of the problem definition.

Table 1-1. Exploring the Problem Statement: Testing Assumptions and Restating the Problem Problem/Challenge: Why are employers unwilling to hire the older job seeker?

Why?	Restatement
Because employers have negative attitudes about the potential contributions of older workers (possible explanation)	How are employers' attitudes related to the hiring of an older job seeker?
Because all older people should be able to choose to work if they so desire (personal value)	
Because older people are less productive than younger workers (possible explanation)	How important is job productivity in age-related employment decisions?
Because younger people deserve a chance to have gainful employment (personal value)	
Because it is more cost effective to hire younger workers (possible explanation)	What costs are associated with hiring different aged workers?
Because the older job seeker exhibits a lack of self-confidence in the job interview (possible explanation)	How are the older job seekers' interviewing skills related the the employers' placement decision?

In this example, the *why* exercise provided two types of information: (1) hypotheses concerning possible explanations for the original problem, and (2) descriptions about the investigator's personal values related to the problem. The problem restatements in this example were developed out of a closer inspection of the possible explanations in the *why* exercise. Each restatement offers a different way of viewing the issue, and one or more of these views may be used in the final statement of the research problem.

It is noteworthy that the *whys* involving personal values actually address a different set of issues, including "Why is this a problem for me?" or "Why is this of particular interest to me?" As in this example, they may not always lead to a direct restatement of the problem. However, they may alert you to possible sources of bias in the future conduct of your investigation and help make your research more scientifically rigorous. For this reason, you should consider all types of *whys* in the exploration of the initial problem statement.

The importance of spending time on the definition of a problem cannot be underestimated. Unfortunately, there are no easy, prepackaged problem definitions in most real-world, applied research situations. In chapter 2, we will discuss how to locate applied research problems and how to present them in such a way that they can be more easily addressed by research.

Alternatives Are Sought

If the problem is viewed as a challenge and the climate is supportive for addressing the challenge, the generation of alternatives can be one of the most exciting phases in the problem-solving process. In this step, different approaches to the solution of the problem are proposed. These approaches provide an opportunity to stimulate our imaginations by directing conscious cognitive activity in the generation of different ideas. As before, we should allow our imaginations to be uninhibited in the generation of alternatives before evaluating the relative effectiveness of each proposed alternative. Exercises for stimulating different alternatives are abundant in the creative problem solving literature and presenting an adequate treatment of them all is not possible here. However, a few general types of exercises are worthy of mention.

Brainstorming.   Brainstorming, popularized by Osborn in his book *Applied Imagination* (1963), encourages a group of individuals to develop as many ideas as possible under the assumption that more ideas will produce a greater likelihood of a creative solution. Brainstorming also assumes that suspending evaluation of ideas and encouraging the elaboration of existing ideas can stimulate ideas and lead to a creative solution of the problem. Some general rules for brainstorming, if the method is to be most successful, are as follows.

1. All ideas are welcome, including the obvious and obscure, uncommon, and silly.
2. Repeating or elaborating on ideas is desirable.
3. No criticism of any idea is allowed.
4. Quantity is desired; the more ideas the better.

Since some of the earlier discussions by Osborn, many others in research and industry have discovered that brainstorming can be very effective on an individual basis as well. The whole purpose of brainstorming is to stretch your imagination and consider all possibilities, usual or unusual, crazy or sane, feasible or unrealistic. The main point to remember is that generating alternatives is meant to be an enjoyable, creative, and nonevaluative activity.

Checklisting. Checklisting takes advantage of the systematic nature of idea generation. An abundance of checklists in our environment can be used to develop alternatives to a problem. For example, if you are faced with the dilemma of buying a birthday gift for someone, a good source of ideas would be a catalog, such as Sear's or Penney's. The catalog can be viewed as a checklist of ideas and can save time and effort in thinking of a variety of gift ideas. Or, suppose you were looking for a group of nursing homes to conduct a survey on housing satisfaction. One place where you might find a checklist of all nursing homes in the area would be the local telephone directory. Although you might miss those that do not have a telephone, usually you would find that this directory is a fairly comprehensive source. Also, the local area agency on aging, the state office on aging, or the lobbying representative for nursing homes in your state might maintain such a list and could be another source for checklists of people or places.

Sometimes, checklists are not readily available. However, it is still possible to generate your own checklists to fit specific purposes. If, for example, you needed to generate a list of all public and private agencies who provided funding for old people in your local area, you could check several different sources (the library, various public records, the staff of larger public agencies or the United Way, etc.) to generate such a list. Checklisting can be useful in generating alternatives at many different points in the research process from the initial selection of whom to study to the different strategies you might take in collecting information.

Drawing Analogies. The ability to draw analogies is considered to be a central element in the development of significant creative innovations. In addition, drawing analogies can be an effective means of developing creative alternatives for everyday problems. One approach to drawing analogies in the creative problem solving literature is known as *bionics*. As the prefix *bio-*

would suggest, bionics refers to a method of drawing analogies between plant or animal life and human beings for potential solutions to real-life problems. For example, suppose you were faced with the problem of assessing the best or most effective methods that older persons might use in protecting themselves from robbery or attack when shopping. In generating alternative strategies, it is helpful to consider how plants and animals protect themselves from their environment and how these tactics might be translated into products or strategies for human self-protection.

Researchers can often generate alternative strategies by considering how they might address the problem if they were the object of the research rather than the researcher. For example, suppose the research problem were to evaluate the effectiveness of a local meals-on-wheels program. Considering the problem from the perspective of the people who receive the meals might be useful. What would they view as the most important outcomes of the program? What information would they consider to be most important to collect?

Checkerboard Method.   The checkerboard method of generating alternatives emphasizes the multidimensional nature of many problems and encourages an analysis of their possible interactions. For example, in considering whether the local adult day care center is meeting its stated goals one decision that must be made is determination of the source of information. The checkerboard method might be useful to see what different information sources can be used for addressing the goals of the day care program. Listing all goals and all sources of information makes it possible to explore all interactions of these two categories to see which source or sources might be most useful for your purposes. In addition, this approach often helps in suggesting new sources. Usually a visual representation is helpful in carrying out this exercise.

As you can see from Table 1-2, using different sources for different goals might result in very interesting (and different) results! This example also illustrates the difficulty of making generalizations about research when the results stem from only one of many possible data sources or settings. This issue of *external validity* is an important one, and will be discussed in detail in later chapters.

In summary, the generation of alternatives can be an exciting part of the research decision-making process. It can be used at all steps in the decision-making process and is meant to develop your creative thinking abilities. The suspension of evaluation is essential to assure that all possibilities are explored before a decision is made. Once you are satisfied that enough time has been spent on the generation of alternatives, it is time to weigh the alternatives in order to make a decision.

Table 1-2. Example of the checkerboard method: Possible sources of information to be used in researching the goals of an adult day care program

	Goals of the Program					
Possible Sources of Information	*Improve Morale among Participants*	*Provide Physical Therapy*	*Provide Nursing Care*	*Provide Socialization Services*	*Give Relief to Social Supports*	*Reduce Likelihood of Institutionalization*
Survey Day Care Participants	X	X	X	X	X	X
Agency Records		X	X	X		X
Survey Staff		X	X	X		
Survey Social Supports					X	
Observation of Participants, Staff and Activities	X	X	X	X		
Survey Control Group	X					X

Alternatives Are Evaluated

Weighing the alternatives in the decision-making process is often the most difficult step because a decision is rarely a clear choice of one alternative over another. Usually there are many alternatives, and each one has a different set of advantages and disadvantages. The final choice is often based on the expectation that the one alternative selected will turn out to be the best in the long run. This step in the APS model is particularly troublesome for students in research methods courses because many would like to see ready-made solutions for their specific research problems. Unfortunately, most research problems must be dealt with by weighing alternatives and making judgments based on the unique circumstances of the project. With some knowledge about the general approaches to designing research, however, this choice is often not as difficult as it first appears. Also, when people use the approach of thinking about the alternatives and evaluating them more systematically, most have a greater feeling of confidence about the decisions made along the way.

How, then, to evaluate alternatives? First, you must develop a set of criteria for weighing each idea. These criteria can be general or specific but must be relevant to the problem at hand. We have found at least four criteria useful in evaluating alternatives at most steps in the research process.

Feasibility. How well could each idea be carried out if it is selected? That is, how well could it be carried out given the political and other real-world contexts of the problem? (In this case, you would look for the greatest chance of complete implementation of each idea.)

Cost. What is the relative cost of each alternative in terms of time, money, personnel, space, and other resources required to carry out each alternative? (Here you are seeking the greatest cost effectiveness.)

Utility. How well could each alternative solve the problem as initially stated? (Here you are looking for the highest probability of usefulness or success of the outcome.)

Impact. How would the selection of each alternative affect others, such as co-workers, clients, and participants? (In this case, you should be looking for the choice that will benefit others maximally with a minimum of disruption.)

These four criteria for evaluating ideas are fairly general and should not be viewed as mutually exclusive. However, each of these criteria is important, and it is useful to consider them separately in weighing alternatives.

A simplified example is illustrated in Table 1-3 to show how to use these criteria in making research decisions. The feasibility of the alternatives in Table 1-3 is difficult to evaluate. First, it is hard to judge just how difficult locating another survey instrument would be. Usually, instruments of this type cannot be found in standard reference sources, such as the public library, and must be obtained through personal contacts or calls to state or federal government sources. A later section of this text describes sources of instruments that may be of use in addressing a wide variety of gerontological research issues. In addition, just how much time it would take to develop an instrument is difficult to measure. It depends on the level of sophistication of the designer, the amount of people and money available for developing and testing the instrument, and so forth. Because these entities are often unknown, you can see how decisions about feasibility are necessarily tentative at this point, as can also be said for the other criteria. The information provided in Table 1-3 therefore represents a best guess about the likely outcomes of the different alternatives. You should consider them in depth, however, to ensure that careful and thoughtful attention is given to the pros and cons of each possible alternative. Your guesses will improve as you develop more experience with and understanding of research methods. You may need to develop other, more specific criteria in evaluating the alternatives to a research problem. In fact, it is important to spend some time thinking about all the different ways your alternatives could be evaluated. One approach is to spend a few minutes brainstorming your evaluation criteria before you actually begin the evaluation process. The four preceding criteria are meant only to stimulate and guide your evaluation efforts. To reiterate, the evaluation of alternatives is one of the most challenging steps in the APS model.

Decision Is Made

Once all the alternatives have been developed and evaluated, a decision has to be made. Again, there are no hard and fast rules on how to make the decision once the alternatives have been weighed. Each of the pros and cons must be weighed in your own mind to form an overall impression about the desirability of selecting the final alternative. Usually, it is possible to rule out alternatives that have impractical or undesirable features. For example, if you estimated that it would take six months to develop a survey instrument, but the survey had to be completed within the next three months, then you probably would look for an existing instrument to serve your needs. Or, if your supervisor told you that she believed only in using standardized surveys, then you would also discard the self-generated alternative, and look only for published standardized instruments.

Table 1-3. Weighing the Alternatives: An Example Deciding on the Use of a Survey Instrument

Alternatives	Feasibility	Cost	Utility	Impact
Use an Existing Instrument	Seems realistic, only difficulty would lie in locating another appropriate survey to fit the needs of the specific project.	Low costs, real costs may come from ordering instrument, making copies of it, and staff time involved in finding and assessing best instrument	Limited to how well items relate to specific study goals, standardized instrument may have more reliability and validity* than a custom-made instrument.	Will depend on length and format, the better organized and short instrument will be received better by those who have to fill it out.
Develop a New Survey	The amount of time required to develop and test the survey would probably take longer, the staff may not have the expertise to design an acceptable instrument.	Staff time (typing and printing, pilot testing, etc.) would likely be higher overall to develop new instrument.	Will fit the specific purpose of study better, but may not have the best characteristics of a good survey (i.e., reliability and validity*).	Same as above, but will have greater control over length and format if custom developed instrument is used.
Combine Alternatives 1 and 2 (a new synthesized instrument with new and old elements)	May be the most difficult to implement, time must be allotted to locate existing measures, develop new ones, and test those too.	Costs would probably fall between 1 and 2 above, but it would depend on what percent of the instrument would have to be developed from scratch.	May have greatest utility, will fit purposes of study and data could be compared to existing survey information for further analyses.	Same as alternative 2 above, however, must guard against instrument looking "patched together" in this case.

*Issues in reliability and validity are discussed in Chapter 4.

Also, there is usually a tradeoff between the ideal decision and the actual decision when it is put within the context of the real world, because what we would like to do or what we view as the ideal approach often requires too many resources, or too much time, or both. Therefore, you should keep in mind that we must usually settle for what is most effective within the given situation, knowing that it will be less than ideal.

Whatever decision is made, a good policy is to let others know of your decision as early as possible to keep those who may be affected by the decision well informed. In fact, if a large-scale project is being implemented at your agency, it is usually advisable to have others assist in the decision-making process whenever possible. Although not all decisions would be the same as you might have made, you will probably find that they depend on the supporting staff's ability and willingness to carry them out. This implementation will be easier if the staff was involved in helping to make some of the most significant decisions with you. Staff can be especially beneficial in the brainstorming and evaluation phases, and you should use these opportunities to draw other people into the research.

One final note is that you should recognize that some of the best-planned decisions do not always work out when viewed in retrospect. (The Monday morning quarterback syndrome is not unique to football; it can also arise in problem solving and applied research.) However, it makes sense to acknowledge mistakes when they occur, and to be willing to learn from them. Monitoring the effectiveness of your decisions and recognizing that no answers are entirely right or wrong will provide you with the foundation to develop and refine your skills at applied problem solving in your research endeavors.

SUMMARY

This chapter has attempted to provide you with an overview of an applied problem-solving approach to conducting research in aging. The Applied Problem Solving model (APS model) includes five basic steps: (1) problem awareness, (2) problem specification, (3) generation of alternatives, (4) evaluation of alternatives, and (5) decision. This approach was presented because it encourages the development of a systematic method for making decisions in addressing applied research problems.

At each step in the research process, you should stretch your imagination in seeking alternatives to meet your research needs by suspending evaluation of your ideas as they develop initially, and using some of the techniques that were illustrated (including brainstorming, checklisting, checkerboard listing, and drawing analogies) to nurture your ideas during this process. It was also pointed out that there are not easy solutions to most applied research problems. Therefore, a rational approach, such as we have suggested in the APS model, is one means of minimizing the overwhelming feelings of inadequacy that many people feel when they aproach research methods for the first time.

Future chapters will look at each step in the research process, from the initial definition of the problem, through the analysis of the data that might be collected, to the reporting of the results. Each chapter will begin with a description of the kinds of problems or challenges that must be dealt with at the given stage of the reseach process. In each chapter we will also be describing the most typical methods that researchers use in their approach to a given research problem (the type of information normally found in most research methods texts). However, we will also be including many examples of research issues that are particularly important when the older population is being studied. We hope that the combination of a problem-solving approach and examples that use applied problems in aging will serve to reduce the anxiety that usually arises among students and new researchers. In addition, we encourage you to apply these research methods to your own research problems because we have found that actively using the information in the development of an individual research project is the single best method for learning and retaining new information.

SUGGESTED READINGS

The readings in the area of problem solving range from simple "how to" books to very sophisticated studies of problem solving techniques and abilities, descriptions of mathematical models, and computer programs designed to assist in solving problems. The following readings are at the practical "how to" end of the continuum.

Carkhuff, R. R. (1973). *The art of problem-solving: A guide for developing problem-solving skills for parents, teachers, counselors and administrators.* Amherst, Mass.: Human Resource Development Press. This book is a very simple introduction to the issues of problem solving. It doesn't offer much detail, but covers most of the basics.

Koberg, D., and Bagnall, J. (1981). *The all new universal traveler, a soft-systems guide to: Creativity, problem-solving and the process of reaching goals.* Los Altos, Calif.: William Kaufman. *The Universal Traveler* is funny and interesting as well as very informative. You will appreciate the entertaining manner in which creative problem solving is presented.

Parnes, S. J., Noller, R. B., and Biondi, A. M. (1977). *Guide to creative action* (rev. ed.). New York: Scribner's. This text offers a more thorough explication of problem solving than the other two. You may decide to read it after you have been through one of the more introductory books.

REFERENCES

Clark, C. H. (1958). *Brainstorming.* New York: Doubleday.

Davis, G. H. (1973). *Psychology of problem solving: Theory and practice.* New York: Basic Books.

Eden, C., Jones, S., and Sims, D. (1983). *Messing about in problems: An informal structured approach to their identification and management.* Oxford: Pergamon.

Koberg, D., and Bagnall, J. (1981). *The all new universal traveler, a soft-systems guide to: Creativity, problem-solving and the process of reaching goals.* Los Altos, Calif.: William Kaufman.

Osborn, A. F. (1963). *Applied imagination: Principles and procedures of creative thinking.* New York: Scribner's.

Parnes, S. J., Noller, R. B., and Biondi, A. M. (1977). *Guide to creative action* (rev. ed.). New York: Scribner's.

Part II

PLANNING AND DOING RESEARCH

2

Choosing and Stating a Research Problem

PROBLEMS TO BE SOLVED

How do I come up with an applied research problem?
How can I find information that will help me to clarify and refine the research problem?
How can I be sure the problem is worth the time and resources necessary to carry out the research?
How can I state the problem so that it will help guide the design and management of the project and the analysis and interpretation of the data?
How can I state the problem so that it will effectively communicate to others the goals and scope of the project?

The starting point in any research project, whether applied or basic, is the recognition of a problem and an interest in solving it by gathering, analyzing, and interpreting information. Research, like any goal-oriented activity, is most successful when the objectives and scope are well understood and clearly expressed at the outset. A clear, precise research problem statement serves as a guide for the design and execution of the project and is crucial to its success. Thus, the problem statement is a key to the remainder of the research.

The ultimate problem will include one or more questions to be answered and/or hypotheses to be tested, as well as a description of the boundaries or scope of the analysis in terms of time, people, and programs. It will communicate clearly what is and is not to be a part of the research. But the actual origin of the problem is often far less concrete and specifiable than the eventual statement. As was discussed in chapter 1, applied research problems often begin with "messes." These messes may be fuzzy notions or

35

ambiguous concerns about the causes or effects of something, or the way some process operates, or the associations among a set of factors. The researcher has the responsibility for focusing these fuzzy notions into researchable problems and then designing and completing the research project. The process of generating fuzzy notions and transforming them into clear research problem statements is the topic of this chapter.

Activities leading to the development of good research problem statements include generating researchable problems, searching for information on each problem, evaluating it, and refining the problem statement. The actual order of these activities is not particularly important; many can be carried out simultaneously. Furthermore, sometimes an iterative process is useful, as you run through several versions of the same problem as you refine it to the point that it can be effectively evaluated, and then revise the problem based upon the evaluation.

Although the ordering of the activities leading to good research problem statements is not a major concern, careful attention to each procedure is critical. Good research must be based upon valuable problems that are well stated. The remainder of this chapter is devoted to ensuring a successful beginning in applied gerontological research by generating and stating effective applied research problems.

SOURCES OF APPLIED RESEARCH PROBLEMS IN AGING

As has already been noted, research problems usually originate with a fuzzy notion or an ambiguous concern. Experienced researchers in applied settings usually have no difficulty with generating plenty of fuzzy notions, but students and beginning researchers may find that getting started is the most difficult part of the entire project, often because too much is expected of a problem when it first emerges. It is rare to find a fully developed, concisely stated research problem awaiting introduction to a beginning researcher. You must actively seek out issues, concerns and notions that will be quite vague and unspecifiable when first encountered.

General Sources of Research Problems

But where can applied research problems in aging be found? Cozby (1981) has described five general sources of research problems, and each can lead to applied research problems in aging. One source, perhaps an unexpected one, is common sense. Research can often be organized to support or refute common-sense notions about the world around us. A second source of research problems is observation. Here we mean the less formal observations that occur as we live out our lives and work at our jobs, rather than the formal observations used as methods of research. In carrying out your work, you may notice trends or situations that raise questions that can become the subject of research. Some researchers feel that informal observations are among the best sources of research problems.

A third general source of research problems is theory. Theories are efforts to organize and explain the observations and findings within a discipline, and they are very useful for generating hypotheses and research questions. Basic research is generally directed toward testing hypotheses and revising or extending theories, but theories can also serve as sources of problems in applied research. For example, program results may appear to be contradictory to accepted theories, suggesting the need for research to examine the apparent contradiction. Or theories may lead to shifts in policies that then require evaluation research. Additionally, theories may suggest potentially useful changes in programs that can become the basis for demonstration/ research projects. For an interesting example of how theory can lead to applied research, see Kastenbaum's (1979) study of the impact of serving beer and wine on the social interaction of geriatric patients.

Past research is a fourth general source of research problems. This source is especially valuable when inconsistencies are noted in the findings of two or more studies addressing a similar issue or when methodological problems are discovered that may invalidate earlier research findings. Past research may also suggest the need for a new study when you wish to learn more about a previously discovered association between two variables. Once you are involved in research, you may find that your own past studies are good sources for generating new ideas (Simon, 1978). It is good practice to keep an eye out for serendipitous findings that suggest new research topics.

A final general source of research topics is practical problems. Applied research is, in the final analysis, research designed to address problems that have some practical consequence (Rothman, 1980). The remainder of this chapter will focus on research issues of this type.

The general sources of research problems just described are useful in showing the range of possible starting points. However, the beginning applied gerontological researcher is likely to feel these sources are too general to be useful for generating research problems. The following sources are likely to be of more direct value in developing applied gerontological research problems.

Special Issues of *The Gerontologist*

The Gerontological Society of America has organized a series of multidisciplinary efforts to describe the state of the art in several subfields of gerontology and to determine the major research issues in each. Some of these have focused specifically on applied research, while others have dealt with research in general, but all are very useful in generating applied research problems. The results of these multidisciplinary efforts have been published in several special issues of *The Gerontologist* (Committee on International Collaboration, 1972; Committee on Research and Development Goals in Social Gerontology, 1969, 1971*a*, 1971*b*). These special issues are highly readable and address critical research problems in a number of areas, including housing, work and leisure, education, social services, economics, minority group problems, health and nutrition. Although several years old, they are by no means out of date.

Requests for Proposals and Grant Announcements

Another source of applied research problems in gerontology is the requests for proposals and grant and contract announcements that are distributed by federal agencies and private foundations that specialize in aging concerns. The agencies and foundations that support research topics should be given priority. Many convene committees of researchers, instructors, and practitioners to help establish the priority research areas. Therefore, even if you never plan to write a proposal for funding, it is worthwhile to review the announcements of major funding organizations of aging research as a source of research ideas. Most of these organizations also regularly publish the titles of recently funded projects, possibly fertile sources for research ideas. The *Federal Register* publishes notices of the most current research funding opportunities in aging through federal agencies. Most grants and contracts offices of colleges and universities have copies of requests for proposals and grant or contract announcements. Appendix 2-1 shows some selected topics from a recent announcement distributed by the Office of Human Development Services of the Department of Health and Human Services. These statements are not presented as examples of well-stated research problems. The Office of Human Development Services expects individual researchers to take these suggestions as the starting points for developing research proposals. It should be relatively easy to generate research ideas from these topics by addressing the problem as it influences your locality or your field of programmatic interest.

Administrators and Staff of Organizations

Another worthwhile source of possible research topics is the staff of organizations that are responsible for legislation, services, and facilities for the elderly. Such individuals are continually giving attention to the issues that lead to research problems and are often happy to share their ideas and concerns. Appendix 2-2 presents a list of the kinds of people you may wish to contact. These individuals can give you new insights that should help you to come up with project ideas. The list is not meant to be exhaustive; you can probably think of others to talk to in your area.

When you meet with representatives from agencies and organizations, do not expect them to have a list of ready-made applied research topics. It is worth repeating that applied research problems rarely emerge fully developed and ready for analysis. You should prepare for your visit by learning some basic facts about the goals and functions of the organization, and you should have a list of questions ready so that you can help the staff member to tease out the research problems. The specific questions to ask will differ from organization to organization, but the following list should be helpful in getting started.

1. What are the major legislative issues that have an impact on the elderly in this locality?
2. What are the two or three areas in which poor information is making it difficult to establish good policy?
3. What are the major problems in service delivery for your agency?
4. What new policies or programs have been recently established or are planned for the future?
5. What kinds of research have been recently carried out on policies or programs for the elderly?

The questions presented in the next section may also be useful in working with the staff members of agencies to develop applied research problems. You should be prepared to probe by asking followup questions that help to clarify the issues that arise. Also, it can be useful to repeat the problem in your own words to see whether you both agree. This procedure will take time, and inevitably some effort will be wasted traveling down unproductive paths. However, overall, discussions with those who plan and implement policies can be a valuable method for getting ideas for applied research.

Generation of Research Ideas in the Organization Setting

As has already been noted, the agency or organization that is involved in services to the elderly is a very productive source of applied research problems. The variety of possible applied research projects is tremendous, but we rarely give careful consideration to them all. The following list, adapted from Brenner (1974), shows the great range of organizational issues that may lead to research problems:

Organizational priorities and objectives

Internal operations

Service delivery and use

Service effectiveness

Program efficiency

Organizational support

This list of organizational issues should be of value to current agency employees as well as to students and others who plan to contact agencies to seek applied research ideas. It is useful for stretching your imagination to areas that you may otherwise overlook, and it should be helpful in ferreting out applied research problems in any organizational setting. Because of its general utility, each issue is subsequently described and some examples of questions that deal with each issue are given.

Organizational Priorities and Objectives.   Organizational priorities and objectives can be the basis for a great deal of applied research. Research on this issue is meant to determine the causes, extent, and magnitude of problems that are of concern to the organization or that should be addressed in the future. The results of this research might be a shift in priorities or a redirection of resources. Research dealing with organizational objectives is often called *needs assessment.* Many in the field of applied research have opposed the use of this term because needs are arbitrarily and (usually) subjectively defined. However, organizations do often find it useful to carry out research that helps to establish new objectives or to bring about shifts in the populations that are covered by services. The following questions address issues of organizational priorities and objectives.

1. What is the extent and severity of various problems as viewed by potential consumers or service deliverers or as determined by an analysis of secondary data sources?
2. What is the etiology of the problem? How does it usually arise and develop? What are the major conditions leading to the problem?
3. What is the epidemiology of the problem? What subgroups of the population are most (and least) likely to experience it? Is the problem usually associated with other problems that may have to be addressed initially or simultaneously? Is the problem more likely to crop up or to be worse in

certain areas or under certain circumstances? Do certain conditions make the problem more (or less) amenable to correction?

Internal Operations. While much research in service organizations deals with current or potential consumers of services, applied research can also focus on internal matters. Organizational efficiency can be substantially improved through research addressing how agency functions are actually (rather than ideally) carried out, how financial and other resources are being allocated, and how the attitudes and qualifications of the staff fit the job requirements. The following specific questions might lead to research in this area.

1. What are the methods for obtaining, storing, retrieving, and processing client information? Do records contain sufficient information and are they complete enough to be of value? Is information being maintained beyond its usefulness or being purged too quickly? How is information generally used by the staff?
2. When new clients are identified, how long is it before eligibility is determined and services are delivered? Is there evidence that this process takes place quickly enough? What are the major causes of delays? Can delays be reduced through staffing or procedural changes?
3. How are client referrals made and treated within the agency and across agencies? Are contracts and agreements with other agencies operating as they should?
4. How well do the activities and responsibilities of staff members match their job descriptions and personnel levels? Do any policies or regulations lead to wasted staff time? Is there an appropriate distribution of the agency caseload? Are eligibility criteria for services understood and consistently applied by employees? Do staff members have the educational background and experience necessary to carry out their job requirements? Would personnel benefit from in-service training on certain topics?
5. What is the level of staff satisfaction and morale? Are employees satisfied with their work environment, potential for advancement, responsibilities, and salaries? What is the rate of turnover, and what are the major causes of turnover? Do the attitudes of personnel influence their work with clients? Are there specific client complaints about the staff?

Service Delivery and Use. This organizational issue covers the connection between the consumer and the agency. The major topics are the characteristics of recipients and the quantity and quality of the service as it is actually delivered. This area and the next two (service effectiveness and program efficiency) encompass the topics that are usually studied in evaluation research. The goal of evaluation research is to determine whether program goals are being met efficiently and effectively. A valuable discussion of evaluative research in programs for the aging has been produced by the Committee on Research and Development (1977) of the Gerontological Society of America. The following specific questions address the issue of service delivery and use.

1. How do those who receive the service differ from those who are eligible but fail to receive it? Might some individuals benefit more from the service than present recipients do, but fail to get it? Do any features of the program, the staff, or the delivery technology discourage or encourage use by certain types of people? How do consumers learn about the service?
2. Do some individuals prematurely discontinue use of the service? Do others remain in the program longer than they should?
3. Is the service being delivered as intended in terms of frequency, quantity, quality, and mandated techniques?

Service Effectiveness.   This issue centers on whether the services provided lead to the intended benefits. The chief goal of research in this area is to determine whether the planned effects have occurred, and, if so, whether they can be reasonably attributed to the service. In other words, is the service successful? The following examples of questions are appropriate to this area.

1. What are the benefits derived from the service as reported by clients, staff members, and others? What problems do consumers experience as a result of using the service?
2. Has the behavior, characteristics, or environment of the client changed measurably in the desired direction?* What is the magnitude and duration of the change? To what extent can the change be attributed to the service?
3. Are some subgroups of users more likely to experience a change than others? Do some subgroups experience changes of greater magnitude or longer duration?

Program Efficiency.   Program efficiency is concerned with the resources needed to provide a unit of service, or more importantly, the resources

---

*It should be noted that many programmatic goals in aging are designed to maintain current status for as long as possible. Thus, the realistic objective of a service may be stability or a slower decline in functioning. These objectives are just as open to research as improvement.

required per unit of outcome. This information is often critical in determining whether a particular service or program will be continued in its present form. Administrators and policy makers have to give careful attention to whether the costs are reasonable, given the benefits derived. The following examples of questions address the issue of program efficiency.

1. What is the cost per unit of service? How does this cost compare to similar agencies with comparable clients? How does the cost vary for different types of clients and in different regions? What are the causes of these variations? How are costs distributed between administrative overhead and direct service provision?
2. What is the cost involved in achieving specific, measurable outcomes, including changes in the client's behavior, environment, or characteristics?

Organizational Support.   Organizations rarely carry out research on current or potential supporters and cooperating agencies. However, studies of this type can be extremely useful, especially among organizations that depend upon charity giving or volunteers. Some questions on the issue of organizational support follow.

1. How is the organization viewed by those who currently provide financial or organizational support or who may do so in the future? Do they know the objectives or the organization?
2. Why do people choose to become involved in voluntary work for the organization? Why do some continue their involvement while others drop out? How large a pool of potential volunteers or financial supporters exists in the community?
3. What are the attitudes and opinions of cooperating agencies, including those who accept and/or make client referrals? Do their attitudes influence their referral patterns or other forms of interchange with your organization?

Activities that Help to Generate Research Problems

Research problems, even those of the fuzzy notion variety, rarely just appear without some effort. Instead of waiting for an idea to materialize, you should actively pursue ideas from sources such as those just described. This section offers a few suggestions on how to actively search for potential research problems.

First of all, you can engage in active, focused note-taking as you review the literature in an area of interest. As you read, jot down interesting findings, questions you have about the research, or important points made by the author. Do not depend on your memory—an idea may "click" only if two points raised by separate readings are connected but may be overlooked if the first point is forgotten. Also, do not read just for content; read with an eye toward the research possibilities. Think beyond the specific passage to how it relates to local programs or how the issue might change if it dealt with a different service or a different group of consumers. Carry out your reading with an inquisitive frame of mind. *Who, what, when, where, why,* as well as *how* and *at what expense* are all issues you should be prepared to raise as you attempt to generate applied research ideas through reading.

The same advice applies when you discuss possible research topics with representatives from agencies. As was noted earlier, you should prepare in advance for your visits by learning about the agency. Otherwise, most of the visit may consist of having the agency staff describe history and goals of the organization. Make a set of questions that fit the organization and be prepared to ask followup questions. Also, make notes during or just after the meeting so that you do not have to depend on memory.

Brainstorming is another method for actively pursuing research problems. If you are already on the staff of an agency, you can use brainstorming effectively with other staff members. This technique not only helps in gathering a large and varied list of possible research topics, but has the added benefit of fostering a sense of involvement in the research process that will probably lead to increased internal support for the research, or at least reduce the likelihood that staff members will set up roadblocks. Students may benefit from brainstorming with other students or scheduling a time when students and instructors can work together at brainstorming research ideas.

SEARCHING FOR MORE INFORMATION ON THE PROBLEM

As soon as one or more possible research problems (still probably in the form of fuzzy notions) have been generated, you should search for information that will help you to clarify and evaluate them. The added information will help you to learn much more about the problem, to see it from a number of different angles, to recognize its major components, to determine its relative importance, and to discover how it can be effectively researched.

People can be an effective source of additional information on a research problem. For example, if knowledge of the problem originally came through discussions with an agency representative, this individual is an obvious source for more detail. You may find that he or she can offer information on the background and development of the problem, describe why it is important, and suggest ways others have attempted to deal with it. You may also find that the staff member can suggest other people to contact to learn still more about the problem.

The literature is another invaluable source of additional information on the problem. Others have probably already carried out research that addresses this or a similar issue, and their experience can help you to clarify and evaluate your problem. Unfortunately, little applied research ends up in the literature for several reasons: (1) the results may be pertinent to a specific population or program and cannot be generalized to other situations; (2) few journals publish articles on applied topics; (3) applied researchers often move directly from one project to the next or carry out several projects simultaneously, leaving little time for writing articles; and (4) many researchers in applied settings are not rewarded for their record of publications. Despite the fact that applied research rarely gets published, you will probably find that the literature is a great resource for learning more about the topic.

How can a review of the literature help? Besides showing that the researcher is well informed on a topic, literature review sections in written works (1) show the historical development of the research topic, (2) describe how the research addresses important theoretical and/or practical issues, and (3) describe shortcomings of earlier research that may be overcome in the present project. But what purpose does reviewing the literature serve when the researcher begins to struggle with a poorly defined research problem? Actually, the review of literature can be very helpful in progressing from a fuzzy notion to a concisely stated research problem. It will help you to organize your thoughts on any number of topics that are important to refining the problem statement (Leedy, 1980). The following issues can be addressed in the literature review.

1. What theoretical approaches may be useful for deducing specific hypotheses or research questions?
2. What kinds of research designs, methods, and analytical procedures have been used in researching this or similar topics? Do some appear to be especially promising?
3. What are the major problems others have encountered in dealing with the topic? Have any suggested ways of overcoming these problems in future research?
4. What is the policy significance of the problem as viewed by past researchers or policy makers? What is its theoretical significance?
5. Given the history of research on the topic, what is the next logical step to be taken in dealing with it? What consistencies and inconsistencies have emerged in past research?
6. Who are the major researchers in this area, and how can they be contacted directly for more information?

While the general print and computerized indexes to the literature will be useful resources for your review of the literature, some specialized sources are briefly described here.

Current Literature on Aging, published by The National Council on Aging, is a valuable quarterly guide to books and journal articles in gerontology. Each item is annotated. Information about this periodical can be obtained from the Publications Office, The National Council on Aging, Inc., 600 Maryland Avenue, SW, West Wing 100, Washington, DC 20024.

Accessions is a monthly publication of the National Gerontology Resource Center of the AARP (American Association of Retired People). It lists all library materials acquired by the National Gerontology Resource Center. All books and other materials listed in *Accessions* are available for loan. For more information, you may write the National Gerontology Resource Center, AARP, 1909 K Street, NW, Washington, DC 20049.

AGELINE is a computerized bibliographic search program that makes it possible for you to locate books, articles, and reports by means of key words. Abstracts and publication information are available for more than 16,000 documents. The *AGELINE* data base is available for on-line searching in many colleges and community libraries through their BRS bibliographic utility. Ask at your local library or contact BRS Customer Service, 1200 Route 7, Latham, NY 12110 for information about the availability of *AGELINE* in your area.

EVALUATING POTENTIAL RESEARCH PROBLEMS

How do you decide whether a potential research problem is worthwhile, or which among a set of possible problems is the one to tackle first? These questions are not easy to answer, but at some point the decision must be made. This section presents some criteria that may be useful in evaluating research problems.

You must have an adequate conception of the research problem before you can carry out the evaluation. A fully developed problem statement does not need to be written, but you should have a good idea of the research objectives as well as some thoughts about the design and methods to be used. These ideas (which should be written down) can serve as the basis for at least a preliminary evaluation. Of course, the more complete and precise the problem statement, the better will be the evaluation. You should bear in mind that even though the evaluation could be more precise as you invest more time and thought in refining the problem and research design, inertia takes over at some point so that it becomes difficult to back out. Therefore, evaluation should be viewed as an ongoing process. Some candidate problems can be eliminated soon after they emerge. Later evaluations, based upon more complete conceptualizations, can eliminate others and help suggest how the remainder can be revised. Thus evaluation may occur before or after you have developed a clear, complete problem statement, and in most instances it should occur at both points as well as during the research-planning phase. As was discussed in chapter 1, you may want to suspend evaluation as you generate ideas, but it is not a good idea to eliminate evaluation entirely. Evaluation is a useful component of the problem selection and design phases of research.

In chapter 1 we presented several criteria (feasibility, cost, utility, and impact) to consider in evaluating alternative solutions to problems. These criteria are also helpful in evaluating alternative applied research problems, because applied research is directed toward resolving a practical problem. Written results of your evaluations will be invaluable as you refine your final research problem statement.

Feasibility

One aspect of the feasibility of a research problem is whether the topic can be successfully addressed by means of research. Is the problem researchable? Not all problems are, and occasionally "research" is used as an excuse to delay or avoid difficult, unpopular, or politically dangerous decisions. Another important issue to consider is whether you and your co-workers can complete the project. Do you have the necessary knowledge, experience, and authority to plan and manage the research? Do you have or can you obtain access to subjects and any needed special equipment and facilities? Will you have the time, personnel, and supplies that will be required? If the research is based upon the analysis of secondary data sources, can you obtain the needed data?

Cost

Every research project requires the expenditure of some resources, and the type of problem as well as the design, sample size, and methods can lead to considerable variations in cost. What is the cost in terms of staff time, equipment and facilities, supplies, printing or duplication, travel, computer usage, agency overhead, payments to subjects, and so forth for this project? It is not always possible at the outset to determine with great accuracy the costs involved in conducting research. However, general estimates (broken down by categories to help ensure that nothing major is omitted) can be useful. Costs must be weighed against available resources if the project is to be funded internally. If there is a chance that some or all of the research will be funded by an outside organization, the likelihood of such funding should also be taken into account.

Utility

Utility is the probability that the research will lead to the desired outcomes. It should be emphasized that this expectation does not merely address whether the research will result in increased knowledge, answers to specific questions, or will be adequate tests of a set of hypotheses, although these outcomes may be desirable. In applied research, outcomes must be taken one step further to consider whether the results will have any practical consequence. Are the issues being subjected to research open to manipulation and revision? Do you understand the mechanisms that will lead to application of the results? What specific steps must be undertaken to ensure that the findings will be used for practical purposes? Do you have control over these steps or some assurance that they will occur? Are there administrative, political, social, or financial conditions that may limit the probability that the research findings will be used?

Impact

Impact is concerned with the importance, degree, and scope of changes that can be expected from the study. In other words, the impact of the research problem is related to the overall significance of the topic, the amount of change that can be expected, and the number of people who will be influenced. Does the research problem address an important issue in terms of planning, practice, accountability, or efficiency? How valuable are the ultimate changes in behavior, the environment, or the mental or physical health that may result from the project? Will the research influence only a small population (perhaps only the persons subjected to the study), or can the results be generalized to a larger group? Ethical issues should also be taken into account here. What potential negative consequences might this research have on the persons being studied? In evaluating the impact of a research problem, you must consider both the short-term and long-term effects and weigh the significance of the project against the specific policy mandates and program objectives of the organization.

The four criteria of feasibility, cost, utility, and impact are never easy to apply to a specific research problem. Answers to many of the questions falling under each category can be only estimated, especially at the outset. But it is important, at some stage in the development of research problems, to make an honest effort at applying these criteria; then you will have a better probability of selecting a worthwhile research problem. These criteria are also useful as you plan the other steps of the research process. Attention to these issues will help to ensure an efficient, effective project.

WRITING THE PROBLEM STATEMENT

During the process of locating, examining, and evaluating possible research problems, you have generated many ideas and accumulated a variety of written notes about the problem you have selected. Now is a good time to draw upon these fragmented ideas and notes as you write a clear statement of the research problem. The problem statement should be a brief, concise, unambiguous description of the research problem. It should describe the limitations or boundaries of the research as well as the specific questions to be answered or hypotheses to be tested. Time and care should be given to writing the statement so that it communicates clearly and efficiently what the research problem is.

Purposes of Problem Statements

Why should so much time and effort be spent on just stating the research problem? Why not save a lot of time by getting started on solving the problem through research? Three very important reasons for taking the time to write a good problem statement are the purposes of conceptualization, communication, and orientation, each to be briefly discussed.

First of all, the process of creating the problem statement forces researchers to clarify their thinking about the research. It helps to ensure a careful review of the exact meaning of words and phrases, and assists in locating weak spots that are less obvious when the problem is unspecified. As already noted, research problems usually begin with a fuzzy notion about something. Necessary detail and clarity are added as time and work proceed. Writing the statement leads to a re-evaluation of the problem as well as a "thinking-through" process that helps you consider the problem in all its facets. If the problem is clear in your own mind, it will be a very simple matter to jot it down. If the problem is not conceptually clear, much can be gained from working on a tight, well-worded statement. The process makes you actively think, helps you identify errors, and helps you develop alternative statements that may more precisely communicate to others the purposes and scope of the project. These results help ensure that the research problem is valuable. If the statement itself is weak, the conceptualization may also be deficient in some way.

A second purpose of the problem statement is to communicate the problem to others with detail and clarity. This communication can be crucial in applied research because the supporters and the consumers of the research are often in a different department or even a different organization from the people who are responsible for carrying it out. It is likely that resources will have to made available, access to subjects will be required, and results will have to be applied by someone other than the researcher. This interdependency necessitates negotiation and cooperation, which can be best accomplished through a clear understanding by all parties of the goals and scope of the project. Enormous amounts of resources can be wasted if the research fails to meet the needs of the consumers.

The political environment that often surrounds applied research makes advance negotiation and agreement on the research problem even more critical. The research findings must be applied if the research is to have any practical value. Whoever will be responsible for applying the findings should be involved with the project from the outset. They are more likely to support the research and use the findings if they have a clear understanding of and a sense of involvement in the project. People in various sections of an organization are likely to view the research from very different perspectives. They may even have different goals in mind for the project. A well-written research problem statement can reduce the likelihood that these varying perspectives will somehow foul up either the research or the implementation of the results (Patton, 1978).

A third reason for writing a good problem statement is that it can be a valuable guide to all the other activities that will lead to the successful completion of the project. A clear statement of the goal of the research and its scope is a very useful reference point. It provides an orientation that will help in making decisions about the design, methods, analysis, and interpretation. As you begin to deal with the many decisions that are necessary to carry out the research, you will therefore find that the problem statement is an invaluable aid.

Characteristics of Well-Stated Research Problems

Well-stated research problems have a number of common attributes that set them apart from poor statements. You should consider the following characteristics as you begin to write your own problem statement (Leedy, 1980). The closer you meet these criteria, the better will be the statement.

The problem statement must be conceptually clear. The statement must convey to the reader in unambiguous terms what you wish to study. Whoever reads it must know what you have in mind. Any difficult or unusual terms should be clearly defined.

The problem statement should be specific. Too often, the problem statement leaves out important qualifications or limitations and may therefore mislead the reader about the target population, time period, the range of effects to be studied, or some other limiting factor. A good statement of a research problem informs the reader of what is to be studied, and it also reveals what is not to be studied.

The problem statement is appropriate for different audiences. In applied research, the problem statement must usually communicate the objective and scope of the project to several different audiences with varying backgrounds and quite different levels of expertise in research methods. Therefore the statement must convey a clear, simple description that just about anyone will understand. Care should be taken to eliminate jargon and complicated sentences.

Typical Faults with Statements of Research Problems

Certain kinds of faults tend to appear again and again in statements of research problems. These faults are especially likely to occur among new researchers because they have had less experience with carrying out projects and seeing how the stated research objectives miss the mark. You should be aware that these mistakes can occur so that you can be on the lookout for them in your own descriptions. The three major mistakes in problem statements (Leedy, 1980) are incomplete statements, statements that are extravagant or irresponsible, and statements that talk about the research problem without ever really stating it.

The common mistake in incomplete problem statements is that they lack necessary detail. Incomplete problem statements are likely to be an indication of inadequate conceptualization, and they are not going to be useful for communication. There must be sufficient detail in the description of the problem so that others will understand what you will do, what questions or hypotheses you will address, and what population you can generalize to. It is probably better to err on the side of too much detail than too little detail.

Extravagant or irresponsible statements are likely to be written by a researcher who has not taken the time to consider the practical limitations of the project. A researcher who wishes to examine the effects of financial incentives for family care of the elderly is probably not going to be able to measure all the intended and unintended effects of all forms of financial incentives in all geographic areas. A more realistic statement would note that the analysis will be limited to the effects of financial incentives of a specific type on institutionalization. Rarely are researchers' objectives that grand; the error is usually due to lack of careful thought about the limitations. However, a problem statement that fails to describe the limitations may lead others to have unrealistic expectations for the project.

In statements that provide information about the research problem without ever clearly stating it many words describe the historical, political, theoretical, or methodological background, or pages are written on the significance of the problem, without ever presenting the research problem itself. Descriptions of the background and signficance are not unimportant, but they are no substitute for a clear, straightforward description of the specifics of the problem. The problem should be stated so that the description is sufficient without the trappings of history and significance. It should not be lost in a maze of peripheral information.

Refining the Problem Statement

What can you do to hone the description of the problem so that it conveys a clear, complete message? First of all, the *why* and *restatement* exercises described in chapter 1 should help you to think through the explanations and justifications for the problem and to produce a variety of different ways of stating it. You should also carefully read and re-read the problem, asking yourself whether it meets the criteria for a good research problem statement or has any of the major faults just described. As you read, consider what others might infer from the statement. Ask yourself whether this inference is exactly what you have in mind. Is the statement complete, to the point, and realistic? Should any phrases be clarified?

Another very useful method for refining the problem statement is to give it to someone else to read and critique. Do not spend time explaining the project before the critics read it; the purpose is to see whether the problem description stands by itself. After the critics have had an opportunity to read the statement, ask them to restate it in their own words. Ask them to tell you what you want to find out. If their rendition of your statement leaves something to be desired, it is a definite indication that more work is needed to clarify the sections that failed to communicate.

If possible, you should choose some critics who have little or no involvement in the project. Their conceptualization of the research will not be influenced by what has been heard or read before. Of course, you should also carry out this exercise with people who will play a role in the research and its application. Their comments will help assure that everyone is starting the project with the same expectations.

Another method for refining the problem statement has been suggested by Leedy (1980). His advice is to break the problem into subproblems.

Subproblems are somewhat independent problems that must be resolved in carrying out the research. In applied research projects, there may be several subproblems, consisting of specific hypotheses or research questions to be addressed. If so, it is helpful to focus on clarifying each one in the process of refining the problem statement. The more specific, the better the problem statement.

Examples of Problem Statements in Applied Research

To give further guidance in writing good, clear statements of applied research problems, two poorly written statements follow, along with examples of how they can be improved.

Poor Problem Statement: What happens when the mentally ill and retarded are deinstitutionalized?

This statement is too broad and lacks specificity. It does not tell us which institutions or which mentally ill or retarded patients are the concern of the research. The problem is also extravagant. We can not possibly learn everything that happens after deinstitutionalization, but the statement offers no way of determining what specific aspects of deinstitutionalization the researcher would like to know about.

Next is a problem statement from the final report of an applied research project addressing the same issue (Joint Legislative Audit and Review Commission, 1979, p. 2). The statement has been revised to change the tense and clarify a few concepts. It offers a better picture of what will be investigated as well as what will not be a part of the study. For example, it is clear from the improved statement that only community services provided by specific state organizations will be considered and that the study focuses upon mentally ill and retarded persons who leave state facilities.

Better Problem Statement

Purpose. The primary purpose of the study is to assess the ability of the State to link clients with appropriate services after seven years of experience with deinstitutionalization. Three major study objectives relate to recommendations of the Governor's Commission on Mental, Indigent, and Geriatric Patients.

1. Review procedures for transferring patients from state institutions to the community
2. Assess the extent to which discharged clients are linked with community services

3. Examine the potential of state-funded community services to meet the continuing needs of discharged clients

Scope. This study will focus on discharge procedures at state institutions for the mentally ill and mentally retarded. It will also examine community services provided to the mentally ill and mentally retarded by the Department of Mental Health and Mental Retardation; the 36 local mental health and mental retardation service boards; the state mental hospitals and training centers for the mentally retarded; the state departments of welfare, rehabilitative services, and health; and the Virginia Housing Development Authority.

Poor Problem Statement: What is the role of Medicaid in nursing home care?

This problem statement also suffers from lack of specificity. In addition, it is conceptually unclear. What is meant by *role?* One role of Medicaid in nursing home care is to provide payments to nursing homes for patients who meet certain income and asset criteria. Because this fact is already known, one interpretation of the question can be answered without carrying out any research. There is certainly very little information about what specific topics should be covered in the research.

Next is a research problem statement that addresses the same issue but provides more detail regarding the scope and nature of the problem (Institute for Program Evaluation, 1983, p. 8). Again, the statement has been revised slightly.

Better Problem Statement

The Chairman of the Subcommittee on Health and the Environment of the House Committee on Energy and Commerce asked us to assess the current role of Medicaid in nursing home care across the states. Specifically, he asked us to examine the characteristics of the population served in nursing homes, including patterns of length and stay; the characteristics of new admissions; and the variability of state program expenditures, bed supply, and reimbursement. The objective of this study is to provide information on these aspects of the program.

It should be noted that the preceding statement also referenced the original letter requesting the research. The letter, from the Chairman of the Subcommittee on Health and the Environment, was published as an appendix to the report. Although it is not reprinted here, it could be considered a component of the problem statement, because it provided a rationale for the study and gave further clarity to some of the research objectives. This inclusion is not good practice because the problem statement should stand by itself. However, when you conduct applied research it is good policy to maintain documentation regarding the background and development of the project.

The two better research problem statements are offered as real-world examples of problem statements by applied researchers. Neither is perfect. You are encouraged to review the characteristics of well-stated research problems and typical faults of research problem statements with the goal of further refining them. However, each of the statements offers a clearer, more complete description of the research goals than did its previous poor example.

As you plan your own research project, taking the time to write down and refine your problem statement is the first major stage in the research process, and it is important to begin from a solid foundation.

SUMMARY

This chapter has dealt with the steps involved in choosing and stating a research problem—the first major stage of a research project. Although applied gerontological research problems are plentiful, first-time researchers are frequently baffled in their efforts to locate one because they often expect the problem to materialize in a form that is readily researchable. Unfortunately, research problems are rarely this accommodating. They tend to start out as messes, fuzzy notions, or ambiguous concerns. If you try to be open to these situations, and do not expect too much of them at the outset, you will be surprised by the number and variety of applied research problems that emerge.

The many sources of applied research problems in aging include special issues of *The Gerontologist,* requests for proposals and grant announcements, and administrators and staff members of agencies that work with older clients. Although students tend to be hesitant about talking to current practitioners, you should plan to do so as at least one part of the search process. Persons who work in the field of aging are excellent sources of research topics. In addition, you will find that most of them will appreciate your interest and offer enthusiastic support in ferreting out good, practical problems.

Part of the process of locating and selecting research topics consists of searching for more information about the problem. People who work in the area addressed by the problem will probably help you learn more about it. The literature can also be a good source of additional information. Be sure to take notes as you gather your information. You will have occasion to return to these notes during other phases of the research process.

You should carefully evaluate each research problem that arises. Application of the criteria of feasibility, cost, utility, and impact will help you to decide whether to continue working on the problem. Careful consideration of these criteria can also lead to insights that will be useful in writing a clear problem statement. In addition, you will find referring back to these criteria useful as you develop plans for the research.

Once you have selected a problem, you should set aside the time to write a concise, unambiguous statement of the objectives of your research. The statement should be conceptually clear, specific, and appropriate for various audiences. The statement will help you clarify your own thinking about the problem, and it will be useful for communicating the problem to others and guiding the remainder of the research project.

APPENDIX 2-1
SELECTED RESEARCH AND POLICY
ISSUES FROM THE 1986 FISCAL YEAR
OFFICE OF HUMAN DEVELOPMENT
SERVICES DISCRETIONARY
FUNDS PROGRAM

Projects are solicited that identify ways to prepare adults in their thirties, forties, and fifties to plan effectively for their social, health, housing, and financial needs in later life. Projects should

Synthesize existing research and information, including the work being done by the National Academy of Sciences and the recent Louis Harris survey, regarding the age-related perceptions of various age groups

Identify the gaps in knowledge that exist in today's various age groups regarding what actions they might reasonably adopt in an early stage of (life) to better prepare for their own aging.

Develop and pilot test approaches for changing both the perceptions and behaviors of differing age groups.

Applications are invited that will demonstrate ways to link available data on the elderly and predictive information on the future needs and benefits of an aging society to the formulation of public policies. Applications should undertake a comprehensive effort resulting in a set (of) monographs that:

Analyze the effects of demographic, social, economic, and other trends on the future status and needs of the older population over the next 25 years

Assess the nature, scope, and types of programs required to meet the predicted needs of the growing number and changing nature of the older population

Identify the kinds and number of personnel required to carry out such programs

Examine the policy issues that must be dealt with in preparing for an aging society

Applications are solicited for manpower studies in the field of aging to answer several or all of the following questions.

How many graduates with special training in gerontology find full-time, appropriate level employment in the field of aging?

How many current gerontology students intend to seek employment in the field of aging?

In what agencies do persons trained in gerontology find employment?

How has training impacted on the work experiences of persons trained in gerontology?

APPENDIX 2-2
PEOPLE TO CONTACT FOR APPLIED
RESEARCH TOPICS

Administrators and staff members of public service agencies (e.g., area agencies on aging, home health agencies, specialized transportation agencies, nursing homes, adult day care sites, domiciliary care units, health and welfare departments, Veterans Administration hospitals)

Elected officials on aging or social service committees and legislative support staff for these committees (e.g., local, state, and federal legislative committees and study groups)

Members of voluntary community service organizations with an aging focus (e.g., church committees with a mission to the elderly, fraternal organizations, United Way, Alzheimer's disease support groups)

Administrators or staff of special interest groups that concentrate on aging issues (e.g., AARP/NRTA, Older Women's League, Gray Panthers, associations representing nursing homes and homes for adults)

Representatives of professional organizations that have a concern for aging issues, especially members of committees or sections that focus on concerns that are of specific interest to the researcher (e.g., the Gerontological Society of America, the American Geriatrics Society, the American Society on Aging, the National Council on Aging, the American Public Health Association, state and regional professional associations such as the Southern Gerontological Society)

SUGGESTED READINGS

Brenner, M. N. (1974). *Mini-study kit: A programmed guide in strategies and methods of research in social services.* Madison, Wis.: University of Wisconsin-Extension,

Center for Social Service. This simple little book provides a step-by-step approach to applied research. It includes an excellent description of sources of research problems in applied settings.

Cozby, P. C. (1981). *Methods in behavioral research* (2nd ed.). Palo Alto, Calif.: Mayfield. Cozby's easy-to-read general text on behavioral research methods includes a section on locating and stating research problems.

Leedy, P. D. (1980). *Practical research: Planning and design* (2nd ed.). New York: Macmillan. This practical guide to research includes a useful section on problem statements as well as exercises designed to help you write effective research problems.

REFERENCES

Brenner, M. N. (1974). *Mini-study kit: A programmed guide in strategies and methods of research in social services.* Madison, Wis.: University of Wisconsin-Extension, Center for Social Service.

Committee on International Collaboration. (1972). International research and education in social gerontology; goals and strategies. *The Gerontologist,* 12 (1:2).

Committee on Research and Development Goals in Social Gerontology. (1969). The status of research in applied social gerontology. *The Gerontologist,* **9** (4:2).

Committee on Research and Development Goals in Social Gerontology. (1971*a*). Research proposals in applied social gerontology: Second report. *The Gerontologist,* **11** (1:2).

Committee on Research and Development Goals in Social Gerontology. (1971*b*). Research designs and proposals in applied social gerontology: Third report. *The Gerontologist,* **11** (4:2).

Committee on Research and Development. (1977). *Evaluative research on social programs for the elderly.* Washington, D.C.: U.S. Government Printing Office.

Cozby, P. C. (1981). *Methods in behavioral research* (2nd ed.). Palo Alto, Calif.: Mayfield.

Institute for Program Evaluation. (1983). *Medicaid and nursing home care: Cost increases and the need for services are creating problems for the States and the elderly.* Washington, D.C.: U.S. General Accounting Office.

Joint Legislative Audit and Review Commission. (1979). *Deinstitutionalization and community services* (special report). Richmond, Va.: Author.

Kastenbaum, R. (1979). Beer, wine and mutual gratification in the gerontopolis. In D. P. Kent, R. Kastenbaum and S. Sherwood (Eds.), *Research planning and action for the elderly: The power and potential of social science.* New York: Human Sciences Press.

Leedy, P. D. (1980). *Practical research: Planning and design* (2nd ed.). New York: Macmillian.

Patton, M. Q. (1978). *Utilization-focused evaluation.* Beverly Hills: Sage.

Rothman, J. (1980). *Social R & D: Research and development in the human services.* Englewood Cliffs, N.J.: Prentice-Hall.

Simon, J. L. (1978). *Basic research methods in social sciences: The art of empirical evaluation* (2nd ed.). New York: Random House.

3

Designing a Research Project

Rosemary Blieszner and Laurie Shea

PROBLEMS TO BE SOLVED

Is my purpose to describe people or situations, or is it either to explain cause
  and effect relationships or to predict relationships among variables—or is it
  more than one of these options?
Do I need to gather data on one occasion or at several points in time?
What technique will best enable me to observe or control or manipulate the
  relevant variables?

Once you have delimited the topic of your study, developed and refined your
research problem statement, and specified the questions to be answered or
hypotheses to be tested, the stage is set for selecting your research strategy.
The design of your research project depends on the comparisons you wish to
make and/or the relationships among variables you wish to assess. You must
consider two aspects of your problem in choosing the best design: whether
you are investigating an existing state of affairs or the effects of an experimental procedure, and the number of occasions on which you need to
collect data.

Before discussing these two issues, it is important to note that the design
of the research influences the validity of its conclusions. Validity is enhanced
by close attention to two general areas of concern—internal and external
validity. Internal validity reflects your degree of certainty that the results of
your research can be explained in terms of the variables you examined and
not others. External validity reflects the extent to which you can generalize
the results of your research from a small sample of people or programs to a
larger group, because assessment of every single person or situation involved

Table 3-1. Potential Threats to Research Validity

Extraneous Variable	Definition
	Internal Validity
History	Events occurring between the first and second measurement
Maturation	Processes occuring as a function of the passage of time per se
Testing	Effects of multiple measurements
Instrumentation	Changes in measuring instrument, observers, or scorers
Statistical Regression	Persons chosen because they are very high or low on a variable will tend to score closer to the mean on the next measurement
Selection	Procedures used to choose participants can result in many extraneous differences among groups
Mortality	Differential loss of respondents from comparison groups
	External Validity
Persons	Associations among variables observed with one group may not apply to others
Setting	Associations among variables observed in one setting may not be found elsewhere
Treatment	Associations among variables based on one set of conditions may not hold true under other circumstances
Measures	Different instruments purportedly measuring the same construct may yield different results
Historical Time	Associations among variables observed at one time may not be found in other periods

Source: After Campbell and Stanley (1966).

in your research problem is usually impractical. Table 3-1 defines various threats to the validity of research. Campbell and Stanley (1966) provide a detailed analysis of research designs and the extent to which each one controls threats to validity.

Internal validity refers to the extent to which the independent variables (those that the researcher controls or manipulates) reflect what the researcher intends them to reflect and not something else. Internal validity is threatened when there are plausible alternative interpretations of the results other than the presumed cause of the outcome. Consider the situation in which a rehabilitation therapist decides to test the effects of a music therapy program on reducing anxiety among patients in an intensive care unit (ICU). The therapist measures the anxiety level of all newly admitted ICU patients on Monday, plays soothing music for them all week, and finds on Friday that these ICU patients are much more relaxed than they had been on Monday. Is the therapist justified in concluding that music therapy reduces anxiety and thus should be used all the time in the ICU? Or are there variables other than the music that might account for the decline in anxiety? The internal validity in this design is jeopardized because the therapist failed to take into account other factors (e.g., the patients' improved health and increased familiarity with the ICU procedures) that may have had more to do with a decline in anxiety than the music per se. There is no way to rule out the confounding influences in this design, but the therapist could change the design to increase internal validity. For instance, the therapist could identify patients of equivalent illness, present music to a randomly selected half of the group and white noise to the other half, make sure patients in both groups had the same number of visitors and similar nursing care, then compare the anxiety levels of the two groups at the end of the week. This altered design would have higher internal validity because the random assignment presumably equates both groups on unobserved variables at the beginning of the study, and both groups received an aural intervention.

External validity refers to the extent to which the findings of a given study can be generalized to other people, settings, treatments, or measurements. High external validity exists when the relationships among variables remain consistent across differing situations. In the case of music therapy for ICU patients, attention to external validity would necessitate checking the effects of music therapy on patients with medical conditions of varying severity, at different times of the year, in hospitals with various types of ICU procedures, in the presence and absence of ICU visitors, and so forth. Although external validity will not necessarily be completely demonstrated in one investigation, it can be confirmed by a series of studies that focus on the same topic but systematically vary key factors.

Procedures that enhance internal validity, such as applying controls to eliminate all plausible explanations but the one in which you are interested, may threaten external validity because your controls might lead to examination of a specialized sample of people or situations that are not representative of the population from which they were drawn. On the other hand, procedures that enhance external validity, such as studying a wide variety of people or situations as they would naturally occur in the larger environment, may threaten internal validity because such procedures might admit a large number of rival explanations into the results. The challenge for researchers is to select a research design that balances concern for both types of validity. Selection of the proper design will be easier if you answer the following two questions with your research problem in mind.

DESCRIPTION VERSUS EXPLANATION

The first question concerns the nature of your research problem. Are you planning to gather descriptive information about a group of people or a certain situation? For instance, perhaps you are trying to decide whether the participants at the local senior citizens center are satisfied with the types of activities available, or whether they would like some new programs. You need descriptive data on their opinions. A hearing aid manufacturer who wants to know whether there are any age or gender differences in hearing acuity, in order to plan an effective marketing strategy, needs descriptive data. Answers to the questions *who, how many, what, when,* and *where* usually provide descriptive information. Descriptive studies may also be called correlational studies when they involve the examination of associations among key variables. For instance, a researcher might collect opinions on a new type of pension plan from a wide variety of workers, divide the responses into groups according to age or gender or income categories, and then determine whether there are meaningful differences of opinion among groups represented by the various categories. Surveys and qualitative techniques are research designs that are well suited to these types of inquiry.

On the other hand, some research problems involve the determination of cause-and-effect sequences or the prediction of future events based on current data. Will a senior citizen fare discount increase bus ridership sufficiently to offset the loss of revenue due to the reduced fare? Why do older men tend to show greater hearing loss than older women? Which caretakers of Alzheimer's disease patients are likely to "burn out" and which will cope satisfactorily? Many of the questions that deal with explanation of observed facts begin with *why.* Questions that deal with prediction ask, "What would happen if . . . . ?" or, "Given these known characteristics of people in this situation, can we anticipate how similar people will react in other, similar situations?" Different research designs (experiments and quasi-experiments) are required to address these problems.

CROSS-SECTIONAL VERSUS LONGITUDINAL RESEARCH

Another decision that you must make concerns the number of occasions on which you will need to gather data. Some questions can be answered with information based on one contact with each person in the sample. Other problems will require you to collect data from each person, or to observe the situation, more than one time. Either descriptive or explanatory questions could be addressed as cross-sectional (one time of measurement) or longitudinal (multiple times of measurement) studies, depending on the topic. For instance, identifying the current physical health status of elderly users of the county health clinic during the fourth quarter of this fiscal year, to prepare a report for the county supervisors' annual meeting, is a descriptive task requiring data from one point in time. However, showing the amount of stability, improvement, or decline in health status of such clients from the beginning of the year until the end is a descriptive task requiring data from multiple points in time. Determining the set of instructions that is most effective in motivating the patients from the clinic to follow their medication regimens could be accomplished by experimenting with different forms of instructions in test groups that meet once. Or, a better answer might be obtained by recording the effectiveness of each type of instruction by measuring patient compliance over a longer period. Estimating community need for a Foster Grandparent program may be accomplished with a one-time survey; assessing the program's effectiveness would require periodic evaluations over months or years.

A research problem that focuses on differences between or among individuals, groups, programs, or situations can probably be answered via cross-sectional techniques. Any research question that asks about stability or change over time in individual characteristics or behavior, or in programs or situations, requires a longitudinal design or at least an approximation to one.

Cross-sectional Designs

In cross-sectional studies, the researcher gathers data from one or more groups of people or types of situations on one occasion. Such data are useful for describing characteristics of people or situations as they are at present, and for comparing groups or situations on variables of interest. Cross-sectional studies are very efficient in terms of time and money. Their internal validity is not threatened by the effects of history or testing, because all participants are contacted only once and at the same time. However, one must guard against selection effects that would render the research sample unrepresentative of the population as a whole. The effects of maturation and instrumentation are of special concern when comparisons are being made among diverse age groups, because life experiences, and not the variables being measured, may account for age group differences.

There are limits to the researcher's ability to interpret and generalize the results of cross-sectional studies. If there are differences among the groups, the reasons for the differences may not be clear. A common type of cross-sectional study in gerontology involves comparing responses of individuals from various age groups. Suppose the results show that younger adults hold one viewpoint and older adults hold another. It would be incorrect to conclude that the observed differences in the two age groups are due to the aging process alone because many other extraneous, unexamined variables may have influenced the results. Because you do not know how the older persons would have responded when they were younger, you cannot determine whether they changed over the years, or simply retained their original viewpoint. Also, the results may be applicable only to the particular group of people or situations that the researcher investigated.

Longitudinal Designs

Longitudinal studies involve collecting data on multiple occasions. They are necessary if the research goal is to determine whether people or programs change over time. Whereas a cross-sectional design involves comparing different groups on one occasion, a simple longitudinal design involves comparing the same people on several occasions. Because of this repeated measurement, longitudinal studies are susceptible to the internal validity threats of testing and statistical regression. They are also threatened by history and maturation, because extraneous events occurring between data collection points may influence the study results in unknown ways. Mortality is a threat to longitudinal studies if participant dropout leads to nonrepresentative or unequivalent groups.

A design modification can improve the internal validity of longitudinal studies. The researcher randomly divides a sample of participants into two groups, to control selection effects. One group provides information today, and both groups provide information in the future. A comparison of time 1 and time 2 data from the first group provides evidence concerning change over time within that group. Also, because the second group is tested only once, the researcher can compare data from the first assessment of both groups to look at change uncontaminated by testing effects. This design is an improvement over simple cross-sectional and simple longitudinal approaches, but the effects of history remain uncontrolled.

It is obvious that longitudinal designs are more time consuming than is the cross-sectional strategy, and the time required to observe human aging as it occurs impedes study of individual developmental processes. However, applied researchers should recognize that many programs operate for months or years, not decades, and longitudinal study of their effects is not only quite possible but can be much more revealing than a cross-sectional assessment. Individuals who have participated in a project for a while may have quite different reactions to it than recent joiners.

Moreover, gerontology researchers can consider using approximations to longitudinal change instead of conducting a study over a long period of time (Baltes and Goulet, 1971). When they studied changes in perceptions of salient personality dimensions, Ryff and Heincke (1983) randomly assigned young, middle-aged, and old adults to one of three conditions: group one young adults rated statements about personality according to their current views, and middle-aged and older adults responded retrospectively as they saw themselves at age 25; group two answered for the middle years, prospectively if young, currently if middle-aged, and retrospectively if old; and group three responded as an old person would, prospectively if young or middle-aged, and currently if old. By using respondents from all age groups and randomly assigning them to focus on different life stages, the researchers were able to simulate perceived longitudinal change. They gained valuable information that was not available from a cross-sectional study. Similar procedures could be used to answer questions about changes in community programs, the effects of new interventions, and other applied problems.

Sequential Designs

Simple cross-sectional and longitudinal designs can be strengthened considerably by employing sequential strategies. Combining a series of cross-sectional and longitudinal studies into one design takes only a little longer than a simple longitudinal study to complete, yet provides much better control over internal validity.

Sequential strategies involve identifying a number of cohorts (people born in the same year or experiencing an event at the same time) and measuring them on the variables of interest on several occasions. Suppose you want to study adjustment to widowhood and decide to focus on women widowed one year or less (W0) and women widowed at least two years (W2). In 1980 you use death records to identify 50 women whose husbands died in 1979, and 50 who lost their husbands in 1978. You interview all these women in 1980 and compare their data for a simple cross-sectional analysis. To continue the sequence, you interview these women again in 1982 when they are W2s and W4s. Now you can make another cross-sectional comparison (this time between women widowed two years and women widowed four years) and also two longitudinal comparisons of changes in adjustment between years one and two of widowhood and between years two and four of widowhood. To round out the design and control for the effects of history (What if a new widow support group was introduced in your community in 1981? Would it affect adjustment?) you should also bring 50 new W0s and 50 new W2s into the sample in 1982. Then you could assess the effects of being a W0 in 1980 as opposed to being a W0 in 1982, and similarly compare the two cohorts of W2s. You would repeat this entire process of reassessing the original participants and adding new groups of similar participants at each time of measurement.

NONEXPERIMENTAL VERSUS EXPERIMENTAL TECHNIQUES

The type of data your research problem requires and the number of data collection occasions determine the appropriate design for your study. Research designs can be categorized as nonexperimental or experimental. If you need to observe and record existing, naturally occurring behaviors, attitudes, or situations, you will choose one of the nonexperimental techniques that ascertain the state of affairs as they are right now. A survey of employers in the region to determine the percentage who favor and would pay for preretirement training programs for their employees falls into this category. So does a review of archival records from the weather bureau and the local hospitals to figure out whether there is a meaningful connection between the combination of high temperature and humidity, and the incidence of heart attacks among elderly persons.

However, some research problems necessitate the control or manipulation of key variables by the researcher. For instance, suppose you want to identify effective instructional techniques for a health course for senior citizens. You gather a group of people for a course, teach the course using, say, the lecture method, and try to evaluate your success in terms of how well the participants score on a final exam. With this approach, you can see if the final scores are high or low, but you still do not know how well the lecture method works or how it compares to independent study, group discussion techniques, or other instructional methods. Maybe one of those other teaching techniques would be even better, but you cannot be sure unless you conduct an experiment. Or, consider the situation of a nursing home administrator who wants to know whether new types of social activities would be a cost-effective way of increasing resident morale. An experimental procedure could be used to estimate, from a small group of residents, the responses of the majority who live there. By testing the ideas on a carefully chosen group before implementing a full program, the administrator could conserve resources, avoid costly mistakes, and make a better planning decision.

The following sections present information about the major nonexperimental and experimental research designs to help you decide which one to employ. Once you have selected the best research strategy for your particular problem, you may wish to refer to references from the Suggested Readings list to gain additional details about the chosen design.

NONEXPERIMENTAL DESIGNS

Survey Research Designs

The purpose of surveys is to determine the incidence and distribution of the variables under study and to identify associations among the variables. National opinion polls covering a variety of topics on aging, such as the polls conducted by Lou Harris and Associates (National Council on the Aging, 1975, 1981) are examples of large-scale surveys. Many other research questions lend themselves to survey designs. Shuttlesworth, Rubin, and Duffy (1982) used written questionnaires to study family members' versus nursing home administrators' expectations about who was responsible for performing essential tasks in the nursing home care process. Waxman and Carner (1984) used interviews to investigate physicians' ability to recognize, diagnose, and treat mental disorders in elderly patients.

Static Group Comparison Design. In this type of study, the researcher examines the variables of interest in different naturally occurring groups—women versus men, people of different ages or races or income levels, and so on. As discussed previously in relation to cross-sectional designs, the results of this type of survey are difficult to interpret because there are unmeasured variables that could also account for any observed differences among the groups.

Panel Design. In panel designs the investigator surveys the individuals involved in the study on multiple occasions. Thus it is possible to examine trends within the groups. A well-known research program using this design is the Panel Study of Income Dynamics (Morgan and Duncan, 1974–1983). Over 5,000 families were interviewed each year on topics such as employment, income, family size and structure, housework, leisure activities, social interaction, and personality. These data are available to researchers who wish to make longitudinal analyses of changes associated with aging, and a number of variables are suitable for applied gerontology research projects.

Validity Issues in Survey Research. In order to control internal validity in surveys, the researcher must be careful to collect sufficient demographic and other information so as to be able to compare groups of respondents on variables that may affect the findings. Then statistical procedures can be used to rule out various alternative explanations of the results. High external validity can be achieved if the researcher is careful to select a representative sample of people, records, or situations to study.

Qualitative Research Designs

Some questions in applied research cannot be answered adequately by experimental, quasi-experimental, or survey methods. When the purpose of your research is to describe existing behaviors or attitudes, to identify the needs of a specific group of older adults as they themselves define them, or to evaluate the impact of a program from the perspective of groups holding different criteria for judgment (e.g., hospital patients, doctors, and administrators), qualitative designs are appropriate.

Likewise, when the behavior you wish to understand cannot be investigated satisfactorily outside of its natural setting or time frame, you must study it when and where it occurs. If, for example, you are evaluating the effectiveness of a recreation program in a senior center, you may need to attend program sessions, observe behavior before, during, and after sessions, and consider program impact from the vantage point of administrators, instructors, and clients.

In addition, sometimes appropriate survey questions cannot be formulated until some exploratory research is conducted because there is insufficient evidence to provide theoretical guidance for the researcher. If your goal is to develop a program to aid older adults in adjusting to life in a retirement community, your first step must be to observe and understand the process of adjustment as it now occurs, and then to target specific areas that might be improved. Or, suppose you are interested in investigating how caring for an Alzheimer's patient affects the family, a subject that previously has not been studied in depth. You will probably need to begin by talking to several such families about their experiences in a nonstructured way in order to let them help you understand how they perceive their situation. The answers they give and the comments they make can then help you to formulate appropriate questions to use in the next phase of your study.

Because qualitative methods are concerned with the *meanings* of action and events to the people studied, they are particularly useful in applied situations where the goal is to introduce innovations with maximum effect and minimum disruption. Qualitative methods may be used alone, in combination with other designs, or as a preliminary step in developing surveys or questionnaires.

Structured Observation.   The purpose of structured observation is to document specific behaviors as they occur. You may be interested in whether or not certain behaviors occur, how often they occur, how long they last, or under what conditions they begin and end. In any case, the behaviors you will observe and record are carefully defined before beginning the study. This methodology is often employed to solve applied problems in natural settings and usually is conducted for the benefit of individuals in that setting. For example, by observing food consumption and wastage in a hot meals program, a researcher could suggest menu changes that would enhance both enjoyment and nutrition.

Participant Observation.   A second type of qualitative research is participant observation, in which you actually enter the field or situation under investigation and experience it as the subjects of your study do. All behavior occurring in the setting is of interest. Data include both detailed field notes, in which you record behavior objectively and precisely, and journal entries, in which you make interpretations and record personal reactions to those observations. Such research is time consuming but exceptionally rich in detail.

Hochschild (1978) describes a participant observation study in *The Unexpected Community*. Hochschild, a sociologist, worked for three years as a recreation director at a senior citizen housing project occupied by 43 older adults, most of them widows. Upon discovering that asking questions was considered impolite, she began to observe behavior in the recreation room. Gradually she took part in recreational activities, drove residents to doctors, church, and shopping, and by sharing their lives came to understand things about their experience that could never have been discovered by survey research or an experimental design. Expecting to find isolation and loneliness, she instead found a community rich in mutual aid, sharing, and resources.

Hand's (1983) study of shopping-bag women in New York City likewise provides unique insight into the subjective experience of a group of women probably inaccessible to a survey researcher. Her report makes it clear that understanding what property, isolation, and public space mean to these women is an essential prerequisite to interventions aimed at improving their situation.

Ethnographic Interviews. Participant observation research will probably include ethnographic interviews, aimed at understanding what people know or believe about a particular subject. These interviews may be structured (researcher asks specific questions) or unstructured (researcher asks open-ended questions and lets the answer to one form the basis for the next). Ethnographic interviews are useful when it is important to know what people are thinking and feeling in addition to, or rather than, what they are doing. For example, research on relationships among older adults has generally asked questions about how many friends people have, how often they are seen, and so on. Because we know little about the quality and meaning of different relationships in their lives, ethnographic interviews might be used to explore this topic. Kivnick's (1982) research on grandparenthood illustrates the unstructured approach. Participants were invited to comment on the changing meaning of grandparenthood as they experienced it over their life course, first as grandchildren, then as parents between children and grandparents, and finally as grandparents themselves.

Validity Issues in Qualitative Research. Because qualitative methods consider the world view of their subjects, they are strong in internal validity. The data are credible and true. The major threats to internal validity are due to the possibility of observer and subject bias, and inadequate sampling of behavior, events, or subjects. Although your goal in doing qualitative research is probably specific to the setting in which you are working, you should remember that your results may not be applicable to any other situation. That is, they probably do not have high external validity.

Even though a researcher using qualitative methods must be careful to document and record the process of the investigation, another researcher conducting the same study in the same place would probably not proceed in precisely the same manner and gather exactly the same data. Because the researcher is actually involved in the research process, some issues of accuracy and consistency in qualitative research result in weak reliability. However, combining quantitative and qualitative strategies to investigate a research problem can enhance the strengths and minimize the weaknesses of both types of designs.

EXPERIMENTAL DESIGNS

True Experiments

The purpose of experiments is to determine the effects of manipulating independent, or treatment, variables on dependent, or outcome, variables. In true experiments, the researcher randomly assigns participants to treatment conditions. After the participants experience the assigned treatment, the researcher measures the effects of each treatment in terms of the dependent variables. Often, one of the comparison groups is a control group that receives either no treatment or an experience other than the experimental treatment. Because treatments always occur prior to their effects, it is possible to establish cause-and-effect sequences with experimental designs. It is also possible to predict responses of a population of individuals based on sample results.

Between-Subjects Design.   One type of experiment involves comparing the treatment effects for two or more groups that differ on the independent variable(s) under study. In the previous discussion of internal validity, the improved design for the music therapy problem represented a between-subjects experimental approach. Another example mentioned was the identification of effective instructional techniques for an adult health course. Because testing the effects of just one teaching method reveals nothing about the usefulness of others, a better decision about which method to use on a large scale could be gained by employing an experimental strategy with a small group. Such an approach would involve randomly assigning course enrollees to one of several classes, each taught by a different technique. The same teacher should lead each group, using the same content, to keep the extraneous factors of teacher personality and content difficulty under control. Another extraneous factor could be controlled by pretesting each group prior to the first lesson, to be sure that all had equivalent health knowledge at the beginning of the course. These procedures should ensure that any group differences on health knowledge observed at the posttest could be attributed to the teaching techniques.

A study by Banziger and Roush (1983) illustrates the experimental approach to evaluating an intervention program. The researchers wanted to find a way to increase the ability of nursing home residents to assume responsibility for their own well-being. They randomly assigned alert residents to one of three conditions: responsibility group, dependency group, and control group. The nursing home administrator met with the responsibility group and reminded them of all they could do to take charge of their own lives and solve their own problems. The administrator then asked each person to decide about taking responsibility for monitoring the seed level of a bird feeder placed outside the resident's window. The administrator also met with the dependency group, but the message to them emphasized how much the staff could do for the residents, and they were not offered the chance to have a bird feeder. The researchers compared posttest measures of the residents' psychological well-being with pretest assessments to check the effects of the responsibility-inducing intervention on happiness and activity levels.

Within-Subjects Design.   This type of experiment is also called a repeated-measures design because the participants are assessed several times. This design is more efficient than the between-subjects procedure because participants serve as their own comparisons. Suppose pharmaceutical researchers are developing a drug to aid older adults with balance problems. They begin the test of a new formula by identifying a suitable group of patients and recording their rates of dizziness and number of falls for several weeks to establish a baseline level of equilibrium for each person. Then the researchers give all of the patients the drug for a week and a placebo for a week. To eliminate any order effects, a random half of the patients receives the drug first while the other half receives the placebo first. Finally, the researchers record episodes of dizziness and number of falls during the experimental period. They compare the baseline (pretest) equilibrium data with the equilibrium data collected under the drug and placebo conditions in order to evaluate the effectiveness of the drug.

Validity Issues in Experiments.   Experimental designs have high internal validity because random assignment assures that members of each treatment group are equivalent on unmeasured variables. Plausible rival explanations of the experimental results are eliminated by random assignment. On the other hand, because experiments require precisely controlled techniques, often administered under unnatural laboratorylike conditions, their external validity tends to be low. They may not provide any useful descriptive data if the experimental sample is not representative of any larger group.

Quasi-Experimental Designs

All of the true experiments just discussed involved manipulation of the variables under study, within very controlled circumstances. However, variables such as age cannot be manipulated, and research problems such as the effects of a community program cannot be explored under laboratorylike conditions. Quasi-experiments are research designs that assess cause-and-effect relationships without randomly assigning participants to treatment and control comparison groups. Campbell (1969) presented examples of quasi-experimental designs for evaluating program effectiveness, and Schaie (1977) discussed quasi-experimental research in aging.

Cornelius (1984) used a quasi-experimental design to study perceived familiarity and difficulty of intelligence tests. The researcher was interested in determining if young, middle-aged, and old adults differed in their ratings of various tests because this information has implications for the types of tests used to assess intellectual abilities associated with aging. Participants could not be randomly assigned to one of the three age groups, but some tests were age-sensitive (tests of abilities showing decline with age) and others were age-irrelevant (tests of abilities showing no change with age). The participants completed each of the various tests and then rated them on familiarity, difficulty, effort required, and adequacy of the time alloted for the test. The researcher compared the ratings across age groups and test types to determine the effects of test characteristics on performance.

Time Series Design.   This longitudinal strategy involves making multiple observations on one or more groups of people, both before and after an intervention or treatment is introduced. The observation-treatment sequence may be repeated several times. This procedure enables the researcher to examine trends in the data before treatment, at the time of the intervention, and after treatment. For example, archival data have been used to assess rates of poverty among older adults before and after the enactment of the Older Americans Act and its various amendments.

Regression-Discontinuity Design.   This cross-sectional technique involves comparing many groups on one occasion instead of comparing the same group over a longer period of time. The researcher identifies a number of relevant groups, some of which receive the treatment and some of which do not. Groups not receiving treatment provide data on differences among naturally occurring groups, while groups receiving treatment supply information about the effects of the intervention. For example, some of the programs developed as a result of the Older Americans Act are targeted to low-income individuals; persons with higher incomes are ineligible for the benefits. Using a job training program for poverty-level older adults as an example, with a regression-discontinuity design it would be possible to compare the employment success of low-income program participants with that of higher-income groups who must seek employment without such assistance.

Pretest-Posttest Nonequivalent Control Group Design.   In this research strategy, there are two naturally occurring groups, one of which receives an intervention. The researcher assesses both groups before and after the time of the intervention, but there is no random assignment to treatment and control conditions. Perhaps you learn that a senior citizen center director has found a dentist willing to do dental screenings at the center. The senior center in a nearby town has not yet introduced this service. This situation would provide you the opportunity to monitor dental health, frequency of dentist visits, and frequency of selected dental procedures among older adults who do and do not receive preliminary screenings.

Validity Issues in Quasi-Experimental Designs. Based on the discussion of the validity of experimental designs, you might be assuming that a potential threat to internal validity in quasi-experiments is the possibility of selection bias. In a sense this assumption is true, but another way to look at the nonrandom sorting of people into the groups under study in quasi-experiments is to consider that the groups actually represent the naturally occurring distribution of people into phenomena within society. Moreover, quasi-experiments have much higher external validity than true experiments. Thus, they represent a compromise between true experiments and nonexperimental designs, and are particularly useful for many of the applied research problems in gerontology.

DESIGNING NEEDS ASSESSMENTS AND PROGRAM EVALUATIONS

A typical applied research problem in gerontology involves identifying the needs of persons or agencies as a basis for planning services and programs. Suppose you are invited to serve on an ad hoc committee of persons interested in hospice care for the terminally ill. Does your community need a hospice? Would doctors, nurses, clergy, and lay people support the development and operation of a hospice program? A needs assessment in this case would take a variety of forms: surveying county or regional health records to determine the number of deaths due to cancer and other terminal illnesses; interviewing medical personnel, counselors, clergy, and others about their perceptions of the need for hospice and their interest in working with a hospice program; and polling a representative sample of business leaders and community members to determine if there is sufficient financial and volunteer support to establish and maintain a strong hospice program. Secondary data analysis, qualitative interview methods, and surveys are examples of research designs for needs assessments. Typically they are conducted at one point in time, but a needs assessment could be designed as a longitudinal study to determine whether particular needs change.

Community programs are designed to solve problems and meet peoples' needs. An important applied research issue involves determining whether existing programs are meeting their stated objectives, are benefiting and not harming people, are cost effective, and so forth. Another way of looking at this issue is to ask, "What would happen if we did not have this program in place?" Evaluation research can be used to assess the effectiveness of any intervention and to improve its quality. The information that is gathered should be used to make decisions about whether or not to continue the program, how to take care of problems within the program, how to improve it, and so on. Experimental and quasi-experimental designs, and comparative studies of several programs, are appropriate research strategies for evaluation studies.

An evaluation study could be conducted one time, or it could be continued over a longer period. A *formative* evaluation is conducted as a program is being developed, a course is being taught, or other process is occurring. It provides feedback that the developers can use to improve the program as they build it. A *summative* evaluation is conducted after a program has been operating for a period of time or at the end of an activity. It provides information about the success of the program and the reactions of participants. A combination of both formative and summative forms of evaluation will provide the most useful information for deciding such issues as whether to change a program, to replicate it elsewhere, or to reallocate funding among its components.

SUMMARY

This chapter presents an overview of research designs available to address your research question. Table 3-2 summarizes the relationship between research problems and designs. If your purpose is to describe people, behavior, programs, or situations, surveys or qualitative designs are appropriate. If you are interested in determining cause-and-effect relationships or predicting population behavior based on sample data, experimental or quasi-experimental designs are more suitable.

You must also decide whether you will gather data once or several times. If data collection on one occasion will answer your research question, cross-sectional designs to compare groups are adequate. If you need to follow behavior or program changes (or stability) across time, longitudinal research is necessary. Cross-sectional and longitudinal procedures can be combined in sequential designs to provide more descriptive and explanatory power in your research.

A third consideration is whether it is necessary to control or manipulate variables. If you simply wish to record behavior as it exists, you will choose a nonexperimental design. Manipulation of variables requires an experimental design conducted under controlled conditions. Assessing the effects of a social intervention would be accomplished best by a quasi-experimental design carried out in the actual setting of the intervention.

Table 3-2. Selecting a Research Design

Examples of Research Purposes	Method	Research Design
To learn what people think	Ask them	Survey: Questionnaire Interview
To find out how people behave in public	Watch them	Observation
To obtain reliable information under controlled conditions	Test people in a laboratory-type setting	Experiment
To assess the effects of a social intervention	Conduct a field experiment	Quasi-Experiment

Source: After Sommer and Sommer, 1980.

Each of the research designs discussed in this chapter has unique strengths and weaknesses and is best suited to answering certain types of questions. When the purpose of your research is multidimensional, combining methods in order to strengthen the internal and external validity of your research can be beneficial. For instance, observations of behavior could be enhanced by adding interviews in which the participants can explain their own behavior. In-depth interviews of a portion of respondents from a large-scale survey might reveal factors useful in interpreting the results. Careful attention to planning the research prior to gathering data will result in information that can be clearly understood and usefully applied to similar groups or situations.

SUGGESTED READINGS

Huck, S. W., Cormier, W. H., and Bounds, W. G., Jr. (1974). *Reading statistics and research.* New York: Harper and Row. This book teaches how to read, understand, and critically evaluate research reports. It includes discussion of good and poor research designs, and information about statistical procedures and hypothesis testing.

Smith, H. W. (1981). *Strategies of social research.* Englewood Cliffs, N.J.: Prentice-Hall. This book covers the topics of research design, measurement, data analysis, and ethical issues in depth.

Spradley, J. P. (1980). *Participant observation.* New York: Holt, Rinehart and Winston. This book presents a complete system for designing, conducting, analyzing, and reporting the results of qualitative research. It includes a discussion of the theoretical underpinnings of participant observation techniques.

Weiss, C. H. (1972). *Evaluation research: Methods of assessing program effectiveness.* Englewood Cliffs, N.J.: Prentice-Hall. This book deals with the application of research methods to the evaluation of social programs in an action context. It includes analysis of the real-life problems and issues that confront researchers who attempt to evaluate programs.

REFERENCES

Baltes, P. B., and Goulet, L. R. (1971). Exploration of developmental variables by manipulation and simulation of age differences in behavior. *Human Development,* **14,** 149-170.

Banziger, G., and Roush, S. (1983). Nursing homes for the birds: A control-relevant intervention with bird feeders. *The Gerontologist,* **23,** 527-531.

Campbell, D. T. (1969). Reforms as experiments. *American Psychologist,* **24,** 409-429.

Campbell, D. T., and Stanley, J. C. (1966). *Experimental and quasi-experimental designs for research.* Chicago: Rand McNally College Publishing Company.

Cornelius, S. W. (1984). Classic patterns of intellectual aging: Test familiarity, difficulty, and performance. *Journal of Gerontology,* **39,** 201-206.

Hand, J. (1983). Shopping-bag women: Aging deviants in the city. In E. W. Markson (Ed.), *Older women: Issues and prospects.* Lexington, Mass.: Lexington Books.

Hochschild, A. R. (1978). *The unexpected community.* Berkeley: University of California Press.

Kivnick, V. (1982). *The meaning of grandparenthood.* Ann Arbor: University of Michigan Research Press.

Morgan, J. N., and Duncan, G. J. (Eds.). (1974-1983). *Five thousand American families: Patterns of economic progress,* vols. 1-10. Ann Arbor: University of Michigan, Institute for Social Research.

National Council on the Aging. (1975). *The myth and reality of aging in America.* Washington, D.C.: Author.

National Council on the Aging. (1981). *Aging in the eighties: America in transition.* Washington, D.C.: Author.

Ryff, C. D., and Heincke, S. G. (1983). Subjective organization of personality in adulthood and aging. *Journal of Personality and Social Psychology,* **44,** 807-816.

Schaie, K. W. (1977). Quasi-experimental research designs in the psychology of aging. In J. E. Birren and K. W. Schaie (Eds.), *Handbook of the psychology of aging.* New York: Van Nostrand Reinhold.

Shuttlesworth, G. E., Rubin, A., and Duffy, M. (1982). Families versus institutions: Incongruent role expectations in the nursing home. *The Gerontologist,* **22,** 200-208.

Sommer, R., and Sommer, B. B. (1980). *A practical guide to behavioral research.* New York: Oxford University Press.

Waxman, H. M., and Carner, E. A. (1984). Physicians' recognition, diagnosis, and treatment of mental disorders in elderly medical patients. *The Gerontologist,* **24,** 593-597.

4

Selecting Measurement Strategies

Jean G. Romaniuk and William J. McAuley

PROBLEMS TO BE SOLVED

What variables will I study?
How will the variables I select be defined and measured?
How will I know if the measures I have selected are good estimates of what I am
    trying to assess?
Are the measures that I select really appropriate for my original purposes?
Should I develop my own measures or should I use existing measures?
How can I construct my own instrument?

Deciding what information to collect brings together several important concepts in research. Much of the discussion in this chapter will be related to what information will be collected, how it will be measured, and how much confidence can be placed in the adequacy of the information that is collected. In research terminology, these questions refer to issues regarding the selection of variables, operationalization of variables, and assessment of reliability and validity. In addition, we will describe where to find existing measures appropriate for gerontological research, and how to assess their usefulness for individual research purposes. This topic is important because applied gerontological researchers often find it difficult or too time consuming to construct, evaluate, and revise their own instruments. By the end of this discussion, we expect that you will be able to make key decisions about the variables to use in your research and how to best measure them.

INTRODUCTION TO MEASUREMENT

Measurement is the systematic observation of the characteristics of people, events, or objects according to a rule or scheme. In all cases, the characteristics or attributes of people or objects are being measured, not the people or objects themselves. Thus, we measure a person's height, or an individual's score on an exam, rather than measuring the person or object per se.

It is important to recognize that our actual measurements are often approximations of what we would really like to be able to measure. Such approximations are sometimes necessary because we are attempting to take discrete observations of something that is continuous in nature. Time, for example, can be measured in hours, minutes, seconds, or even milliseconds. Regardless of what level of specificity we might select, there will always be some imprecision because time could be divided into even finer units than those we have selected.

In addition, many measures are approximations in the sense that they do not assess the attribute directly. These types of measures are known as *proxies* because they "stand in" or "serve in place of" the attributes we want to know about. When using proxies, the presence or absence or quantity of the attribute is being inferred or measured indirectly. Morale is a good example here. Morale is a psychological state that we measure through such proxies as the responses to specific questions on an instrument. Morale is not assessed directly by the responses, but they give us an indication of what the morale of a person may be. The same argument also holds for many other measures, including scores on intelligence or achievement tests. Performance on a series of items is what we actually measure, although we expect (and hope) that the total score is an indirect observation of an individual's underlying ability.

The frequent necessity of approximate (rather than precise) measurements, particularly in applied gerontological research, should not deter you from carrying out measurements. Why? First, because very often, good approximations are sufficient for many purposes. Second, there are methods for evaluating the "goodness" of a measure in terms of its ability to estimate the attribute. Third, the judicious use, evaluation, and refinement of measures will, over time, lead to greater accuracy in our measures. If we were to wait until our measurement techniques were perfect, we would never get around to carrying out research.

IMPORTANCE OF MEASUREMENT

Careful attention to measurement is important for a number of reasons. First of all, because measurement allows you to make systematic observations of what is happening in a situation, you are likely to understand the situation far better than if you depended upon subjective evaluation alone. A good example of the power of this statement is illustrated in the area of personal finances. Often, individuals experience difficulty in managing their money because they do not know where it is being spent. When an accurate accounting of all expenses over a one- or two-month period is made, many people are surprised to find that their subjective feelings or speculations of spending habits are different from their actual spending patterns.

Second, decisions regarding measurement influence the way you will approach and solve all the other problems that arise in completing the research. Deciding what measures you will use to carry out your research is, therefore, a crucial step in the research process. If you carefully select good measures early in the planning phase, you will be more likely to conduct a better research project.

Third, information measured in a systematic fashion allows you to summarize the information more efficiently and is particularly helpful in understanding and interpreting the data collected. In addition, you are able to communicate this information to others in a more succinct, practical fashion, such as in the form of tables, charts, and graphs. As you will learn in chapter 10, potential consumers of research are far more likely to pay attention to the findings if they are presented in an interesting, succinct, interpretable, and useful form.

Finally, as we have stressed in previous chapters, applied research is research designed to have immediate, practical consequences. Usually, the outcome of the research is some sort of decision regarding a program or policy. As Thorndike and Hagen (1977) have pointed out, the more relevant and accurate the information, the better the decision in the long run. Measurement procedures and instruments provide an important set of tools for improving the information available for making decisions, both in terms of the research conclusions, and the eventual impact of these outcomes on policy or program change. However, measurement instruments only give you some of the facts. Researchers (decision makers) must use these facts within their appropriate real-world, political context to decide upon their interpretation and use. Thus, measurement instruments are not ends in themselves, but are merely means to the eventual end (i.e., analysis and interpretation) that can be accomplished only by the researcher, an important fact to keep in mind when reviewing any potential measure for consideration in a research project.

VARIABLES AND THE MEASUREMENT PROCESS

In conducting both basic and applied research, we are interested in describing or explaining variations in the characteristics or environments of people. If variation does not exist on some characteristic, there is probably little value in examining that particular trait. Variation, then, is the key to the meaning of the term *variable*. A variable is a characteristic of a person, event, or object that assumes different levels or values. Almost any characteristic of an individual you can name would probably fit the definition of a variable because it will vary among different people. Here are just a few examples: height, weight, age, sex, intellectual ability, creative ability, fear of snakes, favorite television program, number of brothers and sisters, number of teeth, number of close friends, resting heart rate, degree of life satisfaction, and ability to perform basic daily living tasks. An applied research project in aging may require the measurement of only a few or many different characteristics.

We can divide the types of variables we would consider measuring into seven basic categories—what a person's basic features are, what a person's social and physical environment includes, what a person's inner states and traits are, and what a person is able to do, can learn to do, likes to do, and typically does. This classification of variables could be used to assess the individual's physical, psychological, or social interaction or makeup. Of course, this classification is not unique to the older population, but any one of the categories of variables might be of interest to an applied researcher in the field of aging. Next we will briefly discuss three classes of variables (basic features, social and physical environment, and ability) that are often of concern to persons who carry out applied research in aging.

Basic Features

In the area of basic features of people, gerontologists are often interested in measuring the demographic characteristics of the older population. Sex, race, and marital status are examples of demographic variables used in gerontological research. Also, variables related to the physical health of older persons can be critical in the determination of policy or the evaluation of program benefits. Among the physical health variables that could be measured are temperature, heart rate, visual and auditory accuity, types and severities of circulatory problems, aerobic capacity, range of motion abilities, and so forth.

One of the most interesting variables related to an individual's basic features is age. This variable defines the population in many studies and policies related to the services for the "elderly." Age is normally measured as the length of time, in years, since the birth of an individual. Many misconceptions about the variable *age* should be borne in mind when using it as a variable. Most importantly, it should be clear that age itself does not cause anything. Many changes in the physical and social structure vary with age, but age in and of itself does not cause these things to happen. Age is merely an index for measuring time. There is also a great deal of variation among individuals of a given age. So, even as an index, age is not always the best measure, especially when it is used in reference to physical health.

One interesting topic in the measurement of age and health, which has recently been advanced, is the concept of biological age. An article by Borkan and Norris (1980) discusses the assessment of biological age using a profile of 24 physical parameters including forced expiratory volume, maximum breathing capacity, systolic and diastolic blood pressure, serum albumin, auditory threshold, hand grip strength, and others. These variables were combined to form a biological age composite index. Borkan and Norris were able to differentially predict survival rates for a large sample of older people who varied on this index. In some studies, a measure of functional or biological age may be useful as an adjunct to or substitute for chronological age.

Social and Physical Environment

Gerontologists are often interested in assessing the physical and social environments in which older people live, work, and recreate. Variables in this category might include physical/architectural measures, such as the type of dwelling unit, number of rooms, total square footage, number of bathrooms, amount and types of furniture, number of levels, number of separate units within the structure, number of entry and exit points, distance to services, and so forth. Powell Lawton, for example, has been a pioneer in assessing and describing the physical environment variables that are important in the design of special housing for older people (Lawton, 1970; Lawton, Brody, and Turner-Massey, 1978).

Measures of the social environment can also be important components of applied studies in gerontology. Rudolf Moos and his associates (Moos et al., 1977) have devised scales to measure the social environments of older persons, particularly congregate settings such as nursing homes, day care centers, and so forth. Specific dimensions in measuring the social atmosphere within these settings include support, spontaneity, autonomy, involvement, and various measures of orientation.

Another aspect of a person's social and physical environment, and one that is frequently the object of applied gerontological research, is attributes of programs and services. For example, a program evaluation of a service for older people may examine variables such as the costs of the service, the degree to which the objectives of the program are being met, the growth in the number of new clients being served, the methods used to select clients, or variations in cost-reimbursement policies. All these types of variables, plus others, relate to the organization and delivery of services.

Abilities

A wide range in the types of variables that measure ability and performance is found in the applied gerontological research literature. The specific measures used depend on the substantive topic of the research and the target population. One of the more general areas of ability assessment in the gerontological research is an individual's capacity to carry out the normal activities of daily living, or the crucial abilities that can influence whether an older person is able to remain in the home. Variables used to measure these important life-maintaining and life-enhancing functions include eating, continence, bathing, dressing and grooming, and so forth. Examples of how these variables are operationalized are provided in the Activities of Daily Living (ADL) scales that have been used in many different applied settings. The following ADL items, based upon interview questions, are taken from the Duke University Older Americans Resources and Services (OARS) questionnaire (Center for the Study of Aging and Human Development, 1978, pp. 169-171). The phrases in parentheses add further information that assists the respondent in understanding which category is appropriate.

1. *Can you use the telephone*

_____ without help, including looking up numbers and dialing?

_____ with some help (can answer phone or dial operator in an emergency, but need a special phone or help in getting the number or dialing)?

_____ or are you completely unable to use the telephone?

_____ Not answered

2. *Can you prepare your own meals*

_____ without help (plan and cook full means yourself)?

_____ with some help (can prepare some things but unable to cook full meals yourself)?

_____ or are you completely unable to prepare any meals?

_____ Not answered

3. *Can you dress and undress yourself*

_____ without help (able to pick out clothes, dress and undress yourself)?

_____ with some help?

_____ or are you completely unable to dress and undress yourself?

_____ Not answered

4. *Can you walk*

——— without help (except for a cane)?

——— with some help from a person or with use of a walker, crutches, or other aid?

——— or are you completely unable to walk?

——— Not answered

Researchers can also examine a variety of other abilities such as intelligence, creativity, and mechanical aptitude. Tests of basic mental ability are frequently used in applied gerontological research. For example, a brief measure of mental capacity is included in the first section of the OARS instrument. It helps to determine whether the respondent is competent to answer other sections of the questionnaire.

Selecting Variables

The foregoing discussion provides examples of the kinds of variables that might be used in applied gerontological research. However, your choice of variables will be guided by the research problem. Asking yourself what specific characteristics, events, or objects you need to know about, and what you need to know about them in order to address the research problem will help you identify the variables to include in your research.

OPERATIONALIZATION OF VARIABLES

Once the qualities or attributes of interest have been identified, a set of procedures must be specified that will make those attributes identifiable and measurable. *Operationalization* refers to the process of specifying the actual procedures that will produce indicators of some concept.

An example is perhaps the best way to understand how this important process of operationalization works. Suppose you are interested in assessing the general life satisfaction of a group of older persons who are attending a senior center in your area. In order to measure this variable, you must develop a strategy to assess an individual's life satisfaction. This strategy will be used to help detect different levels of life satisfaction among different people who attend the senior center. In order to do so, you decide to ask a question that can answered in one of two ways:

QUESTION: Are you currently satisfied with your life?

——— Yes

——— No

In addition, suppose that of the 120 people who attend the senior center 95 answer yes and 25 answer no. In this example, you have both operationalized and measured the variable of life satisfaction. Operationalization of the variable took place when you decided how you were going to measure life satisfaction. In the preceding example, the construction of the question with the two-option answer choice constituted an operational definition of the variable, life satisfaction. The measurement of the variable took place when you actually surveyed the individuals in the senior center and determined their responses to the question "Are you currently satisfied with your life?" The results of the measurement process were also analyzed by tabulating the total number of persons who answered each of the two choices.

Measurement of a variable often involves obtaining responses to more than one question. To extend the operational definition of life satisfaction, the following items might be presented to older people.

1. I am as happy now as when I was younger.

_____ Yes*

_____ No

2. Life is hard for me most of the time.

_____ Yes

_____ No*

3. Things keep getting worse as I get older.

_____ Yes

_____ No*

4. A person has to live for today and not worry about tomorrow.

_____ Yes*

_____ No

These questions are a few of the items in an actual morale scale (Lawton, 1972, pp. 152-153). In this case, the operational definition must include the specification of measurement procedures describing how you would use the responses from all four questions to determine overall life satisfaction. Therefore, in addition to developing the set of questions, you need to specify that the procedures for determining overall life satisfaction would include taking the sum of the positive answers (shown with an asterisk) to all four items. Scores could range from 0 to 4.

One final note on operational definitions is that the methods and procedures for obtaining measures of variables could come from a variety of sources. For example, you could survey the individual directly, either through a paper and pencil test or through face-to-face interviews. You could also observe the individuals and rate their behavior without ever talking to them directly. Chapter 5 will discuss how to determine which method of data collection to use. Decisions about measurement and data collection are usually made together, but they are considered separately here for ease of presentation. In deciding how to measure a variable, the following general guidelines are good to keep in mind and will be discussed from different perspectives in remaining sections of the chapter.

Use more items/indices in proportion to the importance of the variable to the central research question or hypothesis.

Use items that have a demonstrated empirical and/or professionally accepted association with the variable of interest.

Use items that are logically related to the variable of interest.

Use items that will yield the same results when applied repeatedly under similar conditions.

Use items whose categories or attributes are exhaustive and mutually exclusive.

LEVELS OF MEASUREMENT

In the previous life satisfaction example, note that the variable was first specified using a scale that divided life satisfaction into two possible response choices (no and yes). Variables can be scaled in many different ways to operationalize and measure them, which is referred to as specifying the *level of measurement*. It is important to understand the different levels of measurement, because the kinds of conclusions you will be able to draw from different scales will not always be the same. Also, the types of statistics that can be appropriately calculated on the data depend on the level of measurement used.

The various levels of measurement are summarized in Table 4-1. As you can see, four basic levels of measurement exist: nomimal, ordinal, interval, and ratio. The numbers assigned to the different categories of nominal variables are quite arbitrary; they serve as shorthand labels for the categories. Many examples of nominal variables are found in the gerontological literature and only a few possibilities have been included in the table.

Ordinal variables represent the next level of measurement and are the first to recognize that variables exist in degree or amount. Ordinal variables are

Table 4-1. Variables and Their Levels of Measurement

Level of Measurement	Properties	Examples in Gerontology	Statistics Typically Used
Nominal Variable	A variable takes on different values, and the numbers which are assigned are arbitrary. Larger and smaller values do not imply more or less of the attribute. Different values represent distinct categories and are not on a continuum.	*Category responses in which different categories are distinct* Sex: 1=Male, 2=Female Car Ownership: 1=Yes, 2=No, or 1=No, 2=Yes Marital Status: 1=Single, 2=Divorced, 3=Widowed, 4=Other	Frequencies, percentages, mode, nonparametric tests
Ordinal Variable	A variable takes on a range of values, and larger numbers indicate more of the attribute while smaller numbers indicate less of the attribute. Different values represent a rank ordering along a continuum.	*Attitudes and opinions, many self-report measures and preferences* Religiosity: 0=Not at all religious, 1=Somewhat religious, 2=Very religious Internal Locus of Control: 1= No control, 2=A little control, 3=Total control Impulsivity: 1=Always plan vacations, 2=Usually plan vacations, 3=Always leave on the spur of the moment	Frequencies, percentages, mode, median, statistics based on rank, nonparametric tests

Interval Variable	A variable takes on a range of values, and numbers are assigned so that equal distances in amount reflect equal differences in numbers which are assigned. The numbers fall along a continuum and have an arbitrary zero point.	*Intervals with arbitrary zero point* Body Temperature: 98°, 99°, 100°	Frequencies, percentages, mode, median, mean, standard deviation, Pearson product-moment correlations, nonparametric and parametric tests
Ratio Variable	A variable takes on different values along a continuum. Equal distances represent equal differences in the amount of the attribute. An absolute zero point is apparent.	*Intervals which have absolute zero point* Number of Children: 0, 1, 2, 3, 4, etc. Number of Trips to the Doctor: 0, 1, 2, etc. Income Per Year (in dollars): $0-millions! Membership in Organizations: 0, 1, 2, etc.	Frequencies, percentages, mode, median, mean, standard deviation, Pearson product-moment correlations, nonparametric and parametric tests

Source: After Siegel (1956).

the crudest measure of amount, however, when compared to interval and ratio variables. Gerontologists use ordinal variables very frequently in their research because many of the variables that assess human conditions and behavior, particularly in the social sciences, cannot be measured precisely. We can only determine whether there is, in general, more or less of them. For example, if you were assessing an individual's state of happiness could you measure the degree of happiness in such a way that the individual could state, "I am 50% happier today than I was yesterday"? Or, if you were trying to ascertain level of impulsivity in a group of older people, would it be realistic to construct an interval or ratio scale and expect individuals to respond in a valid manner? It would probably be difficult to develop such variables and have interpretable results at the end.

Interval levels of measurement are not as prevalent in gerontological research. Temperature is a good example, however, because both the Celsius and Fahrenheit temperature scales have equal increments in the degree of the attribute but have arbitrary zero points. Ratio variables are regarded as the most mathematically precise level of measurement. The major difference between the ratio and interval variables is in terms of the function of the zero point on the scale. For ratio variables, the zero point is real; that is, it indicates a lack of the attribute.

In terms of statistics, you can see from Table 4-1 that different types of calculations are appropriate for different levels of measurement. It is not logical to compute a mean, for instance, on a nominal variable. (For the Marital Status example in Table 4-1, what would a mean of 3.67 tell you?) Frequencies and percentages are usually the most appropriate types of measures. At the higher levels of measurement (interval and ratio), it makes much more sense to compute means, standard deviations, and a wide variety of other valuable statistics (see chap. 9 for more on statistics and level of measurement). For example, the mean number of friends or the mean level of income are numbers that would have an interpretable meaning when applied to a group of data on older persons. This information will become much more important when you begin to decide how you will be analyzing the variables from your own research study.

It is often useful to modify the level of measurement of a variable after the data have been collected. Thus, a ratio variable measuring the number of daily living activities a person can perform without help could be modified into an ordinal variable using a more rudimentary classification (no activities, a few activities, many activities). It is possible to change measures of a higher order (such as interval and ratio) into a lower order after the data are collected. The reverse is not true, however. It is not possible to revise lower-order variables into higher-order variables once the data are collected. In general, therefore, higher levels of measurement have more versatility and flexibility than the lower levels. They can be collapsed into simpler measures, and a wider variety of statistical techniques are available to analyze the data that are collected.

The levels of measurement are intimately tied to the categories or values for a given variable. In constructing or evaluating an operationalized variable, the following guidelines should be kept in mind.

The values of the variable should be *exhaustive*. For example, every possible answer that a person could choose should be represented.

The values of the variable should be *mutually exclusive*. In other words, only one value of the variable should be appropriate for each response.

The values of the variable should be *meaningful and relevant* to the group you are studying; they should be clear and understandable.

DESIRABLE QUALITIES IN MEASURES

As you develop operational definitions for variables in your study, you may decide to make use of measures that already exist, or you might decide to design your own instrument from scratch. Before making this choice, however, you should know about some qualities that are desirable in any instrument which is eventually used. The three most important qualities are reliability, validity, and practicality.

Reliability

Reliability refers to the precision and consistency of a measurement procedure. If, for example, you are measuring an older person's health status using certain vital signs such as heart rate, or body temperature, these measures must be accurate and truly reflect the individual's vital functions. Reliability helps ensure that an individual's score is accurate and would be the same if you took the same measure again under the same exact conditions. Reliable measures also allow you to place more confidence in the changes that might occur in an individual's score over a period of time. For example, if you wanted to measure the extent to which someone's health status gradually changes, you would like your measures to reflect actual change, and not just random fluctuations in accuracy of the measurement instrument. Reliability is an extremely important concept in research. Without reliability, you cannot place any confidence in the accuracy of the data that have been collected and therefore cannot draw any reasonable conclusions.

Three approaches to estimating reliability of a measure are test-retest reliability, parallel forms reliability, and internal estimates of reliability. Each

Table 4-2. Characteristics of Different Measures of Reliability

Estimate	Number of Administrations	Number of Instruments Developed
Test-retest	2	1
Parallel forms	2	2
Internal estimates	1	1

approach can be distinguished by the number of times each individual is measured and the number of instruments that are developed to make the estimate. Table 4-2 illustrates how the different types compare on these dimensions.

Because each of these reliability estimates is obtained using slightly different procedures, the interpretations and potential sources of error among them are slightly different as well. For example, in the test-retest method, the reliability estimate represents the level of association between two sets of scores on the same instrument, which has been administered to the same group on two occasions. This method has two potential problems (sources of error) that can affect the estimate. First, the individual's ability, attitude, and so forth may change from one occasion to the next. Second, the individual may remember items from the first measurement or be influenced in some other way by the initial procedure. This test sensitization may affect responses when the same instrument is administered a second time.

With the internal estimates of reliability, you no longer have the problem of real change or test sensitization affecting the measures because the instrument is administered only once. However, internal reliability estimates have sources of error of a different kind. For example, if an individual is fatigued (often a potential problem with older persons), a whole section or two might not be completed, making the internal estimate of reliability difficult to compute. Thus, parallel forms (administration of two versions of the instrument) are usually considered to be best of all the reliability estimating procedures. However, this method has some major disadvantages from a practicality standpoint, in that two different tests designed to measure the same thing must be produced, and time and other resources must be available to obtain measures from each person twice. In the current state of the art, very few tests have been developed and tailored for older persons, and among these, even fewer have parallel tests available.

For applied gerontological research studies, the most practical types of reliability are internal estimates. The most common estimates include the Kuder-Richardson Formula 20 (K-R 20), the Kuder-Richardson Formula 21 (K-R 21), and the split-half adjusted with the Spearman-Brown formula.

Each is estimated with only one test given on one occasion to one group of individuals.

In any research, it is highly recommended that an internal estimate of reliability be obtained to give others, including the consumers of your study, an opportunity to evaluate the accuracy and precision of the measures you have collected. Also, it is important to look for reliability estimates in any existing measure you are considering. Many applied researchers believe that a value of .70 is a minimum value for a research instrument. (The range of values for reliability estimates is .0-1.0). However, the higher the value above .70, the greater confidence you can place in the accuracy of the measure you are using. For a more complete description of reliability estimates, see Stanley and Hopkins (1972).

Validity

Chapter 3 introduced the concept of validity. There, the focus was on design issues and how they influence the internal and external validity of the conclusions of research. In this section we discuss the validity of a measure.

The *validity* of a measure, while referring to a wide variety of concepts, attempts to assess the *extent* to which a test measures what it is intended to measure. Validity is, therefore, in contrast with *reliability,* which is defined as the *precision* with which a test measures. The validity of a given instrument is always dependent on the people with whom and the purposes for which it is used. Therefore, it is useful to evaluate the validity of any instrument within the context for which it will be used. Three major types of validity that should be considered in evaluating the quality of any measure are content validity, criterion validity, and construct validity. Each type will be described with gerontological examples.

Content validity, sometimes known as rational or logical validity, is concerned with how well the content of an instrument samples the class of situations or subject matter about which conclusions are to be drawn. For example, if you wanted to measure the cognitive ability of a group of adult day care clients using a relatively brief instrument, you would want to include questions that meet some accepted criteria regarding basic mental status. Thus, you might limit your questions to items relating to ability to accurately describe person, time, and place, and ability to handle simple calculations. The major mental status scales in aging emphasize these types of items (e.g., Kahn et al., 1960; Pfeiffer, 1975).

The content validity of an instrument is evaluated using a judgmental, as opposed to statistical, process. In large-scale surveys, content experts are usually asked to comment on how adequately the instrument covers the domain of interest. For small-scale tests, and particularly applied research projects, the researcher usually makes a judgment of the content validity of the instrument independently, but sometimes in consultation with a colleague. Stanley and Hopkins (1972) recommend that the review of content validity contain at least three elements.

Examine the degree of overlap between the items on the instrument and the subject matter being measured.

Assess the degree of consistency between the relative areas of emphasis on the instrument and those relative areas of interest within the subject matter being measured. Are the more important areas given greater emphasis in terms of number of questions?

Examine the degree to which the items in the instrument have been constructed so that they are free from extraneous factors that are irrelevant or incidental to the measurement process.

Criterion validity is an important concept in evaluating a research instrument because it helps corroborate the consistency of the instrument with other measures purported to have a logical relationship to the instrument. At times criterion validity is evaluated with respect to an instrument whose characteristics are understood and accepted *(concurrent validity)*, but criterion validity can also be evaluated by examining how the instrument predicts future related measures *(predictive validity)*. An example should help clarify these facets of criterion validity assessment.

Suppose you had an instrument that was intended to be an estimate of older individuals' satisfaction with a senior citizens' discount ID card program and you developed an attitude survey to assess consumer satisfaction. In assessing the criterion validity of the instrument, and particularly the concurrent validity, you would want to find other measures, in addition to the survey, that would be logically related to consumer satisfaction. Some concurrent validity measures might include observations of the individual to see if higher self-reported satisfaction is related to higher actual use of the card; assessments of individual logs maintained by older persons to record instances of ID discount card use (higher use should be related to higher satisfaction on your instrument); interviews with family or friends to assess their perceptions of the older individuals' satisfaction with the card; and so on. Concurrent validity could be determined by examining the association between the older persons' scores on your consumer satisfaction survey with other instruments that measure the same concept.

If you were concerned about the predictive validity of the consumer satisfaction survey, you would be interested in assessing the ability of the instrument to provide a measure that is able to predict some event or other criterion measure in the future. In extending the preceding example, you might want to see how well scores on the consumer satisfaction survey predict future patronage of retail stores that honor the discount card.

Construct validity, the final area of validity that is useful in assessing an instrument, refers to the ability of an instrument to measure the underlying trait or construct that it was originally intended to measure. Construct validity differs from criterion validity in that the relationships that are sought are based on theories of human behavior. For example, in the previous description of consumer satisfaction with the discount ID program, you could hypothesize that individuals who show high levels of consumer satisfaction with the program do so because they are happier and more satisfied with life in general. This theory about the nature of human behavior would lead you to assess the relationship between scores on the ID satisfaction scale and a general life satisfaction scale, or happiness scale.

Construct validity could also be assessed by looking at predictions about scores on the instrument in response to experimental treatments or interventions. For instance, if the consumer satisfaction survey was a good measure of satisfaction with discounts offered, you would expect that higher discounts (e.g., 10%-25%) would result in higher levels of satisfaction. Again, this hypothesis addresses certain theories about the nature of human behavior and could be assessed by designing an actual experiment that manipulated the level of discount offered and the resulting satisfaction with the ID program that followed.

Practicality

Practicality refers to a wide range of areas that relate to the usefulness of the instrument for your intended purposes. Practicality is often viewed in terms of utility and economy with respect to time, money, or effort. If, for example, you are considering two different instruments to measure depression, you should evaluate the instruments on such factors as total cost for acquiring and/or reproducing a sufficient number of copies, the total time for administration, the relative ease in administering and scoring the instrument, and the adaptability of the measure for the type of analysis you have in mind. These kinds of issues are important, but they are sometimes overlooked by beginning researchers.

Practicality is a very important topic to address when studying older individuals because instruments designed for younger age groups may be inappropriate or impractical when used in a different context. For example, if you were trying to measure general intelligence among a sample of older stroke patients, many timed tests or tests requiring manual dexterity might be impractical and probably invalid as well. Or, a three-hour interview might not be practical for a group of older persons who have diminished energy levels and for whom fatigue might contribute to erroneous and invalid findings.

There are three methods for assessing the practicality of the measures you have selected. First, in a logical analysis, assess how easily and quickly you think the instrument could be administered. Using common sense and judgment, in other words, is one reasonable approach to this issue. Second, ask for the advice and reactions of others concerning the feasibility and practicality of the measures you have selected. In addition, you should note any comments the developers have made along these lines. Third, be sure to test the instrument and other methods on a sample of people similar to those you actually intend to measure as part of your research project. This pretesting is a very important part of assessing the practicality of your entire research procedure and is discussed in more detail in chapter 7.

In summary, this section has reviewed three important qualities in any measures you might want to use in your research. These qualities are reliability, validity, and practicality. Reliability concerns an assessment of how precisely the instrument estimates the values of the variable(s) you are interested in, while validity focuses on how well the instrument measures what you originally intended it to measure. Both are extremely important in evaluating the measures you will devise or select in conducting research. Reliability is especially important, for if you have no confidence in the precision of your measures, then it is impossible to draw meaningful conclusions about the outcomes of research. In other words, without reliability there can be no validity. However, merely having a reliable measure in no way guarantees that it is valid for your purposes. Remember that an instrument or measure must be practical for your intended purposes, for unless an instrument has pragmatic value, data collection efforts could become extremely cumbersome or even impossible to complete.

DECISIONS REGARDING THE SELECTION OR CONSTRUCTION OF INSTRUMENTS

Should you create your own measures or use instruments that already exist? It is very difficult to make the final selection of measures to be used in conducting research. Many factors must be weighed in addition to the reliability, validity, and practicality issues just described. You should be aware of the fact that different researchers have very different viewpoints on these matters. Some believe that issues in quantitative standards must take precedence, and they strongly advocate the use of well-developed, standardized instruments.* They also point to the fact that most researchers do not have the ability or time to develop good instruments and therefore are doing a disservice to their research results through the construction of specially tailored instruments.

On the other hand, many other researchers believe that relevance, sensitivity, and validity are often sacrificed if an instrument that does not truly fit the purposes of the research project is used. In addition, most existing instruments have very little information about reliability, validity, and practicality with older age groups. Therefore, to claim that researchers should only use standardized instruments, when no truly adequate measures are available, can also result in invalid conclusions and be a potential disservice to research knowledge and utilization.

In recent years, a growing interest in issues of measurement in gerontology has led to an improvement in the availability of and information about research instruments and measurement strategies. For example, a three-volume guide to existing instruments covering many important topics in gerontology is now available. These volumes include descriptions of the psychometric properties of many instruments (Mangen and Peterson, 1982a, 1982b, 1984). In addition, a book has recently been published on measurement strategies in long-term care (Kane and Kane, 1983). All of these books are valuable resources for locating and evaluating candidate instruments for applied gerontological research.

In reality, the choice between using an existing instrument versus creating new measures depends upon the purposes and circumstances of the research, and the philosophy of the researcher. It is a good idea to develop a sense of appreciation for both points of view because the applied researcher in gerontology may find it beneficial to select existing instruments for certain problems and to construct new instruments for other problems. Using both existing and new measures within the same study can often be helpful because then you will have measures that are comparable to other studies and that also fit closely your specific purposes.

Evaluating Existing Instruments

Two general areas should be considered when evaluating existing instruments: format considerations and content considerations. In the evaluation of format, the instrument must be well organized and must contain certain

---

*Standardization refers to a process of testing the instrument on many different samples of people and describing their performance. This information can then be used by other researchers to compare the results of their data with similar groups under similar conditions.

basic pieces of information, including a clearly stated purpose, a description of appropriate subjects, instructions regarding administration, examples of how to use it, definitions of any terms that may not be generally understood, good overall descriptions of items, and information about use with older people. If these topics are not addressed, you might use the instrument incorrectly, but certainly many others could also be described. These format considerations are some of the most important ones.

In terms of content considerations, the following topics are important to consider.

Coverage. Are the major dimensions of the instrument adequately covered in terms of the number of items and the content of the items? Do the dimensions address the purposes and hypotheses that you have in mind?

Clearly Operationalized Variables. Are there adequate descriptions of how scores on these dimensions are obtained from the individual responses?

Appropriately Scaled Items. Are the items scaled using generally accepted principles of item construction and evaluation? Do items have such features as being mutually exclusive, exhaustive, and so on?

Reliability. Is information on reliability available? Is such information available on older age groups? Is it within an acceptable range?

Validity. Is information on validity provided? Does the instrument developer describe the content, construct, and criterion validity of the survey? Is a description done for older age samples also? Can you infer from available information that the validity of the instrument is adequate for your study population?

Practicality. Is information on the practicality of the instrument for its intended purposes provided? Are issues such as the feasibility, costs, ease of administration, or time involved in the administration of the instrument described? Will the instrument be practical for your purposes?

Constructing Your Own Instrument

Sometimes you will decide it is best to construct your own research instrument. If you do so, the earlier discussion of issues in operationalization and measurement should be of value. However, several additional issues you should bear in mind are presented in this section (Babbie, 1979; Oppenheim, 1966). More detailed discussions of the methods of questionnaire construction are provided in the Suggested Readings.

Open-Ended Versus Fixed-Choice Questions. Two major types of questions can be asked of an individual. Which type to use depends on the purpose of the research, the type of analysis that will be employed, and the amount of knowledge you have about the concept. In the open-ended question, respondents are given considerable flexibility in their answers. The term *open-ended* is meant to suggest that there is great freedom in the choice, wording, and length of the response. An example of an open-ended question follows.

What are the best things about attending X Senior Center? _____

_____

_____

A variety of responses might result from such a question. Some people might give emphasis to the opportunities for social interaction, others might focus on the ways the Center activities help to pass the hours, others might describe the special talents of the Center staff, and a few might answer the question in terms of how their lives away from the Center have benefited from their attendance.

The great range of possible responses resulting from open-ended questions can be beneficial or problematic, depending upon the particulars of the research topic and plans for analysis. Open-ended questions may be more appropriate, for example, when there is not enough prior research on the topic to allow for the development of a comprehensive set of response categories. In such cases the researcher may want to avoid missing out on important answers due to an incomplete set of responses. Open-ended questions are often used in the first stages of research on a topic for just this reason. Responses to the open-ended question can be examined to determine categories for closed or fixed-choice responses to be used in the later stages of research.

Fixed-choice questions limit the range of responses by requiring the selection of one or more answers from a list that is developed in advance. An example of a fixed-choice question follows.

Overall, how would you rate the services available at X Senior Center— excellent, good, fair, or poor?

_____ Excellent

_____ Good

_____ Fair

_____ Poor

Responses to fixed-choice questions are far more likely to be comparable from respondent to respondent. In addition, these types of questions are easy for the respondents to answer, and the results can be readily prepared for statistical analysis. It also tends to be easier to employ standard techniques for estimating the reliability and validity of fixed-choice questions. On the other hand, fixed-choice questions do force respondents to select from a list of responses, none of which may be entirely appropriate. In fixed-choice questions, spontaneity and variety are sacrificed for efficiency and comparability.

Guidelines for Writing Questions. The following detailed guidelines are intended to help you write effective and pertinent questions.

Consider How Many Questions Are Needed. Sometimes one question will give you all the information you require for a particular attribute. If one does the trick, then there is no need to ask more questions on that topic. Frequently, however, the attributes you want to know about will be global rather than specific. They might even consist of several separate dimensions that you should measure. In this case, asking one question will give you information about only one aspect of the attribute. Additionally, you want to be sure that you have adequately covered the most important attributes in the research. Failure to adequately measure them could mean disaster for the project.

Two rules of thumb are useful in deciding how many questions to ask about a specific topic. First, include more questions to measure complex or multidimensional attributes. Second, use more questions to address the central issues in your research problem.

Make the Questions Simple and Unambiguous. Write each item so that it is as simple and unambiguous as possible. The respondents have to be very clear about what you want to know. It is easy to write questions that are perfectly correct with respect to grammar but still miss the mark because the respondents do not understand them. For example, a question that asks how many siblings (rather than brothers or sisters) the respondent has may lead to expressions of bewilderment rather than accurate information.

Make the Questions Short. When questions are long or complex, respondents may become confused or forget the point by the time they reach the end. Short questions are therefore more likely to elicit appropriate responses.

Avoid Double-barreled and Biased Questions. *Double-barreled* questions ask about more than one thing at a time, so it is difficult both for the respondent to answer and for the researcher to appropriately interpret the response. An example of a double-barreled question follows.

Do you plan to retire and move to Florida?

_____ Yes

_____ No

Does a yes answer mean the respondent plans to retire *and* move to Florida? Or does it mean the respondent plans to retire only, or move to Florida only?

Biased questions are written so that they in some way influence respondents to answer in a particular manner. Leading and loaded questions represent two categories of question bias. *Leading* questions include some phrase within the question that directs the respondent toward (or away from) a particular response. Consider the question "Don't you feel that X Senior Center is doing a good job?" This leading question is worded to suggest that yes is the appropriate answer.

Loaded questions include emotionally laden statements that may influence responses. Quite often, having certain words in a question or response category can be enough to dramatically influence responses. An example of a loaded question follows.

Are you currently receiving any welfare handouts?

_____ Yes

_____ No

Welfare is an emotionally charged word, especially for many older people. Adding the word *handout* makes an even more obviously loaded question. It would be better simply to ask respondents whether they currently receive specific types of services (e.g., food stamps, supplemental security income).

Avoid Negative Items.   When an item includes a negative, two possible problems may develop. First, the negative may be overlooked and the respondent will be answering the wrong question. Second, if the respondent notices the negative, it may result in confusion about the appropriate response. An example may be useful in showing the problems with negative items.

Should older people not receive financial assistance from their children?

_____ Yes

_____ No

If the *not* goes unnoticed, the question would take a different meaning. On the other hand, if the *not* is noticed, it will be difficult for respondents to know how to answer. Does a response of no mean older people should or should not receive financial assistance from their children?

Ask Questions the Respondents Are Competent to Answer.   You must always consider whether the respondents have the appropriate experience, knowledge, and so forth to give a competent answer to the question. For example, it may not be reasonable to expect older respondents to be able to competently answer the following question.

> Do you want to participate in an adult day care program?
>
> _____ Yes
>
> _____ No

Most people would have little idea of what adult day care programs are, and some may have totally incorrect images of adult day care. It may be better to provide as part of the question a brief description of the types of services and activities offered by adult day care. The description would enhance the competence of the respondent and help ensure an appropriate response.

Be Sure the Questions Are Applicable.   It is relatively easy to ask questions that do not apply to some, or even most, respondents. When respondents encounter several of these types of questions they may become annoyed, frustrated, or even angry, and decide not to continue. The problem of asking questions that do not apply can be ameliorated through the use of contingency questions. *Contingency* questions serve to identify appropriate candidates for the questions that follow. For example, consider the following set of questions.

> Have you participated at X Senior Center in the past three months?
>
> _____ No
>
> _____ Yes
>
> What activities do you enjoy most at the center? _____

Whether the respondent is asked about activities that are enjoyed most is contingent upon recency of participation. Persons who have not participated in the past three months are not asked the followup question.

The Ordering of Questions. Experience suggests that placement of questions within the instrument can influence the accuracy and completeness of the responses. In general, it is best to begin with questions that help the respondent to feel comfortable and competent and that foster an interest in the data-gathering process. The first questions should therefore be easy to answer and should address interesting topics. Questions that are potentially embarrassing or that are emotionally laden should come later and should be introduced by means of some less sensitive questions on the same topic. In this way, a positive rapport will be established, and this rapport will smooth the way for the more difficult items.

SUMMARY

All research involves the measurement of some aspect of the world around us. Measurement is sometimes difficult in gerontology and may have to rely on approximations of the phenomena of interest. It is nevertheless important to give careful consideration to issues of measurement because (1) measurement improves your understanding of an issue, (2) decisions regarding measurement influence other aspects of the study, (3) measurement enhances your capacity to summarize information, and (4) good measurement improves your ability to make good decisions.

In conducting research, you will measure one or more variables, which are characteristics of people, events, or objects that take on different values or levels. Before variables can be adequately measured, it is necessary to establish a set of specific procedures that will be used for the measurement. Operationalization is the process of specifying the procedures that will be used. An important characteristic of any variable is its level of measurement: nominal, ordinal, interval, or ratio. The level of measurement influences the type of analysis that can be applied to the information you have collected.

All measures should possess the qualities of reliability, validity, and practicality. Reliability is the precision and consistency of the measure. Validity refers to the degree to which it measures what it is intended to measure. Practicality is the usefulness of the measure for your specific purposes.

The decision regarding whether to employ existing measures or to construct new ones will depend upon two major considerations. First, you should determine the importance of having a standardized instrument. Second, you should examine the format and content of existing instruments to see whether they meet your needs. It is often a good idea to design the data collection so that you can use existing measures as well as measures you develop specifically for the project.

If you construct your own instrument, attention should be given to the types of questions (open-ended or fixed-choice) that will be asked as well as how many questions will be needed to measure each attribute. You should strive to construct items that are simple, brief, unbiased, and applicable to the respondent. Negative items can be misinterpreted or create confusion and should therefore be avoided. Also, each item should be constructed so that the respondents will be competent to answer them. Finally, careful ordering of the items will help ensure that all the questions are answered accurately and completely. You will usually make decisions about measurement in conjunction with decisions about how to collect information.

SUGGESTED READINGS

Stanley, J. C., and Hopkins, K. D. (1972). *Educational and psychological measurement and evaluation.* Englewood Cliffs, N. J.: Prentice-Hall. The book by Stanley and Hopkins is a general review of measurement issues, including tests of reliability and validity.

Mangen, D. J., and Peterson, W. A. (Eds.). (1982-1984). *Research instruments in social gerontology,* vols. 1-3. Minneapolis: University of Minnesota Press. This three-volume set is an outstanding survey of existing instruments in gerontology. Information about the reliability and validity of many of the instruments is presented.

Kane, R. A., and Kane, R. L. (1983). *Assessing the elderly: A practical guide to measurement.* Lexington, Mass.: Lexington Books. This book focuses primarily on existing instrumentation in the area of long-term care. It includes measures of physical, mental, and social functioning as well as multidimensional measures.

Oppenheim, A. N. (1966). *Questionnaire design and attitude measurement.* New York: Basic Books. Oppenheim's book is a simple, straightforward, and thorough explanation of how to write your own interview questions and how to create useful scales.

REFERENCES

Babbie, E. R. (1979). *The practice of social research* (2nd ed.). Belmont, Calif.: Wadsworth.

Borkan, G. A., and Norris, A. H. (1980). Assessment of biological age using a profile of physical parameters. *Journal of Gerontology, 35,* 177-184.

Center for the Study of Aging and Human Development. (1978). *Multidimensional functional assessment: The OARS methodology* (2nd ed.). Durham, N.C.: Author.

Kahn, R. L., Goldfarb, A. I., Pollack, M., and Peck, A. (1960). Brief objective measures for the determination of mental status of the aged. *American Journal of Psychiatry, 117,* 326-328.

Kane, R. A., and Kane, R. L. (1983). *Assessing the elderly: A practical guide to measurement.* Lexington, Mass.: Lexington Books.

Lawton, M. P. (1970). Planner's notebook: Planning environments for older people. *Journal of the American Institute of Planners, 36,* 124-129.

Lawton, M. P. (1972). The dimensions of morale. In D. P. Kent, R. Kastenbaum, and S.

Sherwood (Eds.), *Research, planning and action for the elderly: The power and potential of social science.* New York: Behavioral Publications.

Lawton, M. P., Brody, E. M., and Turner-Massey, P. (1978). The relationships of environmental factors to change in well-being. *The Gerontologist,* **18** (2), 133-137.

Mangen, D. J., and Peterson, W. A. (Eds.). (1982*a*). *Research instruments in social gerontology.* Vol. 1, *Clinical and social psychology.* Minneapolis: University of Minnesota Press.

Mangen, D. J., and Peterson, W. A. (Eds.). (1982*b*). *Research instruments in social gerontology.* Vol. 2, *Social roles and social participation.* Minneapolis: University of Minnesota Press.

Mangen, D. J., and Peterson, W. A. (Eds.). (1984). *Research instruments in social gerontology.* Vol. 3, *Health, program evaluation and demography.* Minneapolis: University of Minnesota Press.

Moos, R. H., Gauvain, M., Lemke, S., Max, W., and Mehren, B. (1977, November). *The development of a sheltered care environment scale: A preliminary report.* Paper presented at the 30th meeting of the Gerontological Society of America, San Francisco.

Oppenheim, A. N. (1966). *Questionnaire design and attitude measurement.* New York: Basic Books.

Pfeiffer, E. (1975). A short portable mental status questionnaire for the assessment of organic brain deficit in elderly patients. *Journal of the American Geriatrics Society,* **23,** 433-441.

Siegel, S. (1956). *Nonparametric statistics for the behavioral sciences.* New York: McGraw-Hill.

Stanley, J. C., and Hopkins, K. D. (1972). *Educational and psychological measurement and evaluation.* Englewood Cliffs, N. J.: Prentice-Hall.

Thorndike, R. L., and Hagen, E. P. (1977). *Measurement and evaluation in psychology and education.* New York: Wiley.

5

Deciding How to Collect Information

PROBLEMS TO BE SOLVED

Will it be possible to use information that is already available, or will I need to gather and analyze new information?
How can different collection strategies influence the cost of the study and the quality and completeness of the data?
Which method or methods should I use to collect the information I need?

Many different procedures are available to the applied gerontologist for gathering information. It would be difficult to list all the possibilities and nearly impossible to provide detailed descriptions and evaluations of each. The variations are almost endless, but it is still unlikely that only one procedure will perfectly fit a given research problem. The results of any one method of data collection will probably provide an incomplete picture of the problem. Furthermore, different methods may lead to at least slightly different results.

The notion that different means of obtaining information may lead to different findings may be disconcerning at first but should not be. A considerable margin for error in all measurement techniques means that different methods will most likely "miss the mark" in somewhat different ways. In addition, applied gerontologists are usually measuring concepts that are very difficult to pinpoint. As was discussed in chapter 4, we are often forced to rely on the measurement of characteristics or attributes that are only indirect manifestations of the real targets of the research. Finally, the issues that are the focus of applied gerontological studies tend to be relatively broad or global. Any one method is likely to provide just one piece of the puzzle. Because each method will lead to somewhat inaccurate and incomplete findings, it is usually best, when possible, to use more than one means of collecting information. The results of the different approaches, taken together, are more likely to provide a better overall understanding of the issue.

An example from a different area of study may be useful in showing how the use of a variety of techniques helps to clarify an issue. Suppose the research problem is to determine the quality and quantity of coal that might be mined in a particular region. Above-ground geological inspections may find useful evidence in the form of rock formations, fossils, or even outcroppings of coal seams. Test drillings could provide information about the content and, to a degree, the extent of any underground coal. The drillings would also produce coal samples that could be submitted to laboratory testing. Seismic tests may further add to the detail by providing information on the location and composition of underground formations. Other tests may also be applied, each offering new information and thereby helping to complete the picture. Of course, the exact quality and quantity of coal in the area cannot be known until mining has been completed. However, the estimates will be improved as additional information, such as tapping different characteristics or manifestations of the underground coal, is collected.

As with the problem of estimating the nature and extent of coal, most research problems faced by applied gerontologists are complex and hidden from direct measurement. Therefore, when possible, more than one method of data collection should be used. The results of each procedure will help to clarify the issue and will lead to better estimates of the issues being addressed. This chapter is designed to assist you in selecting procedures for collecting the information needed to answer a research question.

THE USE OF EXISTING INFORMATION

The analysis of existing information, often called secondary analysis, is a growing but still underutilized method in applied gerontological research. Before collecting new information, careful attention should be given to what data are already available on the topic. Often, all that is needed to answer an applied research question is some time spent in carefully organizing and/or re-analyzing information already gathered by others.

Existing information can be used three ways in research. It can serve as the sole source of data for analysis; it can be used as partial data, complementing information obtained from other sources; or it can be used to examine the validity of information gathered by the researcher. Each of these uses will be briefly described.

Existing Data as the Sole Basis for Research

Often researchers design projects that are based exclusively upon information that already exists. For example, a study to examine the feasibility of congregate housing for older people in an area may use census data to determine the numbers of persons in certain age, income, housing, and household status categories. Information from the state Medicaid program may be used to discover the number of persons in the area who receive Medicaid benefits as well as the kinds of services they receive through Medicaid. This and other existing information can be combined to develop a profile of the elderly population in the target area that would facilitate a decision regarding whether additional congregate housing should be built. As an example, Elwell (1984) used existing data from forms completed by skilled nursing facilities in New York state to examine the relationship between type of ownership and services offered.

Existing Data as One Component of Research

At times, it makes sense to design a research project so that the analysis makes use of existing data as well as new information collected specifically to address the issue. Resources can be used more efficiently by combining information from complementary sources. For example, a hospital social work department, in carrying out an evaluation of its discharge planning program for older patients, may conduct interviews with former patients or their family members. In addition, the researchers may draw upon the hospital's computerized information system for data regarding a patient's age, reason for admission, level of functioning, and length of stay. The pre-existing and newly collected data can then be analyzed jointly to complete the evaluation.

Use of Existing Information for Validation

Existing data can also be used to cross-check various aspects of a research project; one common example is the use of census data to assess whether a sample is representative of the target population. As an example, a sample of persons 65 years or older in a particular community should have distributions on age, sex, income, home ownership, and employment status that closely approximate the census distributions on these characteristics for the same age group in the same area. If the distributions are dissimilar, the nature and extent of the differences may provide valuable clues about bias in the sample selection or data collection procedures.

Sources of Existing Information

Many different types of existing information may be useful for applied research in aging. Because each source has its own special qualities and problems, several of the major sources are discussed separately.

Official Records. Most federal, state, and local government agencies as well as private organizations collect information on a regular basis and store it in a retrievable form. Part of the problem in using this resource is locating the information and obtaining permission to use it. Few agencies or businesses advertise the availability of the information they collect, and many limit access to it. However, you should not give up without trying, because the energy spent in locating and gaining access to official records can be far less than that required to collect new information.

One valuable set of official records is registration information. In our country, records are maintained on births, deaths, marriages, certain communicable diseases, and other important events. These records are administered by the authorities of each state, but efforts have been made to achieve standardization from state to state. Copies of the original forms can often be examined by researchers who are interested in trends in major life events. In addition, compilations of the information are available in printed form or on computer tape from state registrars.

Another category of official records is the varied assortment of documents produced by agencies, businesses, and organizations in the everyday performance of their business. Among the types of information that may be available through these sources are financial transactions, characteristics of clients or customers, the quantity and types of goods or services provided, characteristics of employees, and compliance with regulations. For example, patient records in nursing homes can yield considerable information about their physical status and types of care they receive. The author has used standard forms completed by hospital discharge planners on their Medicaid-eligible patients to examine the characteristics that are most predictive of placement in the community versus long-term care institutions (McAuley, Travis, and Taylor, 1984).

Census documents can also yield a wealth of information for applied research in aging. Information from the census is now available in many different and readily accessible forms, including print, microfilm, and computer tape. Many states have a centralized census data users office that is equipped to help individuals make the most of the huge quantity of facts and figures generated by the Bureau of the Census. A valuable resource for learning about census information is the *Monthly Product Announcement* published by the Bureau of the Census. A free subscription to this publication can be obtained by writing the Data User Services Division, Customer Services, Bureau of Census, Washington, DC 20233.

One drawback to the use of census information is that confidentiality requirements make it impossible to obtain information at the individual level. Only summary information about groups of people are released. On the other hand, the Bureau of the Census has a well-deserved reputation for producing high-quality information. This reputation is the reason why sample and census characteristics are compared to assess the effectiveness of a sampling strategy.

Official records are, as a rule, accurate, complete, and consistent, although these attributes should never be taken for granted. The quality of a specific source should be carefully evaluated before using the information in a research project (Sinnott et al., 1983). Even vital registration data can be biased. For example, cause-of-death information on death certificates often does not give an accurate portrayal of the specific disease that led to death.

When the records of business concerns are being considered for a research project, it is important to take into account the policies, habits, time constraints, and other factors that may lead to inaccuracies in the data. As an example, the patient charts in a nursing home may not necessarily be accurate reflections of patient status or care received (Gubrium, 1975).

An advantage of official records is that the information is usually in a form that is appropriate for analysis. That is, the information is often precoded or precategorized so that few steps are involved in preparing it for analysis, thereby greatly reducing the time and resources necessary to carry out a study.

Previous Studies.   Information from previous surveys and other types of studies can sometimes be reworked to serve a new purpose. A surprising amount of valuable information is available in studies that have been completed by others, or perhaps even by yourself. The application of some creative thinking can often produce new uses for the data. A recent symposium in *The Gerontologist* describes some of the benefits and problems associated with the use of several of the major available data sets (Cutler, 1979; Fillenbaum, 1979; George, 1979; Henretta, 1979). While the topics discussed by the symposium participants tend to be more basic than applied, their presentations point to the value of examining data collected by others.

Fortunately, the field of aging has a number of data archives whose goals are to obtain, prepare, store, and make available information from previous studies. These archives have staffs who can assist researchers in the selection and use of data sets. Three such archives are briefly described next.

The National Archive of Computerized Data on Aging (NACDA), is a special project of the Inter-University Consortium for Political and Social Research and contains data from large national surveys, several longitudinal studies, the census, and much more. Information about this archive can be obtained by writing NACDA, Ann Arbor, MI 48106.

The Data Archive for Aging and Adult Development (DAAAD), a project of the Duke University Center for Aging and Adult Development, contains many state and local surveys as well as data from the Duke Longitudinal Study. Many of the more recent acquisitions are studies that have used the comprehensive Older Adults Resources and Services (OARS) assessment instrument. Information about this archive can be obtained by writing DAAAD, Box 3003, Duke University Medical Center, Durham, NC 27710.

The National Data Base on Aging (NDBA) is a joint project of the National Association of State Units on Aging and the National Association of Area Agencies on Aging. Rather than containing large numbers of data sets, the NDBA maintains information from an annual survey of state units on aging and area agencies on aging. It includes information on expenditures, numbers and characteristics of clients, provider profiles, and much more. Information about the data base can be obtained by writing NASUA, 600 Maryland Ave., S.W., Washington, DC 20024, or by calling a toll-free number (800-424-9126).

Efficiency is one of the key reasons for selecting information from previous studies as the source of data for your own analysis. The information is usually in a form that can be directly analyzed. In many cases, you may request a computer tape and code book that will make it possible to begin analysis immediately. For a reasonable cost, the staff of any of the data archives just described can even complete an analysis, based upon your specifications, and send you the results. Of course, documentation of the methods and procedures should be carefully reviewed to evaluate the quality of a specific data set and to determine whether the methods and procedures used are appropriate for your research problem.

One difficulty associated with using information from previous studies is that the data set may not contain all of the variables needed to complete the analysis as you originally envisioned it. If most of the key items are included, it is probably still useful to analyze the previously collected data as a first step. This initial analysis might go a long way toward answering the questions you had in mind, and the results may very well offer insights that will be useful in designing a new study.

Mass Media Reports.   Reports distributed through the mass media can sometimes be the source of data for analysis. Such reports include articles in newspapers and magazines as well as radio and television news programs or documentaries. These sources can be used to get an idea of what people in general feel about an issue or what people are learning about an issue.

The reliability and validity of mass media reports should be carefully scrutinized because the reports can be influenced by the opinions and values of the individuals responsible for their production. In addition, a considerable amount of effort can be involved in drawing appropriate information from these sources and converting it into a form that can be analyzed. Content analysis, a special procedure for converting recorded works into analyzable data, must usually be applied before, not after, actual data analysis begins. Very specific rules and procedures for carrying out content analysis make it possible to categorize and count various aspects of a program, book, or other source so that the necessary information can be extracted for analysis.

Expressive Material.   Another source of pre-existing information is expressive materials, including autobiographies, novels, letters, diaries, paintings, plays, and films. Such sources offer views that are not readily available elsewhere and can be especially useful for learning what individuals think and feel about issues or problems without being prompted by an interviewer or printed questionnaire. People often do not have an opinion about an issue until they are asked. Thus, it can be valuable to determine what people consider important and how they formulate their opinions *without* having to respond to a set of research questions.

The reliability and validity of expressive material is always an issue, as is generalizability. Because only certain individuals produce these types of materials, there is some likelihood that expressive materials are not representative of the target population. It may also be necessary to weed through voluminous amounts of material to glean a little information that relates to the research problem. Content analysis must frequently be applied to expressive materials in order to create a data set for analysis.

Although many problems are associated with the use of expressive materials, these pre-existing information sources can offer insights and trigger ideas that might otherwise never arise. An example of an interesting use of sources that fall into this category is an analysis of humorous published greeting cards with age themes (Demos and Jache, 1981). Because humor is a powerful medium for arousing, conveying, and reinforcing our images of individuals and groups, such an analysis can improve our understanding of contemporary attitudes about aging. Another example is an analysis of letters to a popular newspaper advice columnist sent by older people or young people about older people (Gaitz and Scott, 1975). These letters offer insights into the age-related concerns and problems of that highly select group of individuals who seek advice from "Dear Abby."

METHODS OF COLLECTING NEW INFORMATION

As has already been noted, there are a wide variety of methods for collecting information, and for any applied research problem in aging several different data collection procedures may be useful. This section offers brief but not complete descriptions of some of the more commonly used procedures. They should provide enough introduction so that you can begin to decide which might be appropriate for the research project you have in mind. You can then turn to more complete descriptions of those procedures that appear to be workable. A number of suggested readings at the end of the chapter offer more thorough explanations and instructions on specific methods.

Face-to-Face and Phone Interviews

Phone interviews and face-to-face interviews (also called personal interviews) are a very commonly used source of information for applied as well as basic research in aging. The major benefits as well as problems of these approaches are related to the fact that both require a high level of involvement on the part of an interviewer. Of course, all forms of data collection that are based upon asking questions of respondents, whether a pencil and paper questionnaire or a personal interview, depend upon establishing an adequate level of communication. However, with face-to-face and phone interviews, the communication is obviously more immediate.

Because of their direct involvement in information collection, well-trained, experienced interviewers can be a valuable resource in gathering quality information. At the very outset, they can encourage potential respondents to participate. They can also assess and report on the context within which an interview occurs. In addition, they can respond to questions or concerns, identify and resolve problems, carry a line of questions and answers to its appropriate conclusion, follow intricate question patterns, and immediately evaluate responses to questions to assure that they are in harmony with the researcher's intent. All of these powerful resources can improve the quality of the information.

On the other hand, because of the time involved in completing personal and phone interviews and the travel or telephone costs involved, this approach can be relatively slow and expensive. In addition, the researcher is very much dependent upon the abilities and motivations of the interviewers, because the interviewers' work cannot be completely scrutinized, and they will have to make snap decisions that might influence the results.

In deciding between phone and face-to-face interviews, a number of factors should be considered. Phone interviews can be more carefully supervised (e.g., by having several interviewers work at a central phone bank with a supervisor on duty). Therefore, it may not be as necessary to spend large amounts of time on training. In addition, the potential for bias due to interviewer style may be lower with phone than face-to-face interviews. However, phone questioning is likely to be inappropriate for longer interviews because it is more difficult to hold respondents on the phone for long periods. Some evidence suggests that older people are more influenced than younger people by length of telephone interviews (Kulka, Herzog, and Rodgers, 1980). Phone interviews are also less likely to be successful when the research design calls for complex questions, such as questions that require lengthy explanations or probes or (obviously) that are best handled with visual aids.

The decision to use phone or face-to-face interviews should also be based upon the need to fully cover the persons in the sampling frame. Some older people live in households that have no telephones. For example, in Virginia, about 5% of persons 60 or more years old have no telephone, while nearly 11% of older nonwhite Virginians do not have phones (McAuley et al., 1980). Therefore, when telephone interviews are the sole source of information, certain elderly people (probably the poorest and some of lower socioeconomic status) will be automatically excluded. In addition, the loss of auditory acuity, which can occur with age, may make phone interviews problematic. In face-to-face interviews, respondents can sometimes compensate for hearing loss by using other cues. On the other hand, field staff in face-to-face surveys may intentionally avoid certain households because of fear or prejudice. Thus, incomplete coverage and selection bias can occur with both formats. However, research suggests that response rates are lower among older people when phone interviews are used (Herzog, Rodgers, and Kulka, 1980).

Cost and time both tend to operate in favor of phone interviews. The time and expense involved in travel to individual households can make face-to-face interviews a very expensive procedure. Phone interviews can generally be completed within a shorter time frame and at a much lower cost than face-to-face interviews.

When an interviewer is needed on location to observe and record, face-to-

face interviews are the obviously appropriate choice. The Annual Housing
Surveys sponsored by the Department of Housing and Urban Development
offer an example of required on-site observations in conjunction with interviews. Interviewer observations provide an objective assessment of the
respondents' homes and neighborhoods. These observations, along with the
survey responses, give a better overall indication of the respondents' housing quality.

Forms Completed and Returned by Respondents

Researchers frequently design their data collection procedures so that potential respondents are required to complete a questionnaire and return it in
some specified manner. The mail-out, mail-back approach is a common
example of this method. In all likelihood you have received many such
questionnaires. Other approaches to distribution include: (1) handing out
the forms in person, (2) placing questionnaires in appropriate locations (e.g.,
evaluation forms on tables in restaurants), and (3) enclosing them in product
packaging (e.g., customer questionnaires that are components of product
warranty registration cards). Besides mail return, forms might be personally
collected by the research staff or placed in a convenient receptacle. All these
combinations of distribution and collection have two common features.
First, they are relatively inexpensive ways of obtaining information. Second,
they place great responsibility on the potential respondent for self-selection,
proper completion of the form, and its return to the researcher.

The low cost of these approaches to data collection makes them very
attractive. Another strong point is that the information-gathering phase can
be completed quickly. These methods of collecting information can be
exceedingly efficient. However, a number of additional factors should be
considered when comparing these procedures to other methods of data
collection. First of all, the response rate tends to be lower than with phone or
face-to-face interviews. Related to rate of response is the fact that certain
types of individuals are more likely than others to respond. For example,
respondents may read and write better than nonrespondents. When older
people are the target group, this problem can be significant because elderly
individuals tend to have less education and poorer visual acuity.

A second consideration in the use of forms that are completed and
returned by respondents centers on control over the selection of respondents. These approaches tend to be more catch-as-catch-can, and self-selection
of respondents can lead to some bias in the sample. Even in those instances
when a mail questionnaire can be addressed to a specific individual, there is
no guarantee that the addressee will be the individual who completes the

form. Furthermore, persons who have more interest in the issues addressed by the survey are more likely to complete and return the forms than those who are less interested. This likelihood means that the results may lead to overestimates of problems, concerns, or needs. In a followup of older nonrespondents to a needs assessment survey by mail, Leinbach (1982) found that respondents consistently expressed greater need than nonrespondents. Furthermore, many of the initial nonrespondents indicated they felt a response was necessary only if they were experiencing a problem.

A third factor to consider is completeness of responses. Respondents who have sole responsibility for reading, interpreting, and answering questions return more "don't knows" and unanswered questions than respondents who are interviewed in person. When mail survey results were compared to similar face-to-face and phone interviews with older people, the proportion of missing observations for the mail surveys was more than four times greater than for the other techniques (Leinbach, 1982).

A fourth consideration is that these procedures can give respondents the time to check their records or to ask others for information. This factor can be good or bad, depending upon the purpose of the study. When questions seek information that is difficult to remember or requires time to organize (e.g., prescription drug information, specific income-by-source information, or the dates of particular events) the added time available for response can be valuable. On the other hand, when more extemporaneous responses are needed, having less control over the time factor may be detrimental to the research project.

The value of information collected by means of forms completed and returned by respondents depends very heavily upon careful advance planning. For example, the introductory materials, such as the cover letter, must be written in a clear, convincing fashion. The value of the data will also be improved by making the instructions clear and simple and by designing the form to be brief and easy to complete and return (Dillman 1978). See chapter 8 for more information on methods of improving responses to mail surveys, a frequently used procedure of this type.

Observational Methods

On certain occasions the best approach to information collection is careful observation and recording of events and activities. Observational studies are an underutilized form of data gathering in gerontology, especially in applied studies. This situation is unfortunate, because (as was discussed in chap. 2) the observational approach can be useful in providing a comprehensive view of an issue and its context.

One problem with observational studies is that they can be quite time consuming. It is therefore difficult to cover a large number of different situations without a considerable outlay of resources. Observational methods are most useful when there is a need to know a great deal about one or a few situations. Therefore, the external validity, or generalizability of results, can be a concern.

Observational studies are a very flexible approach. In designing a study using observations as the main method of data collection, three basic aspects of the approach can be altered to fit the specific situation. First, the degree of structure involved in the observation process can be manipulated. Sometimes the observation should begin with very little structure because the researcher needs to allow the situation and circumstances to direct things. This approach is especially useful when the observations are meant to help develop ideas or construct hypotheses. At other times, a highly structured format is best. It is even possible to design a checklist of specific actions or events to record. When a very specific research question is to be studied, and the action is fast-paced, a more structured approach is appropriate.

The degree of involvement of the observer can be flexible. Observational studies can be designed to make the observer quite unobtrusive, as when observations are made from an out-of-sight location. When circumstances warrant, they can also be designed to make the observer fully involved in the activities being observed and recorded, such as taking a job as a nurse's aide in a nursing home to observe patient-staff interaction. An important factor in deciding upon level of involvement is the degree to which the observer's behavior might influence the actions of others. As a general rule, observers who are more involved are more likely to influence those being observed.

Another element of observational methods that can be varied is the amount of disclosure. The observer may decide to inform individuals of the fact that they are the subjects of research or determine that it is best to withhold such information until later.

Obviously, important practical issues are involved in determining when and how disclosure is made. Under some circumstances the activities will be substantially altered if people know they are being studied. Significant ethical considerations must also be taken into account in deciding about disclosure. See chapter 7 for a more complete description of research ethics.

Observational studies are accurate only to the degree that the behaviors and events are properly recorded. Therefore, it is important to be careful about notetaking. If taking notes as actions occur is not possible, you should plan to take notes as frequently as circumstances allow. In addition the notes should be as complete as you can make them. Efforts to record completely are necessary because it is sometimes difficult to tell at first exactly which behaviors and events are important.

An excellent example of the use of observations is Jaber F. Gubrium's study of the daily activities in a Wisconsin nursing home (Gubrium, 1975). Because he was interested in the everyday lives and social exchanges of the patients, staff, and administration, Gubrium spent several months in the facility. He took on a number of different roles as he established trust and observed the action. He also used other information-gathering techniques to bolster his observational data. His book is an excellent example of how a variety of approaches to data collection is more likely than any one procedure to offer a complete picture of the situation.

Physical Measures

Because many programs designed for older people provide very basic health and personal care services, applied research in aging often requires information on the physical status and health of individuals. Such information is sometimes obtained by means of interviews with respondents or informants. However, sometimes very accurate, objective physical measures must be made. In these cases, it is best to seek the assistance of professionals who can use the appropriate techniques and instrumentation.

An example of an applied research project that could be improved by the use of multiple measures, including physical measures, would be an investigation of prescription drug compliance. Compliance could be measured by asking participants how much and how frequently they took each of their drugs during the past week. They could also be asked to bring in their drug containers for a pill count. Finally, a physical measure such as a blood, urine, or stool sample might be taken for a chemical analysis to determine how much of the drug is in the system.

Applied studies in aging might require electrocardiograms, blood pressure tests, examinations of lung capacity or oxygen intake, or assessments of visual or auditory acuity. They might also require tests of the nutritional content of meals or range of limb motion or measures of physical endurance. The gathering of information in these areas involves procedures that often require special training and experience. Some can only be completed by or under the supervision of a licensed professional. However this restriction does not mean such procedures should be avoided. When these forms of data collection will be required, you should contact the appropriate professionals in advance so their advice and involvement can be planned into the design and execution of the study.

Less Traditional Approaches

While the previous discussion of data collection methods may appear to be exhaustive, many other possibilities may be useful for a particular research problem. It is important to use your imagination to choose a technique that will work well. A valuable book by Eugene Webb and his associates (Webb et al., 1970) describes many unusual approaches to measurement that are likely to stimulate your imagination. They include examining the wear or dirt on pages of library books (to determine which sections are used frequently), measuring wear on floor tiles (to identify the most popular exhibits in a museum), and studying the contents of trash (to learn about liquor consumption in a town where alcoholic beverages are illegal).

Projective techniques, which involve asking people to give their personal interpretations of ambiguous stimuli, are useful clinical aids and may be of value in applied gerontological research (Wolk, 1979). Many types of anthropological techniques also may be of value to the applied researcher, including ethnographic interviews (described in chap. 2) as well as cognitive anthropology, life histories, and social network mapping (Fry and Keith, 1980).

Although it may be difficult for you to directly apply measures such as the ones just described, the point is that we should not be too dependent on the traditional approaches. In the drug compliance study mentioned earlier, the counting of pills is a nontraditional technique that provides valuable new information.

When you are designing a research project you may find it valuable to consider what you would do to gather the necessary information if you could not ask any questions. This exercise may stimulate your creativity, and some of the methods that grow out of this process may become a part of your project.

THINGS TO CONSIDER WHEN SELECTING METHODS

As stated at the beginning of this chapter, it is unlikely that any one method of data collection will perfectly fit your research problem. However, each procedure has characteristics that limit or enhance its value for a specific project. In general, the goal is to obtain the most appropriate, complete, and accurate information, given the available budget, time, and other resources. The following factors should also be considered in the selection of data collection methods. The questions asked in each section should be answered by you as you determine which method or methods to use.

The Research Problem

Before you can select one or more appropriate data collection procedures, you must have a clear idea of the research problem you wish to address. It is important to have a precise understanding of what you need to know at the end of the project. Are you interested in attitudes, social interaction, personal finances, business transactions, demographic characteristics, abilities, physical characteristics, perceived needs, or service use? Do you have a specific research question, or do you need to explore the overall situation so you can learn more about what to ask? Is your research problem one that demands a complex and lengthy data collection approach, or can it be resolved with a simple and straightforward procedure? Should the research topic be examined in its natural setting or can reconstructions or recollections of past events be used? Does the research problem require that certain pieces of information be collected by an unbiased individual or is it alright for people to tell you about the issues? Does the problem require very precise information? Does it require a response from every, or nearly every, person in the sample?

Target Population

It is also important to take into account the specific group you wish to be able to say something about after the research is completed. The nature of the target population may make certain data collection procedures very inexpensive or inappropriate. Is the target population large or small? Is it very compact or widely dispersed? Is there a need to be sure about who responds? Can members of the population read and write? Do they have access to a telephone? Will they be motivated to provide the type of information you need, or will you have to use a technique that will help ensure their involvement? How might their responses be influenced by knowledge of the research? Can you depend upon their ability to communicate, or should you use a method that minimizes communication requirements? Can you realistically expect members of the target population to remember what you need to know? Would responses to questions be influenced by embarrassment about the research topic, a desire to please the interviewer, or other factors?

Resources

A careful consideration of resources that are available for the project and the resources that will be needed to carry out various types of data collection can help to narrow the list of possibilities. How much time is available to complete the project? What funds can be used in support of the research? What staff may be available? What is their experience and training? Will there be the possibility of adequate supervision if interviewers are used? What kinds of facilities and equipment can be used to support the study?

SUMMARY

In the first chapter of this book, we mentioned that all researchers draw from one storehouse of methods and procedures. As you can tell from this brief overview, the contents of the storehouse are quite varied. They include existing information, face-to-face and phone interviews, forms completed and returned by respondents, observational methods, physical measures, and a variety of less traditional approaches. Every data collection procedure has its own blend of characteristics. Selecting a specific procedure or set of procedures requires that you consider the research problem, the target population, and the available resources. Although the traditional interview or mail procedures can be adapted to work for most applied research problems in aging, it is valuable to think about other approaches that may be more appropriate for your problem.

Your research can also benefit from the use of more than one data collection procedure. Using several methods may appear on first thought to make the research project more complex. However, the well-planned use of two or more methods of data collection may actually simplify this phase of the project, reduce costs, and improve the overall value of the information you gather.

SUGGESTED READINGS

Babbie, E. R. (1979). *The practice of social research* (2nd ed.). Belmont, Calif.: Wadsworth. This excellent book covers most of the data collection strategies in the social sciences. It is very readable and logical.

Rubin, H. J. (1983). *Applied social research*. Columbus, Ohio: Charles E. Merrill. Rubin's text is a thorough and easy-to-read introductory research text that reviews and evaluates the basic approaches to data collection.

Sinnott, J. D., Harris, C. S., Block, M. R., Collesano, S., and Jacobson, S. G. (1983). *Applied research in aging: A guide to methods and resources*. Boston: Little, Brown. This book covers the major issues in applied gerontological research and includes a particularly valuable section on existing data sources in gerontology.

REFERENCES

Cutler, S. J. (1979). Survey research in the study of aging and adult development: A commentary. *The Gerontologist, 19,* 217-219.

Demos, V., and Jache, A. (1981). When you care enough: An analysis of attitudes toward aging in humorous birthday cards. *The Gerontologist, 21,* 209-215.

Dillman, D. A. (1978). *Mail and telephone surveys: The total design method.* New York: Wiley.

Elwell, F. (1984). The effects of ownership on institutional services. *The Gerontologist, 24,* 77-83.

Fillenbaum, G. G. (1979). The Longitudinal Retirement History Study: Methodological and substantive issues. *The Gerontologist, 19,* 203-209.

Fry, C. L., and Keith, J. (Eds.). (1980). *New methods for old age research:*

Anthropological alternatives. Chicago: Loyola University of Chicago Center for Urban Policy.

Gaitz, C. M., and Scott, J. (1975). Analysis of letters to "Dear Abby" concerning old age. *The Gerontologist,* **15,** 47-50.

George, L. K. (1979). The happiness syndrome: Methodological and substantive issues in the study of social-psychological well-being in adulthood. *The Gerontologist,* **19,** 210-216.

Gubrium, J. F. (1975). *Living and dying at Murray Manor.* New York: St. Martin's.

Henretta, J. C. (1979). Using survey data in the study of social stratification in late life. *The Gerontologist,* **19,** 197-202.

Herzog, A. R., Rodgers, W. L., and Kulka, R. A. (1980). *Telephone interviewing and age as factors in interview participation.* Paper presented at 33rd meeting of the Gerontological Society of America, San Diego, Calif.

Kulka, R. A., Herzog, A. R., and Rodgers, W. L. (1980). *Age differences in the effect of telephone and personal interviewing mode on the survey interview process.* Paper presented at the 33rd meeting of the Gerontological Society of America, San Diego, Calif.

Leinbach, R. M. (1982). Alternatives to the face-to-face interview for collecting gerontological needs assessment data. *The Gerontologist,* **22,** 78-82.

McAuley, W. J., Arling, G., Nutty, C., and Bowling, C. (1980). *Final report of the statewide survey of older Virginians* (Research Series No. 3). Richmond, Va.: Virginia Commonwealth University, Virginia Center on Aging.

McAuley, W. J., Travis, S., and Taylor, C. (1984). Long-term care patients in acute care facilities: Determining discharge arrangements. *The Gerontologist,* **24,** 27.

Sinnott, J. D., Harris, C. S., Block, M. R., Collesano, S., and Jacobson, S. G. (1983). *Applied research in aging: A guide to methods and resources.* Boston: Little, Brown.

Webb, E. J., Campbell, D. T., Schwartz, R. D., and Sechrest, L. (1970). *Unobtrusive measures: Nonreactive research in the social sciences.* Chicago: Rand McNally.

Wolk, R. L. (1979). Refined projective techniques with the aged. In D. P. Kent, R. Kastenbaum, and S. Sherwood (Eds.). *Research planning and action for the elderly: The power and potential of social science.* New York: Human Sciences Press.

6

Selecting People to Study

PROBLEMS TO BE SOLVED

How many people should I study—everyone I am interested in, or just a few?
How should I select which people to study?
How can I know whether my findings are useful for making decisions about the
    target group?
How can I help ensure the accuracy of my findings?

Occasionally, it is both reasonable and efficient to study every person you have an interest in. For example, if the researcher is concerned about a very small group of people, it might be most sensible to study all of them. Or if the research problem requires having some information about each person in the study population, it would probably be necessary to survey everyone. The U.S. Census is an example of a project whose most important goal is to obtain an exact count. Therefore, some information is required of each person. The Bureau of Census goes to great effort and expense to include everyone, although it always misses the mark by a small fraction.

However, those kinds of problems are the exceptions in applied gerontological research. Usually, there is no absolute necessity for studying everyone. Furthermore, the size of the group that you want to know about is often so large that it would be impossible to study everyone. The only choice is to select some smaller number to represent the total. The process of selection, or *sampling*, is the topic of this chapter.

WHY SAMPLE?

Sampling is a very important step in the research process, but is often given little consideration because people fail to fully understand its purpose and function. In many instances studies involving samples can actually help ensure more accurate and useful information, and in most cases sampling can improve the overall efficiency of a project.

Accuracy

As Babbie (1979) has noted, studies based on samples can yield more accurate results than studies that examine every individual. There are many reasons why working with smaller numbers can improve accuracy. First, it may be possible to examine a few people very thoroughly, using more precise instruments and techniques and better-trained personnel. If many people are included, the time and resources needed to carry out very accurate measurements might not be available. Thus, while sampling means a decreased extent of coverage, this detriment may be more than overcome by increased depth and precision.

Second, the logistical problems associated with studies of entire populations can sometimes lead to errors. More people studied means more interviewers to train and manage, more questionnaires to validate, edit, and code, and more cases to analyze. Control can become a problem under these conditions, and errors can arise. Think for a moment of the multitude of problems associated with identifying, contacting, and interviewing every person sixty-five years of age or older in a moderate-size community. It is very difficult to do, and inaccuracy is very likely to be a major problem.

Finally, sample studies can often be more accurate because they can be completed in a short time. Although we usually think of time in terms of its relationship to project resources (time is money), the duration of a project can also have important implications for the value of the findings. For example, populations change over time, and a study that gets bogged down at the data-gathering stage may, in reality, be examining several different populations without accurately measuring any one of them. In some types of applied gerontological studies, time is, quite literally, of the essence because the loss rate due to mortality or severe illness is very high. The time required to complete full population studies is also important because it might allow for a natural event to occur that could influence later responses.*

---

*Under some circumstances time can be an important and useful part of the study. Longitudinal studies, for example, examine individuals at different points in time to measure changes. However, such planned uses of time (discussed in chap. 3) are quite different from studies that, by default, require data collection over a long period.

Efficiency

The most obvious reason for basing research on a sample rather than the entire population is that sample studies can make efficient use of available resources. Often, the population of concern is so large that enormous funds, staff, and time would be necessary to study every member. In some cases, it may not even be possible to study the total population. However, even when such studies are possible, they may not be warranted because they are too inefficient. *Efficiency* refers to the value obtained per unit of resource expended. Studies of entire populations often require great amounts of resources (time, money, supplies, etc.) without substantially increasing the accuracy, value, or utility of the resultant information. As you will learn later, efficiency is a good guide for determining how large a sample to choose.

STEPS IN SELECTING A SAMPLE

While sample studies can be more accurate and efficient than studies of total populations, they are not necessarily so. Steps involved in selecting a good sample include (1) defining the population, (2) designing a sampling frame, (3) choosing an appropriate sample size, (4) drawing a sample from the frame, and (5) covering each person selected in the sample. Each of these steps will be discussed.

Defining the Population

Populations are the aggregrates we wish to know something about. A clear understanding of the target population prior to selecting a sample is essential. You should be able to describe it precisely and with great detail; otherwise, you will not be able to draw a sample that adequately represents it. Many efforts at sampling are unsatisfactory simply because too little thought is given to the population the researcher wishes to address.

We usually have a sense of what the target population is, and that is a good starting point for developing a more precise definition. Examples of potential populations of interest could include patients in a given nursing home, all older community residents in area X, all elderly users of home health services in your state, and participants in the Y Senior Citizens Center.

At first glance, all four seem to be quite specific descriptions of real populations. The persons who are responsible for the descriptions may have a clear conception of each type of population, and you yourself might have a good understanding of the population each statement represents, but are their and your conceptions the same? Descriptions of populations should be precise enough so that there can be no misunderstanding about who is and is not included. Precise descriptions are necessary for developing a sampling frame and selecting a sample that can represent the population of interest. Let us consider these initial efforts at defining populations to see where ambiguity or misunderstanding could be a problem.

Patients in a Given Nursing Home.   A nursing home is certainly a concrete entity with well-defined boundaries, and it should be easy to determine who is a patient and who is not. However, without further specificity, there may be considerable confusion about which patients are to be included in the population, if the goal is not to learn about all patients. In an interview study, it may not be possible to interview those people who are too ill or who are mentally impaired, and the population description should reflect this probability. Under certain circumstances, the researcher may not be concerned about people who are scheduled to be in the home for only a brief period (respite cases or acute care patients). If such patients are not to be included, this exception should be noted. Specifying a timeframe would also be useful because the turnover rate in nursing homes can be high.

All Older Community Residents in Area X.   Clearly, *older* is a term that people define differently. It could refer to people who are within a specific chronological age range, or persons who view themselves as old, or persons who exhibit certain physical characteristics. The phrase *community residents* is also inexact. To some people, it might mean anyone who lives in the jurisdiction, and others may use it to refer to people who live in noninstitutional settings. In this case, *institutions* must be carefully defined—is a home for adults an institution? Still others may view community residents as anyone whose official residence is in the area of interest; if so, does it include people who are temporarily away? Here again, the issue of timeframe becomes important. People are constantly changing residence, so the population of a community is also constantly in flux.

All Elderly Users of Home Health Services in Your State.   The term *elderly* poses the same problems as use of the term *older*, but *home health* can also be ambiguous. This term has been used to describe different kinds of services, provided by persons with different levels of training, funded through a variety of programs, and offered to quite dissimilar types of people. To reduce ambiguities in interpretation, it is best to carefully describe the type of service, the provider, and the funding source. For example, are users of home health services provided by informal sources (family members, friends, or neighbors) to be included? What about people who purchase home health services privately? A more precise description of *users* is also needed. Does it mean persons who are now on some list of home health users, even if they have not actually received help recently? Does it mean people who have used the service in the last two weeks? Does it include people who use such a service only an hour or so a week as well as those who use it more frequently?

Participants in the Y Senior Citizens Center.   By now, you can probably think of many problems with the description of this population. Certainly, it would be helpful to know whether to include only recent participants, people who participate on certain days of the week, people who participate in selected programs of the Y Senior Citizens Center, and so forth.

These examples are not meant to frighten you into thinking you cannot develop an acceptable description of your population. Instead, their purpose is to show the importance of precision and clarity. Researchers usually begin with a rough idea of who they want to study. Then through careful thought, it is possible to produce a description that fits the research problem and methodology and that clearly communicates to others the extent and nature of the target population. Use of the APS model can help to develop alternative descriptions that can then be evaluated for their use with your specific problem. Ambiguous population descriptions are due most often to inadequate conceptualizations of the research problem and/or of the people who are to be the focus of study. If you begin with any description at all, then think through its implications from a research perspective, it should be relatively easy to improve your description of the population.

Being careful about describing the population is essential for drawing an appropriate sample. Every individual in the sample should be a member of the population. Furthermore, the more traditional probability-sampling approaches (described later) are designed to give each member an equal, or at least a known, probability of being chosen for the sample (Kish, 1965). This careful coverage is possible only when the population description is conceptually clear and unambiguous.

Clarity, precision, and thoroughness in defining the population also help the researcher and others to overcome the temptation to make unwarranted inferences to groups different than the target population. It is important to take the time in advance to develop a complete description of the population of interest and to go over the description with the consumers of the research. In this way any ambiguities and disagreements can be eliminated, and time will not be wasted constructing and selecting a sample that fails to represent the right target population.

Designing a Sampling Frame

Once the population has been clearly and precisely defined, it would seem to be quite simple to choose a few members to represent it. However, some important intervening steps should not be overlooked. An important step prior to the actual selection of cases is to develop a sampling frame. The *sampling frame* is some form of physical representation of the population (e.g., a list) that can be used to select the sample. The most useful sampling frame is one that includes each member of the population without duplicating any members and that contains no one other than persons in the population. In other words, there should be an exact correspondence between the sampling frame and the population. A perfect match is not always attainable, but is something to strive for, because any deviation is likely to contribute to inaccurate results (Kish, 1965).

The simplest and most useful sampling frames are lists that uniquely identify each person in the population of interest. The identification could be through names, identification numbers, or combinations of letters and numbers so long as the list (1) contains a unique identifier for each member of the population, (2) includes no duplications, and (3) has no nonpopulation members. Often, lists are already available or can be created from available information with relatively little effort. For example, nursing homes maintain records of residents that could serve as sampling frames. Usually these records are complete enough so that it is possible to define a population and develop a frame that meets the specific needs of the project. Nutrition projects or congregate meal sites often keep files that may include addresses of participants, information on dates of participation, and so forth. Universities now generally maintain computerized files of students. Such files facilitate creation of a list of students of a specified age that are currently enrolled in certain target courses. Hospital and clinic records may also be the basis for a useful sampling frame. Agencies responsible for providing services to older people in their homes (e.g., companion services, home health, meals on wheels, homemaker, friendly visitors) maintain information that may be readily converted into a suitable sampling frame.

Each of these settings has the advantage of maintaining records, lists, or files that may be useful in the development of a sampling frame. Sometimes they can be used directly as a sampling frame, if checks are made to eliminate duplications. But whether such frames would be accurate reflections of your particular target population is another matter. Nursing home residents differ in obvious ways from the general population of elderly, for example, and a list of nursing home patients would not represent all the older people in an area. Furthermore, considerable differences exist among nursing homes in terms of patient characteristics. Some tend to specialize in Medicaid, while others seek private-pay patients, and still others serve patients with cognitive deficiencies, and so forth. So even when a list is readily accessible, you must carefully consider whether the population represented by the list corresponds to the specific population you wish to know about.

For some target populations, lists are not nearly so readily available as the sources just described. When appropriate lists are not available, much time can be spent in developing one that is appropriate, as when the target population consists of all community residents of a given age. Rarely does any list of community residents specify age, and most available lists are, at best, incomplete. One possible list is the phone book, although it includes only persons who have a phone and who have a listed number. Furthermore, people of a specified age cannot be selected in advance from phone listings. Some localities have city directories (e.g., *Polk* and *Hill* directories) that contain information from door-to-door canvasses of the community. The information may be somewhat out of date and incomplete, but these directories do sometimes include a retiree category that may suffice for some applied research problems.

When lists of individuals are not available for sampling frames, you may need to develop an initial frame that less directly matches the population of interest. Then, through successive stages in the sampling process, the frame can be refined to correspond with the target population. This approach is often taken in community surveys of older people. Because there is no adequate list of older community residents, you may begin by using information on the geographic distribution of all households. Obviously, there is not a one-to-one correspondence between households and the elderly in a community. Some households contain no elderly, while others contain several. However, this starting point (often called a *stage*) does satisfy certain criteria for a sampling frame, in that all elderly—with the exception of transients—are included, and none should be represented more than once. A sample of household groups (e.g., city blocks) may then be chosen based upon some rule about the appropriate probability of inclusion. Then, interviewers could contact all (or a sample of) households in each household group to determine whether anyone living at each selected household meets the age-eligibility criterion for inclusion in the survey. The eligibles would then be asked to participate. This combination of area probability sampling and screening for eligibles is often used when populations are not easily listed.

Choosing an Appropriate Sample Size

Deciding on the number of people to select for the sample can be an exasperating experience. As Simon (1978) has noted, most researchers base their sample size decisions on either the average sample sizes used in past research or the largest number the budget will allow. Each approach has some foundation in logic, but neither guarantees an appropriate sample size for a given research problem.

Earlier researchers studying similar topics in similar settings may have taken great pains in choosing reasonable sample sizes. However, they may also have had severely limited budgets, or they may not have given adequate thought to the issue of sample size. Furthermore, while a budget ceiling can be a valid constraint on sample size, the research methods can sometimes be revised so that the number can be increased by using more efficient procedures in other aspects of the research. Also, budgets are rarely set at the time that decisions on sample size must be made. It is better, when possible, to base the budget on the necessary sample size rather than to base sample size on the budget.

The most responsible approach to selecting an appropriate sample size is to think about it in terms of overall efficiency, taking into account cost versus accuracy. Other things being equal, the larger the sample the more accurate the results will be at reflecting the actual circumstances in the population. Sampling error, or the amount of error introduced by the sample size and method, is inversely related to sample size, but doubling the sample size does not reduce sampling error by half. In fact, it would be necessary to quadruple the sample size in order to reduce sampling error by half! Therefore, as sample size increases, cost increases at a far more rapid rate than sampling error decreases.

It is usually possible to determine, within a small range, the sample size below which accuracy would be unacceptably poor and above which the increased accuracy is unjustifiable, given the cost of the additional cases and the research problem. The sample size should fall within this range because it represents the most efficient use of resources. Table 6-1 shows how sample size as well as the distribution of responses can influence the amount of sampling error in the results. This table shows various confidence intervals for a binomial variable (a measure with two possible choices) at the 95% confidence level. It assumes that a random sample will be drawn from a very large population. You can see from the table that as the sample size increases the confidence interval becomes smaller. Also, as the distribution on the binomial approaches 50/50, the confidence interval increases.

You can develop a rough estimate* of the confidence interval for a binomial measure by finding the intersection of the size of your sample and the distribution on the binomial. For example, if the distribution of yes and

---

*This table does not work in all cases because the size of the population also influences these issues. However, it provides reasonable estimates when the population is very large.

Table 6-1. Estimated Sampling Error at the 95% Confidence Level

Sample size	Binomial Percentage Distribution				
	50/50	*60/40*	*70/30*	*80/20*	*90/10*
100	10	9.8	9.2	8	6
200	7.1	6.9	6.5	5.7	4.2
300	5.8	5.7	5.3	4.6	3.5
400	5	4.9	4.6	4	3
500	4.5	4.4	4.1	3.6	2.7
600	4.1	4	3.7	3.3	2.4
700	3.8	3.7	3.5	3	2.3
800	3.5	3.5	3.2	2.8	2.1
900	3.3	3.3	3.1	2.7	2
1000	3.2	3.1	2.9	2.5	1.9
1100	3	3	2.8	2.4	1.8
1200	2.9	2.8	2.6	2.3	1.7
1300	2.8	2.7	2.5	2.2	1.7
1400	2.7	2.6	2.4	2.1	1.6
1500	2.6	2.5	2.4	2.1	1.5
1600	2.5	2.4	2.3	2	1.5
1700	2.4	2.4	2.2	1.9	1.5
1800	2.4	2.3	2.2	1.9	1.4
1900	2.3	2.2	2.1	1.8	1.4
2000	2.2	2.2	2	1.8	1.3

Source: From Babbie 1979, p. 539, reprinted with permission
How to use this table: Find the intersection between the sample size and the approximate percentage distribution of the binomial in the sample. The number appearing at this intersection represents the estimated sampling error, at the 95% confidence level, expressed in percentage points (plus or minus). Example: In a sample of 400 respondents, 60% answer "Yes" and 40% answer "No." The sampling error is estimated at plus or minus 4.9 percentage points. The confidence interval, then, is between 55.1% and 64.9%. We would estimate (95% confidence) that the proportion of the total population who would say "Yes" is somewhere within that interval.

no responses is 70% and 30%, respectively, and the sample size is 400, the sampling error is estimated to be plus or minus 4.6 percentage points. In this example, the confidence interval for yes responses is between 65.4% and 74.6%, meaning that the proportion of the total population who would respond yes can be expected to fall within the range 65.4% and 74.6% approximately 95% of the time.

The information in Table 6-1 can also be used to obtain a ballpark estimate of adequate sample size. All that is necessary is an estimate of the range of responses in the population for the variable of interest. Then, you can move down the column for that distribution until you find an acceptable confidence interval. The sample size on the same row as the selected confidence interval will be the number of cases to draw in a sample. Thus, if you expect a 50/50 distribution on the variable, and you accept a confidence interval of plus or minus about 6% at the 95% confidence level, you should select 300 cases. But how do you know, in advance, the distribution of responses in the population? Unfortunately, this information is usually not available; if you had it, the study would probably be unnecessary! However, you can base the estimate of the distribution on the results of previous studies, or you can assume the worst distribution (that is a 50/50 distribution), or you might decide to select a distribution that falls somewhere between these two points. Once you have determined what sample size is appropriate, you can estimate the project cost for this number of cases. The results may lead to an adjustment in the sample size as you seek to improve overall efficiency.

The simple procedure just described is not meant to be a formula for determining the sample size. Frequently you may be interested in several variables with different (and perhaps nonbinomial) distributions, you may not plan to use a simple random sample, or the target population may be relatively small. All of these circumstances can affect the sample size you select. However, this procedure can be used as a starting point in selecting an adequate sample. Kish (1965) is a good source for more information on determining sample size under a variety of special conditions.

Drawing a Sample

Once the population has been defined, an appropriate sampling frame has been developed, and the number of cases to sample has been established, the next step is selecting individuals from the frame. These people will then constitute the research sample, and they will, in the aggregate, serve to represent the target population. There are two general categories of samples. *Random* or *probability samples* are those in which each member of the frame has an equal, or at least a known, probability of being selected. Simple random samples, stratified samples, cluster samples, and systematic samples all fall into this category. Samples of this type should be used when tests of significance will be applied to the results or when you plan to make inferences to the population from the sample. *Nonrandom* samples are usually used when inferences to a specific population are unnecessary or when circumstances cause difficulty in drawing a random or probability sample. Nonrandom samples include the snowball technique, purposive sampling, quota sampling, and use of available subjects. All of these major techniques for sample selection will be described further.

Simple Random Sample.   The very useful method of selecting individuals at random from the sample frame so that each member of the frame has the same chance of being selected assures that differences between the sample and the population are randomly distributed. This condition of random distribution of differences makes possible the use of most statistical techniques. In a very elementary sense, statistical tests are designed to determine the likelihood that occurrences in the sample exist in the population. Random samples may be either more or less representative of the population from which they are drawn, but statistics provide a way of determining the chance that the sample findings do not represent conditions in the target population.

Suppose you were interested in studying patients in a certain nursing home. A simple random sample could be drawn as follows:

Target population.   All residents of X nursing home who are rated by staff as physically able to complete the questionnaire and who have been patients in the facility for at least two months prior to the interview period.

Sampling frame.   Names of every patient meeting the target criteria. It should be noted that developing the sampling frame would require at least two steps. First, records would have to be reviewed to cull persons not meeting the criterion for length of stay. Second, staff who are knowledgeable about the patients' status would have to be consulted to determine who is physically able to complete the questionnaire. For convenience, names of patients meeting these criteria are listed in alphabetical order. There are 150 names in all.

Sample size.   The sample will include 50 cases.

Sampling method.   Assign a number (simply a reference number) from one to N to each person in the sampling frame. After determining the sample size (n), go to a table of random numbers and choose the first n numbers that fall between one and N.* The persons who are referenced by these randomly selected numbers will comprise the simple random sample. To complete the example, suppose the goal is to randomly choose 50 of the 150 persons who are listed in the frame. All 150 (N) persons are assigned a number from 001 to 150. A table of random numbers is then consulted to select the first 50 (n) persons whose numbers come up. As can be seen from this example, simple random samples are easy to do if a good sampling frame is available.

Stratified Samples.   The simple random sample has many advantages, but in certain situations other methods may be more appropriate. One potential problem with the simple random sample is that chance will occasionally lead to a sample that is not at all representative of the population. It is possible to improve the likelihood of adequate representation through *stratified sampling.* This procedure requires more than the ability to list the elements of

---

*Tables of random numbers and directions for using them are available in most introductory statistics texts.

the population. The sample frame must also be constructed so that persons with certain characteristics are listed separately. Therefore, stratified sampling requires more advance information about each member of the target population. This knowledge is then used to select a sample that is likely (but not guaranteed) to better represent the population.

Stratified sampling consists of dividing the population into generally homogeneous categories (strata) and then selecting cases according to some scheme within each stratum. Care must be taken in selecting the characteristics used for stratification. The purpose of stratified sampling is to increase the precision of the research variables; thus, it is important to stratify on the basis of characteristics that have some logical relationship to the topic being researched. Some researchers habitually and conservatively stratify on certain demographic characteristics (e.g., age, sex, and race). However, it is best not to stratify on characteristics unless there is a logical reason for doing so.

Suppose you were interested in determining whether employers in your community have active programs of preretirement planning for their employees, and, if so, the nature of the programs.* Companies with more employees probably have more extensive preretirement programs. Therefore, it may be desirable to stratify the sample by number of employees. In this way you could be sure that you do not have too many large companies or too many small companies. A stratified sample could be drawn as follows:

Target population.   All companies listed in the most recent business directory for the target community. There are 300 such companies.

Sampling frame.   The business directory lists the number of employees each company has. This information is used to develop a frame that divides the population into two strata. Stratum A contains 150 companies with more than 25 employees and Stratum B contains 150 companies with 25 or fewer employees.

Sample size.   Eighty companies are to be selected.

Sampling method.   Assign a unique number from 1 to 300 (N) to each member of the sampling frame, beginning with Stratum A and continuing through Stratum B. After determining the overall sample size (n), divide n by 2 to decide how many companies to select from each stratum (this division is feasible in the present example because the population has been divided into strata of equal size). Using a table of random numbers, begin selecting companies from the frame. Continue selecting from both strata until you have the required number ($\frac{1}{2}$ n) from each. In other words, if the sample size is 80, sampling should continue until 40 cases have been selected from Stratum A and 40 cases have been selected from Stratum B.

This procedure will ensure that the sample will contain the same propor-

*It should be noted that this situation is an example of sampling *organizations* rather than people. Often, something other than an individual can be the unit of analysis. The sample design should be appropriate to the unit of analysis.

Table 6-2. Example of Defining Four Strata Based upon Number of Employees and Proportion of Older Workers

	Company Size	
Proportion of Older Workers	*Large (more than 25 employees)*	*Small (25 or fewer employees)*
	Stratum A	*Stratum B*
RELATIVELY FEW (Less than 35% of Workers are Age 50+)	Large companies with relatively few older workers	Small companies with relatively few older workers
	Stratum C	*Stratum D*
RELATIVELY MANY (35% or More Workers are Age 50+)	Large companies with relatively many older workers	Small companies with relatively many older workers

tions of large companies and small companies that exist in the population. Because the size of the company may be an important factor in the availability of preretirement programs for employees, stratification on employment size was used to ensure an adequate distribution of cases on this key characteristic. Although a simple random sample may also result in a sample with an acceptable distribution on employment size, there is no assurance that it actually would. Thus, stratification may require some additional work, but it can increase the overall accuracy and external validity of the results by assuring in advance that the sample and the population have similar distributions on characteristics that are important to the research topic.

The preceding example is a very simple instance of stratified sampling because it uses only one characteristic of the population for stratification. It is possible and sometimes desirable to stratify on several characteristics. For example, it might be useful to stratify not only on number of employees but also on the proportion of employees 50 or more years old. (The information on age of employees is not likely, however, to be readily available. It is always necessary to weigh the advantage of increased accuracy against the resources that would have to be used to carry out the stratification.) If the companies could be reasonably divided into those having a high proportion of employees 50 years old or older and those with a low proportion of employees in this age group, this stratification criterion in conjunction with the number-of-employees criterion would lead to four separate strata: (1) small companies with a low proportion of older employees, (2) small companies with a high proportion of older employees, (3) large companies with a low proportion of older employees, and (4) large companies with a high proportion of older employees. Table 6-2 illustrates how the proportion of older workers and the number of employees can be used to create four strata for sampling.

The more characteristics used for stratification, the more work is needed to prepare the sampling frame. Unless the characteristics are of known or anticipated relevance to the research issue, the extra work is likely to waste time. Thus, it is a good idea to limit stratification to one or two or at most three characteristics that are of central importance.

When the population is equally divided among the strata, and the goal is to choose a sample that represents the entire population, it is not difficult to decide how many units to draw from each stratum. Because all strata contain the same number of elements, the number to be selected from each of the strata should also be equal. Thus, if 100 cases were to be selected from a sampling frame divided into four strata of equal size, 25 cases would be selected from each. However, many characteristics of populations do not so readily produce equal-size strata (e.g., race, rural-urban residence, "old-old" versus "young-old", etc.). When the strata are of unequal size, two different methods of selecting respondents are proportionate stratified sampling and disproportionate stratified sampling. Which method should be selected depends on the overall objectives of the study.

Proportionate Stratified Sampling.   In *proportionate stratified sampling*, the number of cases are selected from each stratum that will result in a sample that reflects the proportions of the strata in the population. In other words, if stratum A contains 75% of the population and stratum B contains 25%, the sample should contain the same proportions (75% and 25%, respectively) of stratum A and stratum B cases. Proportionate stratified sampling is a way of assuring that the same distribution that exists in the population on the characteristic of interest also exists in the sample. The simplest case of proportionate stratified sampling occurs when the strata contain the same number of elements and samples of equal size are drawn from each. Thus, the earlier example of stratified sampling is also an example of proportionate stratified sampling when the strata are of *equal* size. The following example demonstrates proportionate stratified sampling with strata of *unequal* size.

Suppose in the preceding example that the population of companies is distributed so that there are only 100 companies with more than 25 employees, while there are 200 companies with 25 or fewer employees.

Target population.   As before, all 300 companies listed in the most recent business directory for the target community.

Sampling frame.   The sampling frame is constructed as before. However, stratum A of the frame contains only 100 companies with more than 25 employees and stratum B contains 200 companies with 25 or fewer employees.

Sample size.   The sample size is 100.

Sampling method.   Assign a unique number to each company, beginning with 1 in stratum A and continuing through 300 in stratum B. Because 33% of the population is in stratum A and 67% is in stratum B, the sample should also contain 33% from stratum A and 67% from stratum B. Therefore, for a sample size of 100, 33 cases should be selected from stratum A and 67 cases should be selected from stratum B. Actual selection of cases can be carried out with a table of random numbers as described earlier. The objective of proportionate stratified sampling is to make the sample as close as possible to the population in terms of the distribution of cases across relevant characteristics. Because the sample will reflect the population on these characteristics, there is a greater likelihood that it will also reflect the population on the research variables.

When the main goal of the research is to draw conclusions about the entire population, proportionate stratified sampling can be an effective method of improving accuracy. However, sometimes the research objectives require that the sample contains relatively more or fewer members of some strata than exist in the population. In this case, disproportionate stratified sampling can be used.

Disproportionate Stratified Sampling. On many occasions proportionate stratified sampling is not useful because it would lead to too few cases in one stratum to allow for comparisons across strata, or because it would be difficult to carry out separate analysis of some of the smaller strata. In the preceding example, if there were any intentions of examining members of stratum A separately, there may be too few cases for such an analysis.

A reasonable alternative may be to select 67 cases from each stratum. This option is an example of *disproportionate stratified sampling,* because the sample no longer reflects the distribution of the population on number of employees. The term *disproportionate* is used to show that the elements in certain strata were selected in such a way that the sample strata proportions do not equal the population strata proportions.

Disproportionate stratified sampling can facilitate comparisons across strata or allow for in-depth analysis of each stratum separately, but it can create problems when combining the strata for generalization to the full population. In the preceding example, if all elements of the disproportionate stratified sample are combined, there will be too many cases from stratum A to assume that the population is adequately represented by the sample. The stratum A elements will have more impact on the findings than their actual relative distribution in the population warrants. There are two methods for overcoming this problem. First, it may be possible to randomly select elements from stratum A so that the number reflects the proportions in the population. For example, from the 67 stratum A elements, 33 cases could be randomly selected for combination with the 67 stratum B elements so that the combined 100 cases would again constitute a proportionate stratified sample. While this method is perfectly feasible, it means you are failing to use information you have on hand. An alternative approach would be to assign weights to cases. The actual procedures for weighting are beyond the scope of this presentation. Most canned statistics packages (SPSS, SAS, and BIOMED) make it easy to use weights in analysis. However, weighting can lead to difficulty in interpreting statistics. You should therefore consult a statistician prior to selecting the sample if there is a need for a disproportionate stratified sample.

Cluster Samples.   Sometimes it is advisable or necessary to select clusters of population elements rather than individual elements as part of the overall sampling procedure, even when the individual is the unit of analysis. *Cluster sampling* is often carried out in a multistage sampling design in which clusters are first selected and then individuals are drawn from clusters according to some strategy. Most often, cluster sampling is carried out because it consumes fewer resources. It can also lead to a loss in precision unless the clusters are carefully chosen.

Suppose you are interested in some characteristics of current participants in senior centers sponsored by area agencies on aging throughout your state. Due to the time and resources involved, it is not possible to interview people at each senior center or to develop a sampling frame consisting of current participants in all senior centers in the state. Time and expense will be cut considerably if you select a small number (e.g., 15) of senior centers first and then select participants from only the chosen centers.

Target population.   Current participants in senior centers sponsored by area agencies on aging throughout state A.

Sampling frame.   Because there is no sampling frame consisting of all participants, an initial frame will be constructed to include all senior centers sponsored by area agencies on aging in the state. Each area agency on aging is contacted to determine how many senior centers there are and about how many current participants are at each center. The senior centers are actually clusters of current participants.

Sample Size.   Preliminary work with information provided by the senior centers in state A suggests that if 15 centers are chosen, the total number of participants will probably range from 750 to 950.

Sampling method.   Assign a unique number to each senior center and use a table of random numbers to select the sample of 15 centers. Once the senior centers are selected, it is necessary to select participants. If the resources are sufficient, all current participants in the 15 clusters (senior centers) could be included. If a smaller sample size is desired, a sampling frame can be constructed of the names of all current participants at each of the selected centers. A random sample can then be selected from the frame. In this case, the sampling occurs in two different stages—selection of the clusters and then selection of elements within each cluster. This method is an example of two-stage sampling. *Multistage sampling* is merely a sample design that incorporates sampling at more than one stage, or level of aggregation.

Having completed a cluster sample as outlined, it should be kept in mind that the respondents are still not necessarily representative of current participants in the area agency on aging-sponsored senior centers in state A. They are probably very representative of the participants at the selected senior centers, but they may not adequately represent all the statewide senior center participants because people do not randomly choose to participate in a senior center and because the members of any center may therefore be very much like other members of that center. This similarity is called *homogeneity of the units within clusters.* The more homogeneous the membership in a cluster and the less the clusters are like one another, the less precise the cluster-sampling approach. Selecting more clusters and fewer elements from each generally increases the precision. For example, choosing 25 senior centers, rather than 15, could increase the precision even if the overall number of participants selected remained constant.

The precision of the cluster sample could also be improved if stratification were employed in the selection of the initial clusters (Kish, 1965). Stratification is often used when the clusters differ substantially in terms of the number of people contained in each, as is the case in most naturally occurring clusters. If a simple random sample is taken of clusters that differ in size, there may be too many large or small clusters and thus over- or under-representation of their members. However, the clusters can usually be stratified by size, and the proportion of large and small clusters drawn can then be controlled so they will equal the proportions in all centers throughout the state.

In cluster sampling, it is also sometimes useful to stratify on characteristics other than number of elements. Stratification is often carried out at the first stage because easily available information on the clusters greatly simplifies the process. For example, census data are available on minor civil divisions or even small geographic units that can facilitate stratification on population size, median age, education, racial composition, and so forth. Also, agencies generally keep records or aggregate statistics on the clusters they manage. Such sources can make it possible to stratify without knowing detailed characteristics of each member of the population.

To summarize, cluster sampling is used when circumstances make it necessary to carry out research within selected geographic or organizational units. At times it is used when developing a complete sampling frame for the population would be very expensive or difficult. At other times it is used because carrying out research in a few selected geographic areas or organizational units is less time consuming and less expensive than trying to cover the entire geographic or organizational region. Precision increases when more clusters are included and when clusters are stratified on appropriate characteristics, but expenses generally increase as well.

Systematic Samples.   Often used as a basis for selecting elements from a sampling frame because it is simple and efficient, systematic sampling consists of selecting every kth element from the sampling frame, with k representing an interval chosen to cover the entire frame and to lead to the desired sample size. For example, if a sample size of 250 were to be selected from a population of 5,000, the sampling interval (k) would be 5,000 ÷ 250 = 20. The starting point for the systematic sample should be selected randomly, although it should be between 1 and k. Once the starting point is selected, every kth element on the list is chosen for inclusion in the sample.

In systematic sampling, it is important to select a sampling interval (k) that will cover the entire frame. Otherwise, the procedure will be biased against those who are listed later. Sampling frames are usually constructed with some logical ordering of elements (e.g., alphabetical order). Thus, in the preceding example, a sampling interval of 10 used to select 250 cases out of a population of 5,000 would ensure the nonselection of persons whose last names fall in the second half of the alphabet, seriously altering the racial-ethnic composition of the sample and thus leading to biased results.

Systematic sampling can also lead to biased results when the elements in the frame are systematically arranged according to a characteristic that may be important to the study (Babbie, 1979). As an example, a researcher may be interested in the amount of time members of the professional staff in a large nursing home spend with patients. In selecting a sample of patients, choosing patients by room number, beginning with a random start and choosing every kth room as just outlined, may seem appropriate; however, nursing homes are often designed and managed in ways that lead to a systematic distribution of rooms. The selection of every kth room may therefore lead to too many (or too few) patients with one or more of the following characteristics: (1) having rooms closer to the nursing stations, (2) paying for their own care, (3) having rooms closer to the nursing lounge, (4) living in private rooms or in wards, or (5) having severe physical or mental health problems. Because any of these characteristics is likely to be related to time spent with patients, the results of the study may not reflect the actual circumstances in the nursing home. Therefore, the researcher should carefully examine the sampling frame to be sure there is no systematic arrangement of the elements before employing a systematic sampling technique.

As long as no systematic arrangement of elements can bias results, systematic sampling can be a useful method for selecting cases for study. Systematic samples are generally as representative as simple random samples and are also somewhat easier to do. When random starts are employed, systematic samples can be viewed as equivalent to random samples.

Nonrandom Sampling Techniques.   A number of sampling techniques not based upon random selection are most often used out of necessity or convenience. When these techniques are employed, use of standard statistical procedures is rarely appropriate, and the researcher must be careful in generalizing to any population.

Snowball Technique.   In the *snowball technique*, used when it is difficult to identify target cases in advance, the first few individuals contacted are asked to identify others who meet the criteria for research. The process of identification continues until a sufficient number of cases have been obtained. The snowball technique obviously works best when individuals to be studied know persons with similar characteristics. It has been used effectively in studies of illegal drug use and homosexuality, where simple random samples are not feasible. The approach may be useful in applied gerontological research when friendship networks or informal patterns of assistance are the topics of study.

Purposive Sampling.   A method in which individuals are selected on the basis of known population characteristics but without use of random sampling is called *purposive sampling*. This technique is often used in pretests when the main goal is to obtain individuals who reflect the broad range of characteristics that might influence use of a research instrument. For example, in pretesting a questionnaire that is to be used with a sample of noninstitutionalized elderly, it would be useful to select individuals who represent a broad spectrum of functional abilities, health characteristics, educational levels, and living arrangements. Such a range would obviously exist in the population, and the researcher may select a purposive sample of people who have these different characteristics to be sure the instrument is effective across the entire range of possibilities. In this case, the goal is to test the instrument on people who have characteristics that may influence the quality of the responses, not to obtain a sample whose responses can be generalized to the population.

Quota Sampling.   *Quota sampling* relies heavily on interviews and other field staff, because the interviewer is required to obtain a certain number (quota) of interviews with specified characteristics. Quota sampling is often carried out in a multistage sampling design in which small geographic areas are selected first and the interviewer is then asked to conduct interviews in the area until they have reached a specified number or have exhausted all households. Often the interviewer is told to select individuals with certain characteristics such as age, sex, race, or occupation.

As with stratified sampling, the goal of quota sampling is to obtain a sample whose characteristics reflect the characteristics of the population on several important dimensions. Through quota sampling, ensuring that the sample distribution almost exactly matches the population distribution on a set of characteristics is quite possible. If interviewers selected cases in a completely random fashion, quota sampling should yield results very similar to stratified random samples (Stephan and McCarthy, 1965). However, in selecting the quota, the interviewer may make numerous decisions that bias the sample. For example, the sample is more likely to consist of persons who are readily available, nonthreatening, and easier to interview. In a community survey of the elderly, quota sampling would probably lead to a sample containing persons who are more often at home, of the same race and socioeconomic status as the interviewer, more gregarious, better able to hear, and so forth.

Careful control can help reduce such biases. For example, detailed instructions can be provided on how to locate respondents. By narrowing the choices available to interviewers in making their selections, interviewer tendency to select "easy" respondents will be minimized, but not eliminated. These procedures are also likely to increase costs, so that at some point a different sampling procedure may be more practical (Stephan and McCarthy, 1965).

Use of Available Subjects.   Perhaps the most common nonrandom method of all is the use of individuals who are close at hand, readily identified, or otherwise easy to study. Because the selection is based upon convenience, these samples are frequently called *convenience* samples. At times, researchers devise sophisticated methods of sampling within such groups, but this does not improve generalizability to persons outside the groups. For example, in a study of public transportation use among older residents, researchers may randomly sample participants in senior centers in the county of interest. Such a sample could be easily selected, but participants in senior centers are a special group of individuals who are not likely to be representative of all the elderly in an area. They are set apart by differences in physical health, proximity to the senior centers, mobility, and so forth. For similar reasons, you should be careful about using residents of special housing, members of senior clubs and organizations, service users, or other lists of available subjects when the goal is to generalize to a broader population. Clearly, necessity sometimes dictates use of available samples, but it should be obvious by now that the results should be interpreted with great caution.

Covering Each Person Selected

No matter which sampling method is used, steps must be taken to obtain information on every element chosen for the sample. The external validity of the sample is greatest when all the ones selected are studied. People who were chosen but not studied are probably different from those who actually are studied. Additionally, people not chosen but included in the study (e.g., interviewer substitutes) are probably unlike the original sample. In either case, the results are likely to be biased.

There is no response rate (other than 100%) that all researchers accept as adequate coverage of the sample. However, some organizations believe that anything below 75% is unacceptable (Fowler, 1984). It is usually possible to estimate the response rate you will obtain, given your data collection procedure, and then inflate the sample size to compensate. However, you should remember that this inflation simply increases the number of cases in the sample; it will not reduce any bias in the sample resulting from nonresponse. The only way to be sure that there is no bias due to nonresponse is to strive to obtain responses from everyone in the sample.

A number of methods can improve coverage of the sample. First, complete coverage is much easier if identifying information for the sample elements is thorough and accurate. Interviewers must be able to locate and accurately identify the people who are selected. Second, careful training of interviewers can help assure that all persons selected are located and that persons not selected are not included, and can improve the likelihood that contacted persons will participate. Third, a program of multiple callbacks, or multiple waves of mailings in mail surveys, can improve the coverage of the sample.

When possible, the researcher should try to determine who among the sample was not included, what they were like, and why they were not included. This information is useful in determining the way the people covered differ from the ones not covered and can thus serve as an indication of the amount of error introduced by incomplete coverage. The data can also lead to improved plans for future studies. Interviewers can jot down their observations on the sex, approximate age, race, location, housing, and other characteristics of people who refuse to be interviewed. Generally, much less information is available about those persons who are selected but never contacted. Even here, however, some information from the sampling frame may give an indication of possible biases in the sample.

SPECIAL PROBLEMS IN SAMPLING OLDER COMMUNITY RESIDENTS

The older population is growing rapidly, and its proportion of the total population is also increasing, but the fact remains that older people are a relatively small subgroup of the noninstitutionalized population in most communities. As mentioned earlier, there is not usually a totally adequate list of elderly people who live outside of institutions. An excellent method for sampling community residents is an area probability technique using household screenings to determine whether members of selected households meet the age or other criteria that have been established for the sample. Unfortunately, it is also usually very expensive, because household screening is time consuming and requires considerable travel. In addition, many of the households that are screened will yield no cases that meet the criteria. Therefore it is sometimes necessary to use sampling methods that are less costly.

Lee and Finney (1977) developed a method for obtaining a sample of noninstitutionalized elderly while keeping costs low. Their sampling procedure was based on a screening letter that was mailed to households selected by systematic sampling from telephone directories covering the entire state of Washington. The screening letter included a cover letter describing the objectives of the study and asking the recipient to complete and return an attached form that listed the names of all persons in the household who were 60 or more years old. A postage-paid return envelope was also included to facilitate the return of the screening letters. To help keep expenses to a minimum, households without anyone 60 years old or older were asked not to return the screening letter. All persons who were identified through returned screening letters as eligible for the sample were surveyed by means of mail questionnaires. The screening letters identified 1,169 eligible individuals, and a total of 870 completed questionnaires were received.

This sampling approach is very inexpensive. The total direct cost for the project, including sampling and data analysis, was only $5,920. However, some bias was probably introduced because of the sampling and data collection methods used. Not everyone has a telephone, and not all of those with phones have listed numbers. In addition, individuals with certain characteristics may be more likely to complete and return the screening letter and the questionnaire. What kinds of biases might result from such factors? Lee and Finney compared the sample characteristics to census data for the elderly in Washington and found that their respondents were younger, better educated, and more likely to be married. Of course, the sample may also have differed on characteristics not measured by the census but important to the specific research problem.

Gibson and Herzog (1984) have described a somewhat different procedure for sampling. Their method, called rare element telephone screening, was used to locate older blacks, a group that is so rare as to be very expensive to sample using standard strategies. They used telephones to recontact respondents (18-54 years old) who had participated in a national survey.

Table 6-3. Steps in the Sampling Process and Problems That May be Encountered at Each Step

Step	Possible Problems
1. Choose and define a population	Inadequate or imprecise conceptualization of the population
2. Choose an appropriate size	Sample is so small that results are questionable or so large that the research will require too many resources
3. Develop a sampling frame	Failure to match the target population
4. Draw a sample from the frame	a. Chance error (measurable by statistical tests) b. Failure to follow principles of probability sampling
5. Cover the entire sample	Researcher's substitutions, respondents' self-selection (e.g., refusal, unavailability)

These individuals were asked to provide the names, telephone numbers, and addresses of any parents or grandparents who were at least 55 years old. The older individuals who were identified were then interviewed by phone. This procedure led to a high yield of valid phone numbers and a high rate of response when the older people were contacted by phone. While rare element telephone screening may lead to various sorts of bias, it does represent a practical, inexpensive way to obtain a nationwide sample of older blacks.

In deciding whether sampling techniques such as those just described are acceptable, the low cost and enhanced accessibility must be carefully weighed against the need for accuracy. It is worth stating once again that the true test of a sample design is its overall efficiency in addressing a specific research problem.

SUMMARY

Table 6-3 provides a brief summary of the steps involved in sampling and the problems that may occur at each step. First, it is important to carefully define the population so that drawing an appropriate sample will be possible. If the population is not adequately defined, there is no assurance that the other steps in sampling will lead to a sample that represents the population of interest. Second, a decision must be made regarding the number of cases to be included in the sample. If the sample is too small, the results are likely to be inaccurate. On the other hand, too large a sample may stretch available resources to the point where all phases of the study must suffer. Third, a sampling frame (a list or some other physical representation of the sample) is developed. There should be an exact match between the sampling frame and the population, or the results cannot be generalized to the population with any degree of confidence. Fourth, the sample is drawn, following a procedure for sampling determined in advance. The specific technique depends on the type of research question and the need for accuracy. Following the principles of random or probability sampling will help to limit selection biases that might reduce the external validity of the findings. Although with any random sample chance error can lead to incorrect findings, an advantage of random or probability techniques is that the likelihood of incorrect conclusions is calculable. In the final stage of sampling, every effort must be made to cover the entire sample because cases that are not included may be different from cases that are included, and these differences could influence the results.

The older population presents some unique, but manageable, problems in sampling. Two inexpensive methods for drawing samples of the elderly were described and may be of value in some applied research projects. With care and attention, it is possible to obtain a sample that provides an accurate picture of the population without consuming too many resources.

SUGGESTED READINGS

Slonim, M. J. (1960). *Sampling: A quick reliable guide to practical statistics.* New York: Simon and Schuster. As the title suggests, this brief book describes elementary sampling techniques and emphasizes the practical, rather than theoretical, aspects of sampling.

Kish, L. (1965). *Survey sampling.* New York: Wiley. A classic in the area of sampling, this book provides a thorough, detailed description of many different sampling strategies. The theoretical and statistical issues in sampling are also covered.

REFERENCES

Babbie, E. R. (1979). *The practice of social research* (2nd ed.). Belmont, Calif.: Wadsworth.

Fowler, F. J., Jr. (1984). *Survey research methods.* Beverly Hills: Sage.

Gibson, R. C., and Herzog, A. R. (1984). Rare element telephone screening (RETS): A procedure for augmenting the number of black elderly in national samples. *The Gerontologist,* **24,** 477-482.

Kish, L. (1965). *Survey sampling.* New York: Wiley.

Lee, G. R., and Finney, J. M. (1977). Sampling in social gerontology: A method of locating specialized populations. *Journal of Gerontology,* **32,** 689-693.

Simon, J. (1978). *Basic research methods in social sciences: The art of empirical investigation* (2nd ed.). New York: Random House.

Stephan, F. F., and McCarthy, P. J. (1965). *Sampling opinions: An analysis of survey procedure.* New York: Wiley.

7

Planning and Preparing for the Research

William J. McAuley and Cynthia A. Bowling

PROBLEMS TO BE SOLVED

What is an appropriate timeframe for the project?
How can I be certain the methods and procedures I have designed will work?
What characteristics are important in selecting project staff, and what should be
    included in their training?
What ethical issues should I consider as I plan to gather the information?

The perfect research design will be useless unless steps are taken to ensure
that quality information will be gathered. The planning and preparation
stage of the research requires a multitude of decisions and careful attention
to detail. The following major issues in planning and preparing for survey
research will be useful for other types of research also.

PLANNING A TIMETABLE

Exact prediction of the timing for all phases of the research project is
difficult because bottlenecks will arise and unforeseen events will serve to
hasten or (more likely) delay some steps in the process. It is important to
know where such bottlenecks and other scheduling problems might occur so
that extra time can be planned into the timetable.

Time Considerations

In planning the schedule of a research project thought must be given to three major time considerations. The first, and perhaps most obvious, issue is the amount of time available to complete the project. Applied researchers often find themselves working against very short deadlines. In such cases, the design and scheduling of the project must reflect the actual time constraints.

A second time consideration concerns the resources that will be available for the project—money, available staff (their backgrounds, experience, and the amount of time they can devote to this activity), and computer and other facilities. Within limits, the more resources available the more rapidly a project can be completed.

Methodological issues are a third important factor influencing the timing of a project. The size, dispersion, and "interviewability" of the sample; the information-gathering strategy selected; the use of longitudinal versus cross-sectional designs; the kinds of questions asked (e.g., fixed-choice versus open-ended); and the analysis procedures all can have an effect on how long it takes to complete the research.

These time considerations interact to influence the scheduling of a project. Given a specific research design, it is sometimes possible to compress the time allocated to various stages of the study to fit a limited timeframe. But there is always a point at which it is best to revise the basic design and methods to fit the time available. You may want to establish two or more tentative plans incorporating different resource needs and schedules for completion. Brief descriptions of these alternate research plans could be submitted to the sponsor along with an indication of the nature and utility of the results that could reasonably be expected from each plan. Such a procedure will help overcome the tendency for the sponsor to expect too much from a project that is brief and/or underfunded. Through negotiation based upon a realistic conception of what is feasible within a set of time/resource limitations, a practicable research plan and timeframe is more likely to obtain.

Major Phases

Each of seven major phases in most research projects should be given consideration as you establish the schedule. The duration of each phase depends upon the three time considerations just discussed. Many of these phases may overlap considerably so that more than one part of the project is being accomplished at the same time. On the other hand, certain phases must obviously be completed before other phases can begin. Thus, in organizing a timetable you should take into account both how long a particular project component will take to complete (e.g., the number of days, weeks, or months) and also in what order each component should be carried out, compared to other components, so that the project can be completed in a smooth, orderly fashion.

Reviewing, Selecting, and Revising Data Collection Instruments.   If, as part of your planning, you have already decided to use an instrument that has been produced by others, less time will be needed to complete this step. However, if you have only a vague notion about the kind of instrument you will need, it is important to allocate sufficient time to review existing instruments and/or develop your own. This procedure can be very lengthy, depending, of course, on how familiar you are with the subject matter, how concerned you are about the validity and reliability of the instrument, and how simple or complicated the instrument will be.

Regardless of whether an instrument is to be designed from scratch or an existing instrument will be used, time is needed to pretest the instrument and other methods to determine whether they are appropriate for the purposes of the study. After the pretest, revisions may be required, and a new pretest may be necessary to determine whether the revised design will work. If the pretest can be carried out locally by the project staff, and if checks on validity and reliability are deemed to be unnecessary or can be based upon relatively simple procedures, it can be carried out in a week or so. However, if a more dispersed group must be pretested, and there is sufficient concern about the instrument to conduct more formal tests of validity and reliability, the time needed for pretesting could be several months.

Selecting and Training Research Staff.   This phase of the project must include time for the development of training materials and procedures as well as for enlisting and training the field staff. The amount of time needed for these activities depends upon how complicated the data collection procedures will be, how much independent responsibility the interviewers and other data collection staff will be given, and the knowledge and experience of the data collection staff.

In all cases, training is easier and completed faster when experienced interviewers are used. If the data collection staff are not familiar with the collection technique to be used in the research (e.g., when inexperienced interviewers are to be used to complete face-to-face interviews) a certain amount of training time must be devoted to teaching and practicing the techniques. On the other hand, with more-experienced field staff it is possible for the training to focus chiefly on the application of already existing skills and experiences to the current research project, generally reducing the time needed in preparing for and conducting training.

Gathering the Information.   Realistic schedules for data collection take into account time for travel (if applicable), screening and interviewing, callbacks to respondents not reached immediately, and checking the completeness and accuracy of the information collected. It is not possible to anticipate all of the many opportunities for bottlenecks and delays in this phase, nor is it feasible to include enough time to cover all eventualities. However, by taking into account the nature of the population, time needed to complete one case, and the basic types of delays that might occur, it is possible to realistically estimate the length of the information-gathering phase.

The characteristics of the target population can influence the time needed for information gathering in a variety of ways. First of all, some populations tend to be less readily available than others. If respondents are to be interviewed in their homes and most are employed, it may be reasonable to conduct interviews on evenings and weekends. This limitation could lengthen the interview period unless more interviewers are hired. If the population consists of persons who are less healthy, time might be required to locate and interview appropriate informants for some individuals or to schedule return visits for some respondents who will be unable to answer the questions when they are first contacted. Some populations are highly mobile or can be expected to be less available during certain seasons. Older recreation vehicle owners would be a good example of such a group. If such individuals are represented in large numbers in the target population, it is probably necessary to schedule the interviews for a date when respondents are most likely to be available or to plan additional time for recontacts, or both.

When face-to-face interviews are to be used, and the population is relatively widely scattered, weather can cause a real bottleneck. You should, therefore consider possible days lost due to bad weather if travel is problematic in the interview area during the period scheduled for interviews.

With any interviewing procedure, the loss of field staff can lead to substantial delays in the data collection phase. If interviewers quit or are found to be unsuitable, time will be needed to select and train new interviewers; or, if no new interviewers are hired, additional time will be needed to spread the remaining case load over fewer data collectors. Allowances for attrition should therefore be included in the decision regarding the number of interviewers to select and train initially.

Preparing the Information for Analysis.   A number of steps often are involved in preparing the data for analysis (see chap. 9). The editing process of carefully reviewing the data forms to be sure they are accurate and complete begins when the interviewers review the questionnaires or other instruments shortly after they are completed, the best time to identify and rectify errors. In addition to the field edits, a member of the research staff should review each returned form, checking for omissions as well as inconsistent or illogical responses. This step is particularly important when interviews are complex and lengthy. Time must be scheduled for these reviews and any necessary recontact with the interviewer and/or the respondent to eliminate problems.

Two additional aspects of data preparation are categorizing and coding. *Categorizing* simply means creating categories for each variable so it can be readily analyzed. For example, responses to open-ended questions must often be placed into a set of mutually exclusive categories so that the proportion of respondents giving each answer can later be calculated. *Coding* means assigning a symbol (usually a number) to each category. When the information is gathered on forms that are precoded into fixed-choice items, very little time will be devoted to coding, and editing is usually easier and more rapid as well.

Analyzing the Information.   New researchers frequently underestimate the time required for data analysis and tend to assume that the analysis will somehow "take care of itself" or that "the computer will handle the analysis." Unfortunately, neither assumption is true. Data analysis is a crticial, time-consuming phase of the project that will not do itself and therefore must be given a reasonable time schedule for completion.

The time needed for analysis depends on the amount of data collected, how complicated the analysis will be, how thoroughly the analysis has been designed, and whether or not a computer will be used. Obviously, more time should be scheduled for analysis of larger numbers of cases and for analysis that involves more complicated or difficult procedures. On the other hand, use of a computer can help to reduce analysis time, especially with larger data sets or more complicated analytical procedures.

Use of a computer does not always guarantee time savings. For example, with a relatively small sample and a problem whose answer requires only the tallying of simple responses, doing the analysis by hand may be easier and quicker. The computer would make it possible to check the results for various subgroups or to examine the associations among the responses very rapidly, however. In any case, data analysis proceeds more smoothly and is completed more quickly when there is a clear plan for analysis (see chap. 9).

Producing the Report.   The length and amount of detail needed in the report will, to a large extent, determine how much time will be spent on report production. It is important to recognize that two, and sometimes more than two, versions of the report may be needed to address the information requirements of different audiences. For example, a longer, more complete version may be produced for those who are concerned about all the details of the project, while a compact summary may be developed for those who want only the most pertinent aspects, and a very brief capsule report may be needed to give to respondents or the general public.

Disseminating the Results.   All too frequently, no time is allocated for the process of getting the information to the persons who can benefit from the knowledge. The agency that requested the information should receive the findings in an appropriate format (see chap. 10). At times, receipt of a final report may be sufficient, but it may also be useful to plan to give at least one oral presentation to agency staff so they can ask questions and discuss in greater detail the implications of the research. It might also be appropriate to disseminate the results through organization newsletters or professional journals or through presentations at professional meetings. Where possible, such dissemination activities should be scheduled into the initial timetable. When they are part of the schedule they are more likely to be acted upon.

Timetable Format

A well-organized, thorough schedule reflects on the competence and organizational capability of the researcher, so it can be an important bit of evidence of the researcher's ability to handle the project. At times even the project timetable will make the difference in decisions to approve projects. The timetable is always a useful tool for maintaining the flow of events and in meeting project deadlines. Therefore, accuracy and attention to detail are important in developing a timetable.

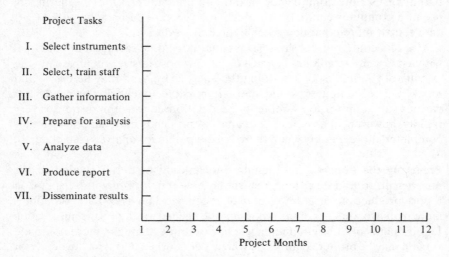

Figure 7-1. Example of a timetable for a research project.

Figure 7-1 offers an example of a project timetable that makes it possible to plot in one location the times required for all the major phases of the project. This type of format is useful because it indicates how much time each phase will consume as well as the date each should begin and the date by which each should end. By reviewing the timetable anyone can see how various components of the project intermesh during the project. It suggests when there may be periods of very heavy effort and periods that will be less pressing and shows the ebb and flow of effort and responsibility.

To begin developing a timetable it is necessary to estimate the time required for each major phase of the project. The phases you use should fit your research plan, and may therefore differ from the ones presented in Figure 7-1. Next a blank timetable covering the entire project period should be drawn with units of time appropriate for the length of the project. For example, for projects lasting several years, it may be reasonable to use quarters (three-month blocks) as the units. For projects of one to two years, months may be used. For projects of shorter duration, months, weeks, or even days may be appropriate. The blank timetable is then filled in by listing the project phases (in appropriate sequence of occurrance) and the times each will cover. The timetable dates should be initially filled in using a pencil, because this process tends to be iterative. Decisions regarding the timing of certain activities will influence the timing of other activities. You will find that work on the timetable will force you to think through the research process and to carefully consider how all the components intermesh. This exercise in itself is valuable.

PRETESTING AND REVISING

No matter how much time is spent in devising ideal research designs and questions, until they are tried out on a sample of the target population, there is no assurance that all phases of the project can be carried out as planned. Pretests serve as trial runs of the research. Pretests of the entire project, sometimes called pilot tests, make it possible to discover and correct problems before they become a hazard to the successful completion of the project.

Reasons for Pretesting

The pretest should be viewed not as an unnecessary, optional frill but as a vital part of the development of the research project. Pretests may be more or less elaborate, depending upon the study, but are always helpful. Babbie (1973) gives the following important reasons for carrying out a pretest.

1.   *The pretest can point out errors or problems that can be corrected prior to full implementation of the project.* Any number of problems may surface during the pretest. Among the things to look for are (1) whether respondents can be selected and located as planned, (2) whether respondents are willing to participate, (3) problems in reading and agreeing to the consent forms, (4) whether skip patterns and directions of the instrument are problematic, (5) questions that appear to be out of order or that seem to be redundant (even if they really are not), (6) questions that are difficult for the respondent to understand or that lead to erratic or inappropriate responses or nonresponses, (7) a tendency of respondents to cut off the interview before it is completed, (8) length of time required to complete an interview, (9) whether responses to open-ended questions can be categorized in an acceptable fashion, (10) whether some portions of the instrument lead to strong emotional reactions, and (11) whether the information that is collected can be analyzed in the manner planned.

2.   *It can be used to determine which specific questions, procedures, or methods to use.* It is often helpful to use the pretest to compare different versions or types of questions. For example, open-ended questions on a topic can be compared to fixed-choice questions. Additionally, face-to-face interviews can be compared with a paper-and-pencil format. Such comparisons can be efficient methods for making the final decisions regarding the methods and procedures to be employed in the project.

3.   *It can help revise your plans about the logistics of the research project.* The experience gained through the pretest can be beneficial in making final plans for the research. For example, if locating eligible respondents takes longer than expected, changes may be necessary in the schedule and/or the budget. If problems develop that suggest the need for additional interviewer training, this extra help can be arranged before the final training session takes place.

4.   *It allows for a check on the validity and reliability of the instruments.* The pretest is an opportunity to evaluate and refine the instrument so you can be sure that it will consistently measure what you want to measure. One particuarly important issue in certain gerontological research is whether information gathered from an informant can be substituted for information gathered from the target respondent. The pretest can be designed so that you can compare results of respondent interviews with those from individuals selected as informants for these same respondents. Such comparisons may lead to changes in the design of the project or to new plans for ensuring that target respondents are used whenever possible.

5.   *It may suggest the need for changes in analysis procedures.* Data from the pretest can be used to determine whether the planned analysis can, in fact, be carried out. If problems appear at this stage, they can be overcome

by changes in the methods so that data appropriate to the planned analysis will be generated or they might be handled by changes in the analysis.

Conducting the Pretest

For the pretest to be most useful, it should be as much like the planned project as possible, but on a smaller scale. Thus, one way of viewing the pretest is as a "mini-project" that will be useful in assuring the success of the research. It is also useful for gathering information from the interviewers and respondents that may not be part of the final study. The pretest should be organized so that you will be able to learn about the reactions of the inter-viewers and respondents to the activities and instruments. To satisfy both of these requirements, four rules should be kept in mind in carrying out the pretest.

1. *Select pretest respondents that closely match the target population for the planned study.* Respondents for the pretest should be similar to the respondents in the planned study along major characteristics such as age, health, education, income, and living arrangement. It is especially impor-tant to select pretest respondents so that they will conform to the study respondents on characteristics that may influence the identification and location of respondents, willingness to participate, and differences in ability to comprehend and react to questionnaire items.

2. *Design the pretest to be as much like the planned research as possible.* The pretest should serve as a trial run of all components of the project. Therefore, it should carefully mirror all the procedures of the project (Babbie, 1973). It may not always be possible to exactly reproduce the final study during the pretest, but every effort should be made to match the planned activities and situations. Therefore, it is often best to hold any questions about the methods used or the instrument until after the planned question-naire items have been completed.

3. *Train the pretest interviewers to document all aspects of the process.* It is important to learn as much as possible about how the planned process is carried out in actuality. Sometimes the differences between the ideal and the actual can be surprisingly large! The Survey Research Center (1976) lists the following items that interviewers should attempt to document during the pretest.

Record the time required to complete each section of the interview. This information will be useful for estimating total interview time as well as for determining whether some sections take up too much time, given their significance.

Take notes on the overall reaction of the respondents to all aspects of their involvement in the interview. These notes may suggest ways of improving the process.

Keep track of questions that do not read well or flow smoothly. Such questions may have to be revised.

Note the location of confusing skip patterns or instructions that might be improved through a revision of the questionnaire or through the training of data collectors.

Be alert for unclear questions. Lack of clarity in questions may be the reason why several respondents ask the meaning of a question, or seem confused, or respond in unplanned or seemingly inappropriate ways. With older people, questions can often be unclear because they incorporate terms that require a higher level of education or words that are currently popular but are not part of their vocabulary.

Record all probes used in the interview because pretest probes can be useful in developing an acceptable set of nondirective probes that can be used in the actual study.

Keep track of problems with available choices in fixed-choice questions. Does the respondent have trouble selecting any one choice? Do all choices seem inappropriate? Much can be learned in the pretest that will help to improve the choices so they elicit the necessary information.

Once the interview has been completed, make notes on any obvious inconsistencies, apparent or real redundancies in questions, or apparent gaps in questions or instructions.

4.   Revise the instrument and procedures as needed and pretest again to determine whether the revisions are appropriate. Often this new testing can be carried out with even fewer respondents than the first pretest. At times, it may be reasonable to include on the second pretest only those questions or other components that required extensive revision. However, because questions have different meanings in different contexts, it is best to use the entire questionnaire. You may find that everything works well or the revisions are so minor that there is no need at all for an additional trial run.

SELECTING AND TRAINING INTERVIEWERS

In projects requiring interviews, the interviewers become the major communication links between the researcher and the respondents. If the interviewers carry out their responsibilities in a professional manner, the information they collect will very likely serve your needs. On the other hand, when interviewers are not carefully selected or are inadequately trained, the quality of the information is almost surely going to suffer. This section addresses five of the most crucial issues in the selection and training of interviewers.

Agency Staff Versus Outside Interviewers

If the research project is going to be carried out by an agency for its internal use, one course of action is to use existing agency staff to conduct the interviews. This option may be viewed as the most practical because of the opportunity for control and the low cost. In many cases, agency staff can be excellent interviewers because they are familiar with the population and the subject matter. However, agency staff may not always be the best choice. A number of factors should be considered in deciding whether to use agency staff as interviewers. First of all, you should determine whether the staff have the experience necessary for the work. Have they carried out similar interviews before? Were they successful?

Second, you should think about how the additional interviewing responsibilities can be incorporated into the ongoing activities of the agency. Does the staff have the time to commit to interviewing? Are they interested enough in the project to do the job well? Will other important agency business be delayed by staff involvement in interviewing? Would "firing" a staff member from interviewing hamper agency morale?

Third, think about whether having the staff members serve as interviewers might bias the results in some way. This possibility may be an issue when the results of the project would in some way influence funding patterns, program goals, employment, or the administration of the agency. It can also be a problem when the study population already knows the agency staff and has learned to deal with them in certain limited ways.

A final issue to consider is whether using the staff for interviewing would interfere with the mission of the agency or alter the staff-client relationships. Current or potential clients may not easily differentiate between the interview and standard agency procedures. For example, if the interviews are to assess needs or evaluate programs, they might build false expectations on the part of the respondents that something will be done quickly. When the survey covers questions that are obviously not a part of the normal staff-client interaction, both the clients and the staff members may find the interviews awkward and uncomfortable. On the other hand, the opportunity for addressing novel topics and working with clients in new ways could actually strengthen staff-client relationships and give new purpose to the staff members' jobs. By carefully considering which staff members might collect the data and how their involvement in interviewing might affect the research, the agency, and the staff-client relationship, the right decision for each situation can be made.

Volunteer Versus Paid Interviewers

If outside interviewers are to be used, another important issue is whether to use paid interviewers or to seek volunteers. One obvious advantage to using paid interviewers is that the payment serves as a strong motivation for the person to obtain complete and accurate information and to follow detailed instructions. Also, when paid interviewers are used, it is generally easier to engage people with prior interview experience. Therefore, the more complex or difficult the task, and the greater the need for complete and accurate data, the more the payment option should be considered. Paid interviewers are also preferable when tight deadlines must be met, because it is not reasonable to expect volunteers to work long hours or during the times that respondents are most accessible (e.g., evenings and weekends). In addition, the turnover rates of volunteers often exceed those of paid interviewers, leading to problems with scheduling, creating the need for special training sessions, and draining resources as new interviewers are sought and screened.

Of course, the main advantage of volunteers is cost. With other things held equal, a research project using volunteers for data collection is less expensive than one that uses paid interviewers. This fact should not be taken to mean that data collection with volunteers can be accomplished with no cost, however. The data collection process is more likely to run smoothly if volunteers are reimbursed for travel, necessary phone calls, postage, and other related expenses.

Modes of Payment

If the decision is to use paid interviewers, there are two traditional ways of organizing payment. Interviewers can either be paid by the hour or receive a certain amount for each completed interview. The cost of the interview phase can usually be controlled best through payment for completed interviews (Hoinville and Jowell, 1978). In establishing an appropriate amount to pay for each interview it is important to consider the total time required to contact and screen respondents, to complete and field-edit each interview, and to maintain records of activities. When face-to-face interviews are used, travel time must be taken into account, although mileage and other travel expenses may be reimbursed separately upon submission of an expense record. In all cases, the payment should be sufficient to motivate an interviewer to complete the interviews accurately and in a timely manner.

Sometimes two or more fee scales should be computed for per-interview payments (Krug and Perkins, 1974), particularly when large differences in the dispersion of the target population occur or when other factors might lead to differences in difficulty or time involved in obtaining interviews. For example, it may be useful to have a payment schedule for rural areas (where respondents are likely to be less concentrated) that is higher than the payments for urban interviews.

A chief disadvantage of the per-interview approach to payment is that interviewers may concentrate on the easy interview prospects. They may be unwilling to make a callback to a home where they have already been and found no one at home or they may decide to omit potential respondents that are far away and would therefore be a "waste of time." Payment by the hour helps overcome the tendency for interviewers to focus on the more efficient or productive cases. Therefore, this approach should lead to more complete screenings and interviews. Payment by the hour is also advantageous when the task is relatively complex, or when a considerable amount of time is spent in locating and screening potential respondents, or when the response rate is expected to be low. Under such circumstances, interviewers who are paid by the interview may become discouraged because their efforts do not lead immediately to payment. The resultant higher dropout rate may actually increase data collection costs and add time to the interview stage.

Payment by the hour helps assure that the field staff will keep working even when cases require considerable time and energy. On the other hand, interviewers who are paid on an hourly basis have little incentive to be efficient. Efficiency can be improved through close supervision and by requiring interviewers to maintain logs of their time spent in the field.

No matter what form of payment is used, the researcher should have a reasonable expectation of how much time it takes to complete an interview. Many researchers depend upon a simple formula for calculating the time that might be allocated for face-to-face household interviews. This formula takes into account time for noninterview tasks such as travel and editing. The number of hours required should, according to this formula, be approximately four times the length of the actual interview (Krug and Perkins, 1974). When the sample design requires that more than one household is screened to locate an eligible respondent, the total number of hours required per interview should be adjusted upward.

Rather than selecting only one of the payment approaches, it is sometimes most appropriate to employ a system based on both the hourly and per-interview approaches. For example, some interviewers may be given responsibility for carrying out less complex and/or more productive interviews and paid on a per-interview basis. Other interviewers (the most experienced and efficient) could be given the difficult cases and paid on an hourly basis. The hourly interviewers might also be given the tasks of "cleaning up" areas, thus helping attain complete coverage of all cases.

Selection of Interviewers

One can never be completely sure that an interviewer will be successful for the specific project at hand, because there are no failproof evaluation procedures to eliminate ineffective interviewers. The best way to learn whether an individual is capable is to see how he or she performs under the specific circumstances that will be used in the project (Hauck and Steinkamp, 1964).

When telephone interviews will be used, Dillman (1978, pp. 256–257) has suggested that the following characteristics be taken into account in selecting interviewers: the ability to read questions fluently, the sound and clarity of the interviewer's voice over the phone, the extent to which the interviewer's voice may interfere with the work of other interviewers, and the ability to respond to questions from the respondent. Such information is obtained best through mock telephone interviews, so plan to use mock interviews as part of the final selection process. When all the interviews will be made in a central location, it will be possible to provide constant supervision and to immediately respond to problems encountered by interviewers. As a result, prior interview experience may be a less critical issue.

When face-to-face interviews are used, Dillman (1978) points out that the skill requirements of interviewers are greater. Face-to-face interviewers must be responsible for locating and screening potential respondents, completing travel reports and other records, planning their use of time, handling their own problems, and so forth. They must therefore be able to work well independently as well as meet the following criteria: good demeanor in dress and manner, experience with older people or at least a desire to gain such experience, efficiency to complete all tasks in a timely manner, patience to locate respondents and to keep them interested in the survey, open-mindedness and ability to meet people, and experience in interviewing.

Number of Interviewers to Select. It is always best to estimate the number of interviewers needed to complete the data collection on schedule and then to add a small cushion so that unplanned problems will not lead to delays in data collection. Krug and Perkins (1974) recommend hiring more interviewers than the projected need, because handling the "problem" of completing the data collection phase a little ahead of schedule is generally easier than being late for meeting deadlines.

How can accurate estimates of interviewer needs be made? Figure 7-2 presents the components of a generic formula for determining the number of interviewers to select. Some estimates will be required to complete the calculations, and some adjustments in the formula may be needed to have it correspond better to your own study. However, application of the formula will make it possible to develop quick and relatively accurate estimates of the number of interviewers required. The formula can also show how changes in one component (e.g., number of weeks scheduled for data collection) will, other things held equal, lead to changes in interviewer requirements.

Generic Formula

A = Number of completed interviews anticipated.

B = Number of weeks allotted to complete interviews.

C = Number of interviews needed per week to reach goal. (A ÷ B)

D = Time (in hours and fractions of hours) needed per interview (includes travel, editing, etc., using rule of thumb of 4 times the actual interview time).

E = Number of hours per week an interviewer will be hired to work.

F = Number of interviews one could reasonably complete in a week. (E ÷ D)

Then:

1. C ÷ F = Number of interviewers needed to complete the task.

2. Multiply the above by 1.1–1.2 (depending on the task) to account for turnover and select this number of interviewers.

Example

A = 1000 interviews anticipated.

B = 5 weeks timeframe for data collection.

C = 1000 ÷ 5 = 200 completed interviews per week.

D = 4 hours needed per interview (the actual interview takes about an hour)

E = 40 hrs/wk each interviewer will work.

F = 40 ÷ 4 = 10 interviews completed each week per interviewer.

Then:

1. 200 ÷ 10 = 20 interviewers needed to meet weekly quota.

2. 20 x 1.1 = 22 interviewers to be hired.

Figure 7-2. How Many Interviewers to Select.

Recruitment Strategies.   The most common method for recruitment of interviewers, particularly when they will be paid, is newspaper advertisements. The advertisement should be specific regarding qualifications needed and the method and location of data collection. For example, it should note whether face-to-face or telephone interviews are needed; whether the study will be in respondents' homes, nursing homes, or other locations; whether experience is desired (and if so, how much and of what type); whether the interviewer must drive his or her own car; the expected hours per week; and duration of the study (Hoinville and Jowell, 1978). Professional interviewers often scan the help-wanted sections for employment opportunities, so an ad can be a good source of prospects.

Another source of professional interviewers is national, regional, or local survey research firms. The larger firms maintain lists of professional interviewers living in various locations and usually have current evaluations of performance. We have found that these research companies are often willing to share lists because they want to keep the interviewers involved in survey work so they will be available the next time a firm has a project in the area.

Volunteers are probably recruited best through clubs, benevolent and service associations, or colleges. A good place to begin is with the individuals in charge, who might be the presidents of clubs and associations or the instructors of classes. If such leaders can be convinced of the value of a project, they can help assure that others will volunteer. Being clear about the details of the study and the qualifications of interviewers is perhaps more important when recruiting volunteers than when recruiting paid interviewers. The goal is to find individuals who are willing to commit the time and energy to this particular study; otherwise, turnover may be greater than desired, and substantial delays may result.

Screening Techniques.   Now that a pool of potential interviewers has been identified, the next step is to select those who will be most successful in gathering the information and carrying out the related activities. One stratgey is to have all those interested in interviewing complete a questionnaire that requests information about prior interview experience, familiarity with various activities involved in data collection, experience with older people, and so forth. References should also be requested, and the references should be contacted. The questionnaire should be designed for screening interviewers for your specific project, and it should be completed whether volunteers or professionals will be used. You should also personally interview the candidates so that you can see how they present themselves.

The training session may be used to make the final selection of interviewers (Krug and Perkins, 1974) and will be an opportunity to see how they perform during practice interviews. If the final choices are to be made during training, it is important to select a sufficient number to allow for the anticipated reductions. It is also best to inform applicants that the training will be the final phase of selection and to pay those who attend for their involvement in the training.

Training of Interviewers

The main functions of the training are to familiarize the field staff with the purpose of the project, to review their responsibilities, and to learn and practice all the procedures associated with data collection. In many instances, the training session will be the only time for extended personal contact with the interviewers. Consequently, all the elements must be covered in a clear and thorough manner.

An interviewer's manual is a very useful aid in training. The manual should cover all procedures completely and clearly and include information about the target population and special problems or approaches that might be most successful in gaining complete and accurate interviews. For example, given the target group, are there likely to be special problems regarding hearing, vision, mobility, and so forth that might influence the interview process? How can these situations be handled? If the manual can be distributed prior to the training session, it can give interviewers an opportunity to prepare for the training and can serve as a comprehensive outline during training. It can also be used later as a reference manual when interviewers are in the field.

For face-to-face interviews, it is best to plan a two-day training session to cover all the topics. The evening between the first and second day will provide time for the trainees to review training materials and uncover problems or questions that can be brought to the second session. Time should be scheduled for breaks, because fatigue will hamper learning. See Figure 7-3 for a sample training agenda. Although the agenda must be modified to fit the methods and procedures of your project, it gives some guidance in planning your own training session.

One aspect of this training outline, the supervised interview, is often difficult to arrange and schedule but can be very useful in honing the skills of the interviewers and in identifying those who may not be successful. Furthermore, this approach almost always leads to new questions that can be handled prior to actual field work. If supervised interviews cannot be scheduled during training, perhaps each interviewer could carry out one or more supervised interviews shortly after training but before the field work begins. Another alternative is to schedule members of the project staff to sit in on the first one or two interviews of each interviewer.

ADDRESSING ETHICAL ISSUES

Applied research is a process with potential for great harm as well as considerable positive value. Ethical concerns are therefore always a part of any applied research project. Unfortunately, ethical issues are too often not given careful, objective consideration. Under these conditions, they still exist but simply go unrecognized. Therefore, situations can occur that the researcher would not tolerate if he or she knew what was happening. It is, therefore, very important to be aware of the ethical issues in a project as it is being planned and conducted so they can be dealt with in an effective, professional manner.

There are few, if any, ethical absolutes in research. On the other hand, some well-accepted standards can guide individuals in making ethical judgments regarding their projects. Most professional organizations have com-

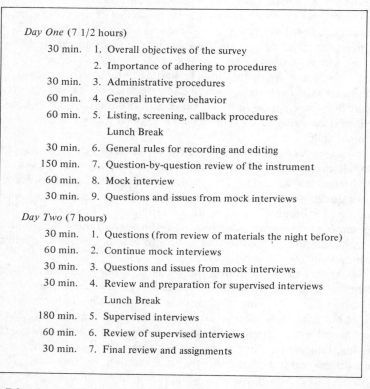

Day One (7 1/2 hours)

30 min.	1. Overall objectives of the survey
	2. Importance of adhering to procedures
30 min.	3. Administrative procedures
60 min.	4. General interview behavior
60 min.	5. Listing, screening, callback procedures
	Lunch Break
30 min.	6. General rules for recording and editing
150 min.	7. Question-by-question review of the instrument
60 min.	8. Mock interview
30 min.	9. Questions and issues from mock interviews

Day Two (7 hours)

30 min.	1. Questions (from review of materials the night before)
60 min.	2. Continue mock interviews
30 min.	3. Questions and issues from mock interviews
30 min.	4. Review and preparation for supervised interviews
	Lunch Break
180 min.	5. Supervised interviews
60 min.	6. Review of supervised interviews
30 min.	7. Final review and assignments

Figure 7-3. Sample Agenda for Interviewer Training (after Krug and Perkins, 1974).

missions that deal with such matters. The American Psychological Association (1981) has codified their ethical standards in a publication entitled *Ethical Principles of Psychologists,* a useful guide for all researchers as well as people who serve as counselors or consultants. Another useful document on ethics in research is the *Code of Professional Ethics and Practices* of the American Association for Public Opinion Research (cited in Babbie, 1979).

Both of these guidelines emphasize that the principal investigator must accept responsibility for all the ethical decisions and their outcomes in a research project. This responsibility cannot be transferred to the agency for whom the research is conducted or to the other staff of the research project. The principal investigator should strive to plan the project to reduce the risk that others in the staff will handle some phase in an unethical fashion. Checks should be designed into the study to assure that the project meets basic ethical principles.

The following five major categories of ethical concern should be kept in mind during all phases of the research project, from planning through reporting (Babbie, 1973; Strain and Chappell, 1982).

Obtaining Informed, Voluntary Consent

The individuals selected for a research project should not be forced or coerced into participating. They should be informed that their involvement is fully voluntary and that they can refuse to answer certain questions or engage in certain activities and can end their involvement in the research at any time they wish. Researchers may not want to be so open in describing the voluntary nature of participation because it may mean less than complete coverage of the sample. In many applied settings, it is often possible to directly enforce participation or to subtly imply that participation is required in order for the subject to receive (or continue receiving) services (Reich, 1978). The temptation to use such tactics can be great, because adequate coverage of the sample is a key factor determining the utility of the results. You should be careful not to succumb to such temptations. Potential participants in research projects are usually willing to cooperate if they feel comfortable about the research topic and believe they can responsibly answer the questions or carry out the other activities required by the study. Chapter 8 offers some hints on ways of improving the response rate while maintaining the respondent's right to voluntary participation.

There are, of course, some instances when it is not possible to obtain informed consent prior to participation in the study. For example, certain types of observational studies could not be conducted effectively if the respondents knew in advance that their behavior was being monitored. In circumstances that do not allow for prior consent, it is important to debrief the participants as soon as possible after the research.

In order to gather assurance that potential participants have been informed about the study and are freely volunteering to participate, many agencies and institutions require that a consent form be completed by those who do agree to cooperate in the research. Figure 7-4 is a facsimile of a consent form. Because the researcher often depends upon others to gather the information, requiring this evidence of informed consent is a valuable aid in ensuring that the respondents are, in fact, participating on a voluntary basis. Another useful check is to include questions about how cases were asked to be involved in the study when callbacks are conducted. Interviewers should be told during training about these callbacks. When interviewers know that some checking will be done on their means of obtaining interviews, they are less likely to resort to deceit or intimidation to obtain respondent cooperation.

RESPONDENT CONSENT FORM

Statewide Survey of Older Virginians
Investigator: William J. McAuley

I,   , agree to participate in an interview about one hour in length in which I will be asked questions concerning my opinions about services and my ability to do things and take care of myself.

I have been told that all the information I give will be held strictly confidential. I understand that none of the information will be used for any other purpose than this research project. I realize that I may withdraw at any time.

The interviewer will be happy to answer any questions you may have.

_____   _____
Respondent's Signature   Date

_____   _____
Interviewer's Signature   Date

Figure 7-4. Facsimile of respondent consent form.

Protecting Privacy

It is always important, on ethical grounds, to use whatever means are available to protect the privacy of participants in research projects. When possible, the research should be organized so that the responses are fully anonymous. *Anonymity* means that the information provided by an individual cannot in any way be linked to that individual. Because, in most applied research there is at least some potential for the researcher to link responses to individuals, total anonymity of responses is not often possible.

It is more likely that the *confidentiality* of respondents can be protected, meaning that the researcher will exercise care so that others will not be able to find out which participants gave which responses. The difference between anonymity and confidentiality is important and no more than can be delivered with respect to protecting the privacy of research participants should be promised. It is also important to carefully design the data collection, editing, entry, storage, analysis, and reporting phases of the project so that confidentiality is, in fact, protected to the extent possible. Interviewers, in particular, should be cautioned not to discuss with others what they have learned from participants.

The necessary use of records from agencies or facilities is another area in which the protection of privacy is an issue. The researcher and representatives of the organization should discuss these matters openly and reach agreement in advance regarding what, if any, information about the agencies or facilities will be made public. The Code of Conduct of the American Association for Public Opinion Research contains a clause that serves as a useful guideline in these matters: "We shall hold confidential all information obtained about the client's general business affairs and about the findings of research conducted for the client, except when the dissemination of such research is expressly authorized" (Babbie, 1979, pp. 66-67).

Avoiding Harm

The researcher must carefully plan and conduct the study so that it minimizes any potential injury to the participant. In many forms of applied research in gerontology, the risk of harm to the participant is low, but research can occasionally produce harm to individuals. The kinds of harm that might result from participation in applied research projects are so varied that they defy categorization. Some examples should help you to become more vigilant. First of all, some projects may cause actual physical harm. Research that involves experimentation with new drugs may improve a patient's health, but it could also lead to severe illness or death due to unknown side effects. Studies involving physical exercise, situations that provoke high levels of anxiety or embarrassment, the taking of blood or tissue samples, or the use of special diets all obviously have some risk of physical harm.

Other types of harm can result from investigations. For example, certain survey questions might force a respondent to confront a problem in a way that could result in considerable mental anguish (Babbie, 1973). Investigations of environmental changes in nursing homes could result in the disorientation of some patients. Participant observation studies could lead to shifts in the friendship networks of older people that might be detrimental to certain individuals, particularly if the researcher becomes an essential part of the network and then withdraws when the study is concluded. Without care in maintaining the confidentiality of participants the presentation of results can sometimes lead to embarrassment or even the loss of services or legal problems for the targets of research.

As a conscientious researcher, you should always be on guard for the potential harm that may result from participation in a study. You can then determine ways of minimizing the chance of harm. You should also consider whether the benefits that can be derived from the study make it worth the risk of harm to the participants. There will never be a completely objective, foolproof procedure for making this determination, but writing down your estimates of risk of harm, including the specific types of harm that participants might experience as well as the specific anticipated long-range and short-range benefits of the study, can help. Often, review committees for funding agencies and institutions of higher education require this inventory of risks and benefits as part of the proposal review process (Makarushka and McDonald, 1979) because it can be difficult for researchers to be fully realistic in evaluating the risks and benefits of their own research. If there is no such review committee for a project, you could ask colleagues to consider these issues and perhaps suggest a project design having less risk of harm and greater potential benefit.

As part of the informed consent process, potential respondents should be told of any risk of harm resulting from their participation. In most cases, going into great detail is not necessary, but actual informed consent is not possible unless the prospective participant is told about the possible hazards of participating. As a general rule, more detail about potential risks should be offered in those studies involving greater risks.

Maintaining Honesty

Researchers should strive for honesty in all phases of a research project. The need for honesty begins with the initial work with the sponsors of the project. Being truthful about the researcher's qualifications and the potential utility of the results is important. The researcher should also be honest in informing potential participants of the risks or hazards involved as well as the voluntary nature of participation. Honesty is also an issue in the reporting phase of the project. The American Psychological Association statement of *Ethical Principles of Psychologists* (1981, p. 1) includes a section addressing the issue of honesty in reporting. This section, quoted subsequently, is a valuable guide for anyone responsible for presenting the results of their research to others.

[Psychologists involved in research] provide thorough discussions of the limitations of their data, especially where their work touches on social policy or might be construed to the detriment of persons in specific age, sex, ethnic, socioeconomic or other social groups. In publishing reports of their work, they never suppress disconfirming data, and they acknowledge the existence of alternative hypotheses and explanations of their findings. Psychologists take credit only for work they have actually done.

The quotation stresses the special need for honesty in the reporting of research that may influence social policy (i.e., applied research). Individuals who conduct applied research in gerontology should always keep in mind that the results of their investigations will, in all likelihood, be used to make decisions about programs, policies, and procedures that will influence the lives of older people. Honesty in all phases of the research project is essential under these circumstances.

Meeting the Needs of Participants

Another ethical issue, and one that can be of particular concern to those who work with the frail or vulnerable older population, is the responsibility of the researcher for meeting the requests and needs of those who are participating in the research project. This responsibility becomes especially evident in applied research designs that are set up to provide assistance to some individuals (the experimental group) and to withhold it from those who serve as controls.

One set of guidelines for this sort of situation has been proposed by Cathleen Yordi and her associates (Yordi et al., 1982), based upon their research into a health services project for vulnerable older people in a large urban area. These researchers contend that it is morally wrong to ignore certain types of service needs discovered in a control group, but that the type of need and the individual's request for assistance can be taken into account in determining whether and how to provide assistance. Table 7-1 describes the major components of their strategy. They suggest that when service needs are of an emergency nature (e.g., when they are life-threatening or when the health of the individual is at stake), assistance must be offered. When service needs are not emergencies but are merely requested by the

Table 7-1. Responsibilities for Intervention with Control Group Members

Service Needs	Intervention Responsibilities
Emergency Needs	
Expressed by participant	Required
Unexpressed	Required
Nonemergency Needs	
Expressed by participant	Optional, limited
Unexpressed	None

Source: After Yordi et al., 1982, p. 73.

control group member, the overall situation must be examined to determine whether to delay the service until the research is completed, to offer limited assistance, or to offer no help. When a researcher discovers a nonemergency need that is not requested, there is no obligation to provide assistance.

The authors stress that any actions or interventions provided to members of the control group must be carefully documented so they can be taken into account during the analysis and reporting phases. In addition, some cases may have to be eliminated from the control group because of the interventions they receive. If this situation can be anticipated, it would be best to inflate the initial size of the control group to accommodate the loss. Strain and Chappell (1982) provide an extensive discussion of how the issue of research participant needs can appear and be addressed in survey research.

SUMMARY

Careful planning and preparation establish the foundation for successful data collection. Planning begins by constructing a timetable. The timetable takes into account the amount of time required for each phase of the project as well as the dates it should begin and end. The process of constructing a timetable forces you to think about how the various aspects of the project fit together temporally and logically. When the project is under way, it will also help you monitor your progress.

Another step in preparation for data collection is pretesting the methods and procedures. Pretests serve several purposes, including (1) pointing out unexpected problems while they can still be corrected, (2) establishing final procedural details, (3) revising project plans, (4) evaluating validity and reliability, and (5) planning analysis. To be most useful, the pretest should mirror the various aspects of the research as closely as possible.

Many researchers require help in collecting the information. But how do you decide who should be responsible for interviewing? Two very basic issues to consider are whether to use agency staff or outside interviewers and whether paid or volunteer interviewers should be sought. If paid interviewers are used, per-interview payment procedures will probably help to control costs, but hourly payments may lead to better coverage. Criteria for selecting and training interviewers should be established by taking into account the specific requirements of the project, including the degree to which interviewers will be required to act independently and make decisions on their own.

Although they may go unrecognized, ethical issues are part of any applied research project. By examining the procedures of your project with respect to five basic categories of ethical issues, you should be assured of meeting generally accepted ethical principles. These basic issues are (1) obtaining informed, voluntary consent, (2) protecting privacy, (3) avoiding harm, (4) maintaining honesty, and (5) meeting the needs of participants.

SUGGESTED READINGS

Dillman, D. A. (1978). *Mail and telephone surveys: The total design method.* New York: Wiley. This book is an excellent guide to hiring and training interviewers as well as other phases of the research process. As the title suggests, it deals chiefly with mail and telephone procedures, but you will also find much useful information on other techniques.

Cadell, D. M., Krug, D. N., and Sohr, M.A. (1974). *Interviewer training manual for the Older Americans Status and Needs Assessment Survey.* Washington, D.C.: U.S. Administration on Aging.

Krug, D. N., and Perkins, W. M. (1974). *A survey guide to accompany the Older Americans Status and Needs Assessment Questionnaire.* Washington, D.C.: U.S. Administration on Aging. These guides provide practical details on most phases of the research process. The information on selecting, training, and paying interviewers is particularly useful.

Reich, W. T. (1978). Ethical issues related to research involving elderly subjects. *The Gerontologist,* **18,** 326-337.

Strain, L. A., and Chappell, N. L. (1982). Problems and strategies: Ethical concerns in survey research with the elderly. *The Gerontologist,* **22,** 526-531. *The Gerontologist* has published many articles addressing ethical issues in applied research. These two cover many important points.

REFERENCES

American Psychological Association. (1981). *Ethical principles of psychologists.* Washington, D.C.: Author.

Babbie, E. R. (1973). *Survey research methods.* Belmont, Calif.: Wadsworth.

Babbie, E. R. (1979). *The practice of social research* (2nd ed.). Belmont, Calif.: Wadsworth.

Dillman, D. A. (1978). *Mail and telephone surveys: The total design method.* New York: Wiley.

Hauck, M., and Steinkamp, S. (1964). *Survey reliability and interviewer competence.* Urbana, Ill.: University of Illinois Bureau of Economic and Business Research.

Hoinville, G., and Jowell, R. (1978). *Survey research practice.* London: Heinemann.

Krug, D. N., and Perkins, W. M. (1974). *A survey guide to accompany the Older Americans Status and Needs Assessment Questionnaire.* Washington, D.C.: U.S. Administration on Aging.

Makarushka, J. L., and McDonald, R. D. (1979). Informed consent, research and geriatric patients: The responsibility of institutional review committees. *The Gerontologist,* **19,** 61-66.

Reich, W. T. (1978). Ethical issues related to research involving elderly subjects. *The Gerontologist,* **18,** 326-337.

Strain, L. A., and Chappell, N. L. (1982). Problems and strategies: Ethical concerns in survey research with the elderly. *The Gerontologist,* **22,** 526-531.

Survey Research Center (1976). *Interviewer's manual* (rev. ed.) Ann Arbor: University of Michigan Institute for Social Research.

Yordi, C. L., Chu, A. S., Ross, K. M., and Wong, S. J. (1982). Research and the frail elderly: Ethical and methodological issues in controlled social experiments. *The Gerontologist,* **22,** 72-77.

8

Gathering the Information

Cynthia A. Bowling and
William J. McAuley

PROBLEMS TO BE SOLVED

How can I locate respondents?
What can I do to obtain the cooperation of as many respondents as possible?
How can I be sure to gather complete, accurate, unbiased information?
How should I handle special circumstances that may be encountered when
    interviewing older people?
When and how should I gather information from an informant?
How can I be sure to obtain good participation when using the phone or mails
    to gather information?

Once all the methods and procedures have been developed and tried out and
the groundwork has been completed, it is time to start the data collection
phase of the research. A high response rate is imperative to ensure the
accuracy and utility of the data. As was discussed in chapter 6, valid, reliable
estimates of the population of interest (external validity) depend upon
gathering information from each person in the sample. In addition to good
response rates, care should be taken to ensure that each respondent in the
study is interviewed in the same manner and that responses are recorded
uniformly. Otherwise, varying strategies for interviewing or recording may
contaminate the results.

    This chapter will offer some guidelines and steps to assure a high response
rate and more consistent data collection techniques. Much of this chapter is
concerned with collecting information by means of face-to-face interviews, a
common method in applied research. However, other approaches will be
mentioned, and you will find that the strategies that are described for
face-to-face interviews can be adapted to other forms of data collection. The

major steps in the data-gathering stage can be summarized as follows (Cadell, Krug, and Sohr, 1974).

1. Have all the necessary materials handy (i.e., maps, questionnaires, consent forms, letters of introduction, identification, pencils).
2. Locate the correct dwelling, identify yourself, and determine who, if anyone, in the selected household is eligible for your study.
3. Explain the general purpose of the survey.
4. Have the respondent sign the consent form.
5. Conduct the interview, recording the starting and ending time.
6. Review the questionnaire for completeness prior to leaving the respondent's home.
7. When outside or at home, edit the questionnaire carefully and complete any paperwork related to the interview.
8. Return all materials to the researcher on a regular basis.

No matter what the format for gathering information may be, the success of this stage of the research project depends upon the ability to create a friendly, permissive atmosphere of trust and confidence. It is important to keep in mind that surveys, whether accomplished through face-to-face or telephone interviews or through the mails, are methods of seeking information that depend on establishing a social relationship between the target respondent and the interviewer or researcher. Each participant approaches the situation with different motivations and different criteria for measuring success and failure. This relationship is crucial in obtaining good information, and even *any* information! Those who are not convinced thus should consider the results of having someone knock on a stranger's door and ask questions from a standard questionnaire without any introductions, or of mailing a questionnaire that is accompanied only by a return address. The flexibility available for establishing a friendly, permissive atmosphere of trust and confidence differs across data-gathering techniques, but it is always important to use fully what resources are available to create such an atmosphere.

LOCATING RESPONDENTS AND OBTAINING PERMISSION TO INTERVIEW

The techniques described in this section will be useful in locating prospective respondents and in building rapport with them quickly so they will agree to the interview. People are usually willing to participate in surveys that are presented to them as legitimate, worthwhile, and nonthreatening. Well-trained interviewers who know what to expect when they contact prospective respondents are a valuable component of the research team. As representatives for the researcher, they must initiate and carry out a complex social exchange with respondents. Their appearance, dress, and conduct can all be factors in determining whether complete, accurate responses are obtained. Discussion of some methods for dealing effectively with the first steps in the interview process follows.

Contacting All the Respondents

Interviewers must make every reasonable effort to find all the individuals selected for the sample in order to help assure that the sample data can reasonably represent the population. A number of strategies can increase the efficiency of locating respondents. First of all, interviewers should review maps and other documentation of their areas of responsibility so they can plan their trips to maximize the number of calls they can make during a single trip. Interviewers should also drive by the interview sites to get their bearings and to find any clues regarding when respondents in the area may be at home. Additionally, if no one is at home during the initial visit, the interviewer should try to learn when someone is likely to be there and should leave a personal note that will facilitate introductions during the next visit.

Many types of problems can arise in locating and contacting prospective respondents. For example, in our own experience, interviewers have tried to locate roads on published maps that no longer (or perhaps never did) exist. Others have followed narrow, treacherous dirt lanes that crossed apparently unfordable streams. Still others have met dogs that exhibited special enmity toward interviewers. One interviewer was even met at the door by a shotgun! Fortunately these experiences are rare, so special consideration can be given to ways of managing such problem cases.

Problems with locating dwellings can often be resolved by recent maps or by asking local residents for assistance. Workers at local post offices, service stations, and fire stations are often good at helping clarify addresses. Problems with physical barriers, unfriendly animals, and unfriendly people must be dealt with creatively and cautiously. Interviewers must act responsibly when they encounter such situations, doing nothing that might cause (or increase) the threat to themselves, and trying to act in ways that might retain the possibility of obtaining the interview at a later time. In most cases, it is best to leave and immediately contact the researcher for further instructions.

Perhaps a more common problem with locating respondents is interviewer concern about entering particular neighborhoods or approaching certain homes. This fear can be very damaging to the research because, unlike the problems described earlier, interviewers can be hesitant about expressing their fears and may try to conceal their feelings by recording call attempts that do not occur. It is best to recognize that such an attitude might be a problem and to inform interviewers that they should tell you about areas or homes they do not care to contact. You can then decide whether to send interview teams for these cases or to handle these cases personally.

Callbacks, or return visits to a dwelling, can be necessitated by a variety of circumstances. They are required when the eligible respondent is not at home or when the eligible respondent is home but cannot be interviewed at the time of the visit. Good callback strategies are especially important with surveys of older persons because inadequate callback procedures may lead to over-representation of homebound or retired people. Some recommendations for callbacks are given in Cadell, Krug, and Sohr (1974).

Visit each sampled household at least four times or until an interview is completed or a definite refusal is obtained.

Only two of the four calls should be scheduled during working hours on weekdays. Others should be made during the evening hours or on weekends to locate people who work or have other activities that take them away from home during working hours.

Calls should be at least four hours apart unless there is a valid reason for returning earlier.

Following the second unsuccessful call, interviewers should attempt to obtain information from neighbors regarding when members of the target household are likely to be at home.

Obtaining Clearances and Identifications

After the target respondent is located, a number of steps can be taken to increase respondent cooperation. These steps can do much to create an atmosphere of trust and confidence in the interviewers. Although some might be completed prior to the interview phase, they are discussed here because they are all logically related to the issue of identification and clearances. Having the proper clearances and identification can in some instances mean the difference between a refusal and a completed interview. Although most people are willing to cooperate in a survey research project, increasing numbers of people want some sort of evidence that the study is legitimate and the interviewers are actually representatives of the project. This assurance is an especially important issue with older people who are frequently viewed as easy marks for con artists and thieves and who may, therefore, be hesitant about allowing people into their homes or agreeing to answer questions about themselves. The following six steps have been found useful in overcoming fear and increasing cooperation.

Contact local authorities (police, sheriff) to learn whether any special requirements exist for persons who plan to interview in an area (Krug and
Perkins, 1974). The letter should briefly describe the study, give the
names of the interviewers, and give the beginning and ending dates of
the interviews in that specific jurisdiction. Sometimes the law enforcement agency will contact you to request that the interviewers come in to
register. Interviewers should comply with this safeguard for both the
target respondents and the interviewers.

Write a letter of introduction for interviewers to carry with them at each visit
(Krug and Perkins, 1974). The letter should briefly explain the purpose
and importance of the research project and, if possible, should be
signed by someone the respondent would be expected to know by title
or name. A good idea is to provide interviewers with multiple copies
because target respondents often want to keep a copy.

Distribute identification cards to the interviewers. The cards should have the
interviewer's picture, the signatures of an official and the interviewer,
the title of the study, and an expiration date (Krug and Perkins, 1974).

Ask local newspapers and radio and television stations to provide brief
descriptions of the research projects (Krug and Perkins, 1974). Often
these organizations are willing to do so as part of their public service mission.

Have available a toll-free number that potential respondents may call to
check the legitimacy of the research. This number can be included in
the letter of introduction. Although only a few people will actually call
the number, having it available has, in our experience, helped assure
potential respondents that the study was genuine.

Write local religious organizations to request that they include a brief
announcement regarding the study in their bulletins or their services.

One additional technique used successfully in our own research is to send
an advance letter to potential respondents. This step is not always feasible,
because specific addresses may not be known prior to the field work, but
when it is possible, it can be a useful technique. The letter should be mailed
so that it will arrive three to seven days in advance of the initial contact
effort. It should contain a brief description of the study, a mention of the
length of time of the interview, information about confidentiality, the importance of full participation, the name of the interviewer who will be calling on
the respondent, and a person to contact in case of questions. The letter
should be typed with large type and/or double spaced for ease of reading. If
the name of the respondent is known, address the letter directly to that
individual because personalized correspondence tends to have greater impact.

It is not necessary to use all of these approaches in every study. Some approaches fit better into certain research designs than others. You should tailor the activities designed to improve compliance so that they are appropriate for the sample and the methods being planned.

Handling the Initial Contact

Besides convincing the respondents of the legitimacy of the study, interviewers must be prepared to overcome objections or questions that often arise prior to the interview. Appearance and demeanor at the initial meeting can often be key elements in obtaining the interview. Therefore, interviewers should be dressed properly, be pleasant, and have a confident, positive attitude about the survey. All of these elements should be discussed in training. In addition, practice in greeting the respondent and in fielding the kinds of questions that normally are asked at the door will help reduce any anxiety the interviewers may have about greeting potential respondents.

During the initial contact, interviewers must be able to size up the situation quickly and to act responsibly. The first few minutes are often of considerable importance, as during this period the respondent decides whether to participate in the interview. A good strategy is for interviewers to answer general questions about the study but not to get too specific about the contents of the interview until the potential respondent has agreed to participate and has allowed the interviewer inside.

Most respondents' questions are related to feelings of inadequacy about their ability to answer questions or their curiosity about how they were selected. Interviewers should be given training about the common questions and concerns respondents have and appropriate ways of handling them. Some typical questions or objections (Cadell, Krug, and Sohr, 1974) are:

"I don't have time for an interview right now."

"Why did you choose me? Are you talking to my neighbors too?"

"What's this all about?"

"What good will this do me?"

"I don't want people to know how I feel about things."

All of these questions and concerns can usually be dealt with by explaining the broad goals of the research, describing in general terms how respondents were selected, discussing the value of having responses from all those chosen for the study, reassuring the respondent that there are no right or wrong answers, explaining that the respondent's own views on the questions are being sought, and describing procedures for assuring confidentiality. One experienced and successful interviewer has told us that she approaches each potential respondent with the view that "this is the most important case in the entire survey." By giving respondents a feeling of importance and competence, she is almost always successful in obtaining agreements to be interviewed. Neophyte interviewers should be careful not to produce a negative atmosphere by being hesitant or timid about the survey. Interviewers who are more assertive, but positive, are likely to have better results.

Handling Refusals

Occasionally, target respondents will refuse to participate regardless of advance notices, letters, identifications, and the appearance and demeanor of the interviewers. Even the best interviewers experience a few refusals now and then. With experience, interviewers can tell the difference between a true refusal and an apparent refusal that actually represents a desire on the part of the respondent to give more thought to the request. It is important to always leave the door open for another try at a later date, and it is even more important to be careful not to allow someone else to refuse for the respondent. Members of the household may attempt to protect older people by refusing on their behalf (Hoinville and Jowell, 1978). It is good research practice to plan for all refusals to be contacted one last time. Usually, the researcher either assigns another interviewer to the case or makes the contact directly. Efforts at converting refusals are more likely to be successful when the person making the initial contact records the circumstances of the refusal as well as any other factors that might be helpful to the conversion (Krug and Perkins, 1974). Under any circumstances, refusals should be accepted courteously and without pressure.

CONDUCTING AND ENDING THE INTERVIEW

Some guidelines to be followed during the interview can help to ensure the quality of the information.

Beginning the Interview

If at all possible, the interview should take place in a comfortable setting with both parties seated, facing each other. This arrangement is not always possible, though, and interviewers should be trained in how to handle less than perfect circumstances. Preferably the interview should take place without an audience, because respondents are more likely to answer questions truthfully if other people are not listening (Cadell, Krug, and Sohr, 1974). One step in beginning the interview should be to describe the confidentiality of all answers and to assure the respondents that they can refuse to answer specific questions or terminate the interview at any time. Once they begin the interview very few respondents will actually stop before they reach the end. Another step in beginning the interview is to have the respondent sign and date the consent form, if it is a part of the procedures.

Asking Questions

To assure the validity and reliability of the responses, each respondent must be interviewed in the same manner. The following suggestions are designed to ensure that the responses will be accurate and useful (Cadell, Krug, and Sohr, 1974).

Always remain neutral. Do not make statements or offer nonverbal cues that might suggest that a particular response is correct or incorrect, good or bad, similar to or different from other respondents. Be careful not to show surprise at certain responses, because this reaction might suggest that that response is unusual or inappropriate.

Ask the questions exactly as they are worded. Deviations from the original wording, even subtle ones, can lead to changes in the responses.

Read each question slowly and in a clear voice. With practice, it is possible to read the questions in a conversational tone that helps to maintain the respondent's interest.

Ask the questions in the exact order they appear. Be careful to properly follow any skip patterns (certain questions may be skipped because of responses to contingency questions). Ask every question, with the exception of those that the instructions require you to skip.

Repeat questions that are misunderstood or misinterpreted, by reading them again exactly as worded.

Discourage the respondent from rambling, perhaps by asking the next question, or by repeating the last one if an appropriate answer has not been provided.

Shield the questions from the respondent's vision, unless instructed otherwise. Respondents tend to try to read ahead and look at how past responses were recorded, and these actions tend to make them less attentive to the questions being asked.

Do not attempt to explain words, phrases, or entire questions unless instructions allow for doing so. It is generally best to repeat the question and to allow respondents to make their own interpretations.

Before accepting a "don't know" response, use a neutral probe to help stimulate an answer. Appropriate ways of using probes are described in the next section.

Using Probes

Many times respondents say they do not know the answer to a question when, in reality, they are still thinking about it. At other times, they give answers that do not really seem to fit the question or give answers that are very general when a more specific response is required. On these occasions a neutral probe should be used to help the respondent to answer or to get back on track (Babbie, 1973). Neutral probes are questions or actions that are meant to encourage a response, or a more complete response, without suggesting what the answer should be. The following ways of providing neutral probes are useful (Cadell, Krug, and Sohr, 1974).

Repeat all questions that are misunderstood or that lead to "don't know" responses.

Give the respondents time to answer. An expectant pause can signal respondents that a more complete response is needed and give them time to organize their thoughts.

Ask neutral questions, such as "Do you have more to say about that?" or "Is there anything else?"

If the question has specific response categories, read the categories and ask the respondent which is more appropriate to them or which fits them best.

Ask the respondent to provide further clarification, such as "Would you mind telling me a little more about that?" or "Would you explain that a little further for me?"

Probes must not give the respondent any clues about what the response should be. Probes that begin "Don't you think that ...," or "Most people have told me ...," or "I assume what you're trying to get at is ...," all serve to direct respondents toward particular answers, and the response is less likely to represent the respondent's true feelings.

Recording Responses

Just as interviewers should ask questions in a similar manner, they should consistently and accurately record the answers. Consistency in recording responses is important because if interviewers are allowed to develop their own recording procedures, codes, and patterns, their notations will be difficult to decipher after the survey is completed. In addition, interviewers' personal attitudes and values can color the recorded responses if there is no consistent method for recording information. The most important rule to follow is to *consistently* follow the researcher's instructions for marking responses to fixed-choice questions and writing out answers to open-ended questions (Cadell, Krug, and Sohr, 1974). Any deviation from the instructions could lead to problems. Therefore the researcher must carefully plan these details in advance. If deviations in recording responses do become necessary, the deviation should be recorded and the reason should be jotted down. The following suggestions for recording responses are also useful (Cadell, Krug, and Sohr, 1974).

Write responses so they can be easily read by others.

Record responses as completely as possible during the inteview, rather than depending upon memory.

For open-ended questions, write down the respondent's exact words. Do not try to paraphrase or summarize the responses.

Make notation of all probes used and all changes made in questions.

Do not leave blanks on the interview form without providing an explanation. When questions are skipped (because instructions require skips), a slash through them lets the researcher know why there are no responses. Write out (or abbreviate) "not applicable," "don't know," or "refused to answer," so the researcher can determine what happened with a particular question.

Closing the Interview

Two tasks must be accomplished at the end of the interview. The first is to quickly review the interview form in the presence of the respondent. Any questions that were inadvertently overlooked can be covered, and any scribbles that no longer make sense to the interviewer can be clarified. Spending a few extra minutes at the close of the interview taking care of minor problems is better than having to make a followup call. The second task is to thank the respondent for participating in the study. This final activity of the entire interview process should leave the respondent with a feeling of accomplishment.

Editing the Responses

As soon as possible after leaving the respondent, the interviewer should thoroughly edit the entire interview form by a much more meticulous procedure than the quick review that was completed in the presence of the respondent. The purposes of this process are (1) to identify and correct or explain errors or omissions in the recording of the interview, (2) to learn from mistakes so they will not be repeated in subsequent interviews, and (3) to clarify handwriting and write out any abbreviations that might be misinterpreted (Cadell, Krug, and Sohr, 1974).

If, during the editing procedure, a question occurs about how to properly record an answer, a note should be composed for the researcher to examine this interview carefully. In this way a problem can be resolved before it becomes a major difficulty. Any other interviewer comments should also be written at this time, while the memory of the interview is still fresh and less likely to be confused with others.

PROBLEMS THAT MAY ARISE WHEN INTERVIEWING OLDER RESPONDENTS

Interviewing older respondents is basically the same as interviewing persons of any age. However, considerable variation exists in the older population—at least as much as in other age groups. Most older persons residing in the community will be willing and able to respond to the questions in the survey, but occasionally interviewers encounter older people who have difficulty with the traditional interview format and for whom some adaptations must be made. These difficulties can be due to problems with hearing, vision, speech, mobility, mental status, or some other health or functional deficit. Such problems are more likely to appear in research projects that focus on certain subgroups of the older population, such as clients of adult day care centers; patients in long-term care, psychiatric, or acute care facilities; or users of home health or personal care services.

Mary Schmidt (1975) has described six potential challenges that may arise when attempting to interview the "old old": intermittent confusion, chronic confusion, dysphasia (language problems), problems with sight and hearing, unwillingness, and overprotective relatives or caretakers. Her cardinal rule in interviewing such respondents is to approach the interview slowly, allowing the respondent time to assess the interviewer and the situation. She also stresses the value of a well-constructed instrument. Instruments should be brief, varied, and clear and employ familiar terms whenever possible. These guidelines are good to follow in the construction of research instruments for any population.

Martin Bloom and his associates (Bloom et al., 1971) have discussed some very useful strategies for interviewing older people having specific health problems. He has also described behaviors that are indicative of various types of limitations. Table 8-1 is an adaptation of the strategies used by Bloom and his colleagues to overcome some of the most commonly encountered limitations of older people. If these strategies are needed and they result in deviations from the researcher's instructions, the strategy and reason for its use should be thoroughly described.

In a few cases, it will become apparent that even with adaptations the respondent is not intellectually, physically, or emotionally capable of participating in the full interview. This inability occurs in surveys with all age groups, although it is more likely to be a problem in certain subpopulations of older people, such as those mentioned previously. Rather than basing the decision to discontinue the interview upon incorrect answers to one or a few questions, it is usually better to make the determination on the basis of general trends in responses that suggest the interview session will not lead to meaningful information about the respondent. Some questionnaires are constructed so that they begin with a series of questions whose responses can be used to decide whether to continue with the respondent or to seek an informant (e.g., Center for the Study of Aging and Human Development, 1978). This strategy is useful when the sample is likely to include a relatively large number of target respondents who may not be able to provide useful information.

You should prepare specific instructions to interviewers regarding whether and when informants should be used and how an informant should be selected. For certain types of research (e.g., those concerned primarily with attitudes and values) use of an informant may not be appropriate. Under other circumstances, an informant may be used to supplement information provided by the respondent. For example, respondents might be asked the more subjective questions, while informants are asked the more factual questions. In still other cases, use of an informant might be appropriate for all of the information regarding the respondent. You should determine when and how informants should be used as well as the criteria for selecting them before data collection begins. Thus interviewers will know how to handle these situations as they arise in the field.

It is usually best to select as an informant a relative or close friend who lives in the respondent's household. In rare instances, an informant may be a family member, friend, or paid helper who lives elsewhere but who spends a large block of time with the respondent during most days. The relationship of the informant to the target respondent should be recorded, as should be the reason for using an informant.

Table 8-1. Strategies for Interviewing the Ill Aged

Limitation	Behavior	Strategies
Hearing	Presence of hearing aid or person seems inattentive or has strained facial expressions or leans forward with "good side."	1. Speak in normal, clear voice directly to person so he/she can read your lips. 2. Speak slowly without accentuating words and wait longer for a reply. 3. Allow respondent to read questions if necessary and use nodding as a reinforcer.
Vision	Presence of thick or dark glasses, a cloudy film over the eyes, or discoloration in eyes.	1. Hold objects respondents are required to read so they are clearly visible. 2. Use a calm, reassuring voice and speak clearly and distinctly. 3. Do not touch or shake hands with the respondent until you have spoken first. 4. Sit where there is no glare and the respondent can see you best.
Language Function	This limitation is immediately evident as the person trys to speak. The respondent knows what he/she wants to say, but may be unable to form words. Persons with this problem are especially sensitive to the attitudes and moods of others and may become irritated over minor incidents.	1. Give the person time to respond without pressure and be attentive. 2. Try to give as many nonspoken cues and gestures as appropriate. 3. Keep words as short and as clear as possible.
Fatigue	Characteristics of fatigue may be diffuse physical weariness, low level of energy, postural changes, changes in facial expression, sighing or grunting sounds, and sleepiness. There also may be lowered motivation and mental dullness and inattentiveness.	1. Try to identify source of fatigue to discern if a short break is needed or another appointment should be made. 2. Timing of the interview is important. Try for optimal times during the day—not too early in the morning, not too close to meal times, or when other appointments are due, and not after exhausting exercises or treatments.

Source: After Bloom et al., 1971.

Even when informants serve as the source of information, interviews should be conducted in private. Older people who cannot be interviewed can usually still understand conversation and should therefore not be within hearing range of the interview with the informant. To avoid confusion, the interviewer should make it clear that the questions are to be answered *in terms of the target respondent,* rather than the informant.

MONITORING AND RECORDKEEPING

During the information-gathering phase, you should keep a watchful eye on the progress and products of the interviewers. Researchers who make the mistake of allowing the data collection to go unmonitored are likely to be disappointed by low response rates, useless information, and high costs. Two interrelated procedures, monitoring and recordkeeping, help to ensure that the data collection process does not run out of control.

Monitoring

Monitoring includes supervising and reviewing the various aspects of data collection and providing feedback to the interviewers. Monitoring is valuable because it makes it possible to identify and rectify problems in data gathering, thereby ensuring that this phase operates smoothly and efficiently (Krug and Perkins, 1974). Frequent (at least weekly) contact should be made with interviewers in person, or, if necessary, by phone. During these contacts recent activities can be summarized, and problems as well as issues related to efficiency can be discussed.

Another aspect of monitoring is the careful review of data collection instruments and other forms as they are submitted by the interviewers at frequent intervals as scheduled (Krug and Perkins, 1974). Otherwise, problems might go unnoticed too long, and a loss of the materials in transit could be disastrous. The questionnaire should be examined to ensure that (1) the correct household and respondent were contacted, (2) the questionnaire is complete, (3) the responses were properly recorded, and (4) there are no inconsistent responses.

Monitoring also consists of followup interviews with a sample of each interviewer's respondents. Most of these verifications can be accomplished by phone, if the phone number was requested as part of the questionnaire (Babbie, 1973). Followups can accomplish several purposes. First, they can serve as a check on whether the interview actually took place. Second, they can provide a check on the accuracy of the information collected by the interviewer. For this purpose, it is best to ask the respondent selected key questions so the verification responses can be compared to the original survey responses (Babbie, 1973). Third, they serve as opportunities to check on the procedures used to obtain the interview (were they ethical?) and the overall reaction of the respondent to the interviewer (was he or she courteous and pleasant?). Interviewers should be informed about followup procedures as part of their training. If they know about this process, they are more likely to be careful about attending to detail.

Recordkeeping

Monitoring and recordkeeping go hand in hand to control error and ensure efficiency. The best way to monitor the field work is to have an organized recordkeeping system that can accomplish several objectives (Krug and Perkins, 1974): (1) providing information that can be used to compute the survey response rate, (2) monitoring and controlling field work progress, (3) ensuring efficiency of the data collection phase, and (4) monitoring the quality of the field work. In a large survey many different forms may be needed to keep records on various aspects of the project. The following forms are crucial in meeting the four objectives just described.

Master Log. The master log book is the centralized location where key aspects of the entire field work phase and its progress are recorded (Krug and Perkins, 1974). It is usually the only place where the respondents' names and their unique assigned identification numbers are found together. In all other places, only the respondent's identification number is used, to maintain the confidentiality of the answers. All attempted and completed contacts should be written and dated in this log. You will want to keep track of all contacts until an acceptable outcome is achieved. Acceptable outcomes include the following situations (Krug and Perkins, 1974).

The interview was completed.

Four attempts were made and the respondent never was contacted.

The respondent refused.

The respondent was unable to participate and no one was available to participate on his behalf.

The sampled house was vacant or could not be found.

The log should also be used to record the date an assignment is made and which interviewer is assigned so you can encourage interviewers to complete several in-process interviews. Other information that may be maintained in the master log include the dates when the forms were edited, when followup calls were made, and when the form was prepared for analysis.

Callback Form.   A callback form should be completed for each household or respondent in the sample. This form is a legend of the dates and times as well as what happened each time each household was contacted to participate (Krug and Perkins, 1974). It is maintained by the interviewer until an acceptable outcome is achieved. Researchers use this form to make sure every effort was made to secure an interview and that the calls were made at different times of the day. They may also use the information recorded on the form when they try to convert an earlier refusal (a good reason for requiring that all forms be filled out completely).

Time and Expense Sheet and Daily Progress Report.   These two forms go together (Cadell, Krug, and Sohr, 1974). The time and expense record summarizes the hours spent (or interviews completed if payment is per interview), the mileage driven, and other expenses related to the project, and serves as the interviewer's request for payment. Researchers can also use it to monitor progress and costs. The daily progress report shows the actual hours worked, the type and amount of work completed, the miles traveled, and the miscellaneous expenses incurred during each day of effort. The daily progress report is used by the interviewer to account for time and to complete the time and expense sheet.

MAXIMIZING PARTICIPATION IN TELEPHONE AND MAIL SURVEYS

Most of the procedures described for face-to-face surveys are similar for conducting telephone and mail surveys. The key is to design and conduct the data collection phase in ways that will ensure that the information is collected as completely and accurately as possible. Again, the goal is to estalish an atmosphere that encourages the potential respondent to complete the data-gathering phase and to answer each question as accurately as possible.

Telephone Surveys

This format is very similar to face-to-face interviews. The major exceptions are, of course, that the situation does not allow for eye contact or the immediate presence of the interviewer. These exceptions reduce the opportunity to fully evaluate the situation, to use visual cues to determine potential problems in the interview format, and to use visual stimuli to convince a potential respondent to participate.

Telephone interviewers should be instructed in procedures for locating respondents and in using callback procedures as well as how to properly administer the questionnaire. They should be prepared to handle questions and concerns regarding the purpose of the study, how the respondent was selected, and whether the respondent is capable of answering the questions.

One useful way to increase participation in telephone interviews is to send advance notice letters so they will arrive three to five days prior to contacting the respondents (Dillman, 1978). Such notice is not always possible, particularly when random dialing procedures are used, but it can increase the response rate and should be used when feasible. The letter should include the same items of information that are included in a letter to potential respondents in face-to-face interviews.

When conducting telephone interviews, telling the respondents that you need a few moments to record responses is sometimes helpful because they are unable to see the responses being written down.

Mail Surveys

Mail surveys differ most from face-to-face interviews in that personal contact with respondents is totally lacking. Therefore, establishing a friendly, permissive atmosphere of trust and cooperation and encouraging the participation of respondents rests entirely with the cover letter and the questionnaire. The cover letter should therefore be constructed very carefully (Hoinville and Jowell, 1978). It should do a good job of "selling" the survey to the recipient. Remember also that the easier it is to complete and return the questionnaire, the more likely potential respondents will do it. No one will be there to help with instructions, probe for an appropriate answer, or encourage the respondent to complete "just the last few questions." Brief and simple questionnaires are more likely to increase the respondent's willingness to cooperate. For older respondents, large type and the use of double spacing is likely to encourage higher response rates because the forms will be easier to read. A stamped, self-addressed envelope should be enclosed, or alternatively, the questionnaire itself can be designed to be self-mailing (Dillman, 1978). Some surveys that use the mails go so far as to include a pencil so that this detail is worked out for the respondent.

As Babbie (1973) has discussed, a general rule for mailed surveys is that the longer the respondents delay in answering the questionnaires, the less likely they will complete them. He recommends three separate mailings to increase participation. The first mailing includes the original questionnaire and a letter of introduction/explanation. The second and third mailings, if necessary, should be spaced two to three weeks apart. Because most potential respondents who fail to complete the earlier waves will have discarded the materials, it is best to send the questionnaire and the cover letter (revised as needed) each time. When possible, telephone followup calls may also help increase response rates.

SUMMARY

Obtaining complete and accurate information depends upon establishing a permissive atmosphere of trust and confidence, no matter which technique is used to collect the data. In order for the results to be useful, an effort must be made to contact and obtain information from all the individuals selected for the sample. Careful planning and creative problem solving in the field can overcome many obstacles to locating cases. The researcher should be aware of the possibility of interviewer resistance about contacting certain households or entering some neighborhoods and develop plans for dealing with these issues. A strategy for callbacks should also be designed to help ensure coverage of all the cases.

Steps to be taken in preparation for the initial contact with potential respondents include contacting local authorities, composing a letter of introduction, issuing identification cards, planning news announcements, establishing a toll-free phone number, contacting religious organizations, and mailing an advance letter. Using some of these steps, as appropriate, will reduce respondent concerns about the interview, limit the chance of legal problems, and, in general, smooth the way for the interview.

Upon initial contact, the interviewer should rapidly size up the situation and act responsibly. The impression that is made in the first few minutes will often be the key element that determines whether the respondent agrees to the interview. An assertive, positive attitude on the part of the interviewer can improve the response rate. Refusals should be accepted courteously and without pressure, but interviewers should be wary of family members who seek to protect their older relatives by refusing for them.

The actual interview goes more smoothly when both parties are comfortably seated and no one else is nearby. The questionnaire should be carefully followed as to order and wording and the interviewer should strive to avoid cues that might bias responses. When the interview is completed, the interviewer should conduct a quick edit and then thank the respondent for participating. A more thorough edit should be completed as soon as possible after the interview.

Interviewing older respondents is the same as interviewing other people, in most instances. However, occasionally circumstances may arise that require special interview strategies, especially when certain populations of older people are the subject of research. Informants may also be required in some cases. When exceptional interview strategies must be employed or informants used, all the details should be recorded.

Monitoring procedures will help ensure that the field work phase operates smoothly and efficiently and that the information is accurate. Monitoring is accomplished through frequent contacts with interviewers, careful reviews of questionnaires and forms on a regular schedule, and completing followup verification interviews on a sample of each interviewer's cases. Recordkeeping works in conjunction with monitoring to control errors and improve efficiency. Good recordkeeping will help to (1) calculate response rate, (2) control the timing of the field work, (3) ensure efficiency of information collection, and (4) enhance the quality of the field work.

Telephone and mail surveys are in many ways similar to face-to-face interviews with respect to the issues discussed in this chapter. However, each procedure has special features that should be considered in gathering complete, accurate information. Advance letters, when feasible, help increase response rates in phone interviews. The quality of the cover letter in selling the project and ease of completion and return are major factors that will improve responses in mail surveys.

SUGGESTED READINGS

In addition to the Suggested Readings presented in chapter 7, the following article is recommended.
Bloom, M., Duchon, E., Frires, G., Hanson, H., Hurd, G., and South, V. (1971). Interviewing the ill aged. *The Gerontologist*, **11**, 292-299. This article provides practical advice on identifying the limitations of ill older people that might require special interview strategies. It also describes how to obtain successful interviews with people having limitations.

REFERENCES

Babbie, E. R. (1973). *Survey research methods.* Belmont, Calif.: Wadsworth.
Bloom, M., Duchon, E., Frires, G., Hanson, H., Hurd, G., and South, V. (1971). Interviewing the ill aged. *The Gerontologist*, **11**, 292-299.
Cadell, D. M., Krug, D. N., and Sohr, M. A. (1974). *Interviewer training manual for the Older Americans Status and Needs Assessment Survey.* Washington, D.C.: U.S. Administration on Aging.

Center for the Study of Aging and Human Development. (1978). *Multidimensional functional assessment: The OARS methodology* (2nd ed.). Durham, N.C.: Author.

Dillman, D. A. (1978). *Mail and telephone surveys: The total design method.* New York: Wiley.

Hoinville, G., and Jowell, R. (1978). *Survey research practice.* London: Heineman.

Krug, D. N., and Perkins, W. M. (1974). *A survey guide to accompany the Older Americans Status and Needs Assessment Questionnaire.* Washington, D.C.: U.S. Administration on Aging.

Schmidt, M. G. (1975). Interviewing the "old old". *The Gerontologist, 15,* 544-547.

9

Making Sense of the Information

PROBLEMS TO BE SOLVED

How do I prepare my information for analysis?
What kinds of analyses are appropriate, given my research problem and the type
   of information I have gathered?
How can I summarize and describe the characteristics of my sample?
How can I use my information to make inferences about the target population?

Having gathered the information for your research project, the next step is getting it ready and analyzing it. Although the analysis phase usually comes late in the research process, plans for data analysis cannot wait until the press of the other phases of the study has subsided. Analysis should not be an afterthought, because the analytical techniques to be employed depend upon the research problem and the nature of the information you have gathered. If you wait until the end to think about it, you may discover that carrying out an analysis that meets your needs is difficult. Therefore, you should plan the analysis before data collection begins. In this way you can be sure that you will have the kind of infomation needed to perform an analysis that will answer the research question.

This chapter describes the issues involved in preparing information and carrying out the analysis. It will give you brief descriptions of some of the many, many analytical tools that are available to the researcher. The goal is to give you some background in data analysis so that you can make decisions about what to do under different circumstances. By the end of the chapter you should have a better idea about which analytical techniques to apply in your situation. The suggested readings can provide more detail on specific methods of data analysis.

GETTING THE INFORMATION READY

A number of procedures are involved in preparing the data for analysis, including editing, reviewing, categorizing, and coding. Each of these aspects is described next.

Editing

Editing is the process of carefully examining the information to locate and correct errors, omissions, and other problems. Editing should begin as soon as possible after the information is gathered. These first edits are often called *field edits* because they take place in locations where the information is initially gathered. Field edits can make best use of the memory of the person who collected the data as well as the original source of information (whether a document or an individual). Brief but thorough examinations of schedules, notes, or forms just after they have been completed are an important line of defense against problems in the data set.

Field editing can influence the quality of the information in several ways. First, it can help ensure that all the information has been recorded as completely as possible. Omissions can be found and taken care of, and terse, hastily composed notes can be "fleshed out." Second, field edits can help assure that the schedules or forms were properly administered and all the requirements of data collection were adhered to. Were skip patterns properly followed? Were probes asked? Was the appropriate selection process used? Third, editing at this phase can make it possible to locate and correct errors in recording information. If the data collector remembers the response to a question is *satisfactory*, while *unsatisfactory* is the recorded response, time is available to return to the respondent or other data source for clarification. Finally, this initial phase of editing will help ensure that all the information can be read and understood by others. Are written responses legible? Are all the *x*s dark enough to see?

While field editing is a very important technique for ensuring the quality of your information, editing can also occur at later points in the research process. For example, a member of the research staff may be responsible for examining each form for problems. Editing at this stage can uncover omissions as well as illogical or illegible responses. Often, problems discovered at this stage are best rectified by returning to the person who collected the information or to the original source of information. When correcting is not feasible, the problem information may have to be excluded from the analysis.

Reviewing

In preparing for analysis, it is valuable to thoroughly review the raw data. Give yourself some time to become familiar with the information in its most unrefined form. You will find that your knowledge of the information will help you anticipate and rectify potential problems in the analysis phase. It will also be of use in deciding how to categorize responses. This review may even result in useful hunches about your original research problem or serendipitous insights that will launch you into new avenues of research.

How you go about getting to know your information depends upon the nature of the data you have gathered. If the information is chiefly quantitative or is precategorized, reviewing frequency distributions (which are actually summary statistics rather than raw data) may be helpful. If you have a very large data set, you will probably have to depend heavily on summary statistics for individual variables as a way of learning about your information. However, even with large data sets based upon quantitative or precoded data, going over some of the completed data collection forms individually is valuable. Studying the individual forms will be a step toward understanding (on an intuitive level) how the variables fit together.

If the raw data are nonquantitative, such as responses to open-ended questions or field notes from an observation study or another of the many qualitative strategies described in chapter 3, getting to know the information requires reviewing the actual responses or notes. As you read through the recorded information you will probably be surprised at its variety, depth, and richness. No matter how carefully we plan our research and no matter how diligently we strive to anticipate what people will do or say, some individuals manage to act or think in unexpected ways.

Whether your information is chiefly quantitative or nonquantitative, you are likely to find the process of reviewing the raw data one of the most interesting phases of the project. As a matter of fact, it can be so much fun that it is difficult to pull yourself away, because each piece of information is new, and you have helped to bring it to light. However, the information in its raw form is not likely to be of much value in the real world. It is, therefore, necessary to continue moving toward making sense out of the raw data.

As you come to realize that you are responsible for analyzing and interperting this wealth of information, your excitement may turn to anxiety. The data may seem so diverse and complex that there is no way to effectively move beyond it. Remember that your goal at this point is to immerse yourself in the information so you become thoroughly familiar with it. Later sections of this chapter are designed to help you make sense out of your data.

Categorizing

Categorizing is the process of creating categories for each variable so that the information will be useful for analysis. It is usually necessary to categorize or recategorize at least some of your information prior to analysis, even if you worked diligently to precategorize all the variables.

Some recategorization of precategorized variables may be necessary because cases are not distributed across the original categories in a way that will facilitate analysis. As an example, suppose you gathered interview data regarding annual family income from 50 elderly respondents. Responses were precategorized into six response categories. In reviewing the information prior to analysis, you discovered the following range.

Number	Percent	
32	64.0	Less than $15,000
13	26.0	$15,000 to $29,999
4	8.0	$30,000 to $44,999
0	0.0	$45,000 to $59,999
0	0.0	$60,000 to $74,999
1	2.0	$75,000 or more
Totals 50	100.00	

A quick review of the number of responses for each category of the variable shows that there are few cases with incomes higher than $29,999. Therefore, for an analysis that required separate examinations of people at different income levels, it would probably be necessary to collapse the six levels into only two—less than $15,000 and $15,000 or more—simply because there are not enough cases to allow us to consider more detailed income groups.

This hypothetical example suggests two important things about precategorized variables. First of all, careful thought should be given to how cases might be distributed across categories. In this case, it would be best to develop categories that provide greater division of the income levels below $30,000 because relatively few older people have high incomes. Second, when possible, it is best to obtain very specific information rather than depending on a few very broad categories. If the respondents had been asked to give their actual family incomes or to place themselves into many reasonably small income categories, the information could have been categorized later into any number of different groups. The data can always be rearranged so there are *fewer* categories than you started with, but it is not possible to create *more* categories than were originally established for the information collection phase.

Responses to open-ended questions, observational notes, and other forms of qualitative information will also have to be categorized if they are to be subjected to quantitative analysis. A technique for categorizing responses to open-ended questions is described next and can be modified to categorize other forms of qualitative information.

To create categories out of an open-ended question, you should plan to review a reasonable portion of the responses. It is helpful to write each different response on an index card. Repeat responses can be noted by jotting down the number of repetitions on the card where you recorded its first occurrence. Hash marks are a useful method for keeping track of multiple occurrences.

After you have written down responses for forty or so cases, you will find that you are getting fewer new responses and more repeats, a good indication that you have nearly exhausted the possibilities. Your earlier review of the data should also give you clues about whether you have begun to exhaust the range of different responses.

Once the responses are on cards, the next step is to place them in stacks that contain similar types or categories of responses. Several attempts may be required before you decide upon a set of stacks (categories) that are mutually exclusive (each response fits in only one pile), exhaustive (all the responses can be placed in one of the piles), and logically related to the research problem. These characteristics of good measurement were discussed in chapter 4, and they are just as important when you are refining your measure through categorization as they are when you operationalize a variable. To make the stacks exhaustive, be sure there is an "other" stack for responses that do not seem to fit into any of the stacks of similar responses.

The stacks are likely to be most valuable if they represent the range of substantially different kinds of responses, without including every minor detail. The research problem ought to offer some guidance regarding the appropriate number of categories. Is it a problem that stresses the range of different responses, or is it one that requires the examination of a few broad categories? Do not lose track of the research problem, because it may establish guidelines for specific types of response categories you will need to carry out the analysis.

Once you have established the working categories, you can go through all the remaining responses to the question to determine which category fits each response. You may need to revise the categories slightly because a new set of responses emerges, one response catgory is getting so few repeats it will need to be added to the "other" group, or the "other" group is being used too frequently.

When the categories are fairly well established, have someone other than yourself attempt to categorize some of the responses using your classification scheme. If you discover that the categorizations of responses do not match, you probably need to re-examine your method of organizing the responses into groups because the scheme you have established may not be as logical as you thought.

As you begin to place each response in a category, you will find that a shorthand way of referring to the various categories is useful. Coding, described in the next section, is a procedure for devising and assigning such shorthand labels.

Coding

Coding simply means assigning a symbol (usually a number) to each category of a variable. The number can then be used to refer to that category. These shorthand labels make many of the other phases of data preparation and analysis more efficient. For example, it is easier to write down a number by a response to show which category it fits than it is to write down a long description of the category. These shorthand labels save space and time and are especially valuable when computers are used for data analysis.

If you have more than five or six variables, you should plan to construct a codebook to help you keep track of the codes you assign as well as other pertinent information about each of the variables in your data set. The codebook is a kind of reference book for the variables. The more information you include in the codebook, the more valuable it will be to you. When you have a question about a variable, you can simply refer to the codebook for the answer.

The codebook should include the following items of information about each variable: (1) the number of the question or item on the original data collection form, (2) the original question or item, or a descriptive summary, (3) the location of the variable in your data set and a label for the variable (these items are especially important when the data are computerized), (4) the categories of the variable, (5) the codes for each category, and (6) any additional information that might facilitate the proper use of the variable. It is also convenient to include a copy of the data collection instrument in the codebook so that others can see the specific items that led to the information.

Figure 9-1 presents a small section from a codebook showing one way of organizing information about the variables so that it can be easily accessed. The question number is valuable in referring to the specific item on the questionnaire. The card number, column number, and variable label make it possible to locate the variable within a computerized data file. A summary of the question serves as a useful reminder about what led to the response. Finally, each of the categories of the variable is associated with its code. You may decide upon a different format for presentation, but this kind of information is always useful to incorporate into a codebook.

ANALYZING THE INFORMATION

Now that the information has been prepared, it is time to begin the analysis. Analysis, whether quantitative or nonquantitative, has as its goal the reduction, description, and interpretation of the information that has been collected. Too much information is in the data set to simply give it, as it is, to other who want to know the results of your investigation. Also, the information in its raw form probably would not make much sense to anyone else. You must make sense out of the raw data by summarizing it, identifying and presenting important issues or trends, and in most cases, drawing inferences from the sample to the target population.

For most applied research projects, you will use some form of quantitative or statistical analysis. Statistics use numbers both to describe the sample and to make inferences from the sample to the population. The subsequent sections describe some of the many statistical techniques that may be appropriate for applied research in aging. Toward the end of the chapter there is a discussion of the analysis of nonquantitative information.

Descriptive Statistics

Descriptive statistics are ways of describing various characteristics of the sample through the use of numbers. They help you to summarize individual

			Variable	
Q. #	Col. #	Question	Label	Code
94	73	Past 6 months, additions or departures from household (exclude deaths)	VAR473	0 = No 1 = Yes 9 = DK/No answer
95	74	Past 6 months, problems with serious family disagreements	VAR474	0 = No 1 = Yes 8 = No family 9 = DK/No answer
96	75	Past 6 months, moved	VAR475	0 = No 1 = Yes 9 = DK/No answer
97	76	Past 6 months, helper moved away	VAR 476	0 = No 1 = Yes 8 = No helper 9 = DK/No answer
98	77	Past 6 months, major changes for worse in your neighborhood	VAR477	0 = No 1 = Yes 9 = DK/No answer

CARD NO. 4

Figure 9-1. Example of a page from a codebook.

variables, examine associations between variables, explore differences in the same variable from one group to the next, and so forth. Descriptive statistics are valuable because they make it possible to reduce a great deal of information to a few numbers, based upon a set of generally understood rules and assumptions (Blalock, 1960).

An important set of rules in statistics has to do with using statistical techniques that match the type of variable you have. In chapter 4 the characteristics of nominal, ordinal, interval, and ratio variables were described. Statistical techniques have been designed to fit each of these types of variables. Different techniques are required because, as was discussed in chapter 4, the numbers assigned to the categories of variables having different measurement levels yield different amounts of information about the attribute that was measured. With nominal variables, the numbers assigned to the categories are arbitrary and tell us nothing about what the categories are like. It makes no difference whether the number *1* is assigned to males and *2* to females or vice versa. As a matter of fact, any two numbers could serve as codes for the categories of sex. The numbers assigned to the categories of ordinal variables tell us whether there is more or less of something, but they do not tell us how much more or less, because the intervals between the numbers are not equal. We can, therefore, use the categories only to rank cases. Interval and ratio variables give us far more information because equal differences in the numbers reflect equal differences in the attribute. It is important to keep these differences in levels of measurement in mind, because they are one factor that determines the type of statistic that can be applied.

Describing Individual Variables.   No matter what the research problem may be, summarizing the characteristics of each important variable in the data set is nearly always useful. These statistical summaries of each variable can give you a broad picture of what the data are like and can be helpful in organizing the remainder of the analysis. Rarely do they represent the end of your analysis, but they can be a valuable beginning point.

Statistics may be used to summarize a number of characteristics of variables. Two of the most basic characteristics are measures of *central tendency* and *dispersion*. Measures of central tendency provide information about the most frequent, middle, or average case. Measures of dispersion inform us about the spread of scores across the range of values.

Central tendency.   Three basic measures of central tendency are the mode, the median, and the mean. The *mode,* an appropriate measure to use with nominal data, is simply the most frequently occurring category for the variable. Suppose you asked a group of older respondents about their current employment status and obtained the following results.

Category	Number of Respondents
Employed full time	26
Employed part time	7
Retired	35
Never worked	6

In this sample, *retired* is the modal category for current employment status. When two categories have equal numbers of cases that are more than all others, the distribution is *bimodal* (having two modes).

The *median* is a measure of central tendency that divides the sample so that half the cases have a higher value and half have a lower value. The median is useful with ordinal variables, but cannot be used for nominal variables because the notion of higher and lower makes no sense at the nominal level of measurement.

The *mean* is a measure of central tendency that is appropriate for interval or ratio data. It is the arithmetic average of the scores on the variable and is computed by adding all of the individual scores and then dividing by the total number of scores. Suppose a sample of participants at a nutrition site for older people were asked how many times they visited the nutrition site in the past four weeks. The following responses were obtained.

Respondent	Number of Visits
A	1
B	4
C	3
D	8
E	3
F	13
G	2
H	6
Total	40

The total number of visits was 40, and there were 8 respondents. Therefore the mean is 40 ÷ 8, or 5 visits.

Table 9-1. Measures of Central Tendency Appropriate for Different Levels of Measurement

Level of Measurement	Appropriate Measure of Central Tendency		
	Mode	Median	Mean
Nominal			*
Ordinal		*	*
Interval-Ratio	*	*	*

When selecting measures of central tendency, always keep in mind that some measures are inappropriate for certain levels of measurement. Table 9-1 shows how to select the correct measure of central tendency, a general trend that is true for all statistics. It is possible to use a statistical measure or test associated with a level of measurement lower than that represented by the variable, but it is not possible to use measures that are appropriate for higher levels of measurement.

Dispersion.   Measures of dispersion give us additional information about the variables by telling us about the spread of the scores. With nominal variables, few single measures of dispersion are truly useful. An index of qualitative variation can be computed (Ott, Mendenhall, and Larson, 1978). This statistic is the percent of all possible variations that actually occur in a given variable. Because this measure has little intuitive value, the dispersion of a nominal variable is best summarized by presenting the entire frequency distribution for the variable to give the reader an opportunity to review the number and percentage of cases within each category.

The *range* is a simple measure of dispersion that is appropriate for ordinal or higher levels of measurement. The range is most appropriately expressed as the difference between the highest and lowest score for the variable. In the example of visits to a nutrition site, the range would be 13 − 1, or 12. The range is also sometimes described by presenting the highest and lowest value. We might therefore say that the number of visits ranged from 1 to 13.

A common statistical measure of dispersion, but one that can be used appropriately only with interval or ratio variables, is the *standard deviation.* The standard deviation is a valuable statistic, because it is the foundation for many other descriptive and inferential statistics. The standard deviation, based upon the mean, is calculated by subtracting each score from the mean, squaring this deviation, adding up all the squared deviations, dividing by the number of cases, and finding the square root of the result.

Because the standard deviation is such a commonly used statistic, it may be useful to see how it is calculated using the example of number of visits to a nutrition site.

Respondent	Number of Visits	Mean Minus the Number of Visits	$\left(\dfrac{Mean\ Minus\ the}{Number\ of\ Visits}\right)^2$
A	1	$5 - 1 = 4$	16
B	4	$5 - 4 = 1$	1
C	3	$5 - 3 = 2$	4
D	8	$5 - 8 = -3$	9
E	3	$5 - 3 = 2$	4
F	13	$5 - 13 = -8$	64
G	2	$5 - 2 = 3$	9
H	6	$5 - 6 = -1$	1
TOTALS	40		108

To calculate the standard deviation, the number of visits for each case is subtracted from the mean number of visits (which we already determined to be 5) to give us the deviation of each score from the mean. These individual deviations are then squared. The squared deviations sum to 108. This sum of squared deviations is divided by the number of cases ($108 \div 8 = 13.5$). This statistic, called the *variance,* also has a number of uses in other statistical procedures. The standard deviation is then determined by finding the square root of 13.5, which is 3.7.

Examining Associations.   Many applied research problems in aging are concerned with whether one characteristic is associated with other characteristics. For example, is frequency of interaction between nursing home residents and staff associated with the residents' reported level of satisfaction with the facility? Is more frequent use of personal care associated with lower levels of functional capacity? Measures of association describe the degree to which we can know about one variable based upon what we know about some other variable. If associations are discovered, one does not necessarily cause another; it simply means that they vary together. We cannot infer cause because there are many different possible explanations for associations among variables. However, knowledge about how variables are associated can be a powerful tool in understanding the data. The appropriate statistic to use for examining associations depends upon the level of measurement.

Associations between nominal and ordinal variables are generally based upon contingency tables. Contingency tables, also called cross tabulations, show the joint distribution of cases on two or more variables. Suppose you want to know if the sex of a sample of 100 older community residents is associated with whether they feel there is someone who would be able and willing to take care of them indefinitely if they become sick or disabled. The distributions of sample responses are given in the following table.

Sex	Number	Percentage
Male	40	40%
Female	60	60%
Have an Available Caregiver	*Number*	*Percentage*
Yes	50	50%
No	50	50%

Knowing the distribution of each variable does not help us to learn whether the two variables are associated. A contingency table displaying the joint distribution of the variables does provide some valuable information about whether and how the variables are associated. A hypothetical contingency table for these two variables follows.

		Have an Available Caregiver		
		Yes	No	
	Male	50%	50%	100% ($n = 40$)
		($n = 20$)	($n = 20$)	
Sex				
	Female	50%	50%	100% ($n = 60$)
		($n = 30$)	($n = 30$)	

An examination of the joint distribution of cases suggests there is no association between sex and respondents' feelings about whether they would have a caregiver if they became sick or disabled. Men are just as likely as women to feel they will have a caregiver. It should be noted that percentages in contingency tables are usually computed within categories of the *independent* variable. Independent variables are the variables that are assumed to lead to or be the cause of or to be a dominant influence of dependent variables (Rosenberg, 1968). In this case, sex was viewed as the independent variable, so the percentages who felt they had and did not have an available caregiver were computed separately for the male and female groups.

What if the contingency table showed the following joint distribution?

		Have an Available Caregiver		
		Yes	No	
	Male	75%	25%	100% ($n = 40$)
		($n = 30$)	($n = 10$)	
Sex				
	Female	33%	67%	100% ($n = 60$)
		($n = 20$)	($n = 40$)	

In this case, men appear far more likely than women to feel they have an available caregiver. Although the table suggests an association exists between the two variables, it would also be useful to calculate a single number that can be used to summarize the association between the two variables.

One useful measure of association for nominal variables is Goodman and Kruskal's lambda. Lambda may range in value from 0 to 1. A value of 0 means that knowledge of the independent variable is of no value in determining where the cases might be on the dependent variable. In the first example of the joint distribution of sex and availability of a caregiver, knowledge of the respondent's sex was of no help in estimating which category of the other variable the respondent would select. A lambda value of 1 indicates that knowledge of the independent variable makes it possible to predict with no error where the cases will be on the dependent variable. When considering use of lambda, you must remember that it is a *directional* measure of association, meaning that the value of the statistic may differ somewhat depending upon which variable is selected as the independent variable (Mueller, Schuessler, and Costner, 1970).

Goodman and Kruskal's tau is another useful measure of the strength of association between nominal variables. Tau also ranges from 0 to 1, and the interpretation of the values is similar to that for lambda. Tau, like lambda, is a directional measure of association, so decisions regarding which of the two variables is the independent variable will have some effect on the calculated measure (Mueller, Schuessler and Costner, 1970).

Because the numbers associated with categories of ordinal variables contain information about the order or rank of each category, this additional information can be employed to calculate measures of association. Gamma is an appropriate measure of association to use with ordinal variables because it tells us how predictable the order of one variable is, given the order of another variable. Unlike the measures just described, the value of gamma does not depend upon which variable is selected to be dependent and which is independent. Gamma ranges in value from −1 to +1. The minus and plus signs are an indication of the direction of association. For example, a gamma of −1 means that there are no errors in predicting the order of all untied pairs of cases and that the two variables are associated in such a way that the order on one variable is associated with the opposite order on the other, sometimes called an inverse association. A gamma of +1 means that there are no errors in predicting the order of untied pairs and that the order on one variable is the same as on the other variable, often called direct association. It is best to use gamma only when there are a reasonably large number of categories for both variables, because this statistic disregards tied pairs (Mueller, Schuessler and Costner, 1970).

Kendall's Tau b and the Kendall-Stuart Tau c are two additional measures of association between ordinal variables. Kendall's Tau b should be used when the number of categories is equal for the two variables. Therefore, when you examine a contingency table presenting the joint distribution of the two variables, the number of rows should be equal to the number of columns. When the two variables have different numbers of categories, the Kendall-Stuart Tau c is the appropriate measure (Liebetrau, 1983).

Spearman's rho can also be used with ordinal variables. Rho is used to determine the association between two rank orders, so the information must be converted to ranks first. The question answered by rho is how well can a set of ranks on one variable be used to predict the ranks on another variable? Rho ranges in value from −1 to +1, but this full range is not possible with large numbers of tied ranks. Special computational formulas, however, can correct for ties. The value of rho is the same no matter which variable is chosen as the dependent variable.

When the variables are at the interval or ratio level of measurement, more information is available for the calculation of associations. The most basic measure of association for interval or ratio level data is the Pearson product-moment correlation (often called the Pearson r). The Pearson r is a measure of the linear relationship between two variables and ranges in value from −1 to +1. A value of −1 means that all the values of one variable can be predicted by knowing the values of another variable and that as the scores on one variable increase, the scores on the other variable decline. A zero r indicates that there is no linear association between the two variables. An association may exist, but it does not conform to a straight line. The value of r does not depend upon which of the two variables is selected as the dependent variable.

Pearson product-moment correlations are best understood by thinking of two ratio variables that have a large number of categories. One way of examining the association between the two variables is through the use of a scattergram. Scattergrams are simply graphs that show the location of individual data points for two variables. A hypothetical scattergram for income and out-of-pocket expenditures for health care in a small sample of respondents is displayed in Figure 9-2. Each point on the scattergram represents the out-of-pocket health care expenditures and level of income for one case in the sample.

The pattern of points on the scattergram seem to suggest an association between the income and expenditure variables. In this case, the association is positive, a higher annual income tends to be associated with higher out-of-pocket health care expenditures. The association is not perfect, however, because knowledge of income would not allow you to determine, without error, an individual's out-of-pocket expenditure on health care. The Pearson *r* is a measure that tells how well we can predict one variable knowing the values of another variable.

To carry this hypothetical example one step further, we can draw a line that seems to fit the general trend in the points of the scattergram. While a reasonably good line could be drawn by vision alone, a mathematical formula has been developed to determine the characteristics of a line that fits

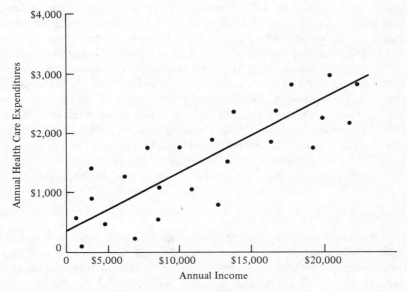

Figure 9-2. Hypothetical scattergram.

the data points extremely well. This line, called a *regression line,* is calculated to minimize the vertical distances between the data points and the line. The Pearson *r* summarizes how well the regression line actually fits the data points. If the regression line comes very close to all the points, the Pearson *r* will be close to $+1$ or -1, with the sign being dependent on the direction of the association. When the line does not fit the data points well, the Pearson *r* will be close to 0.

Examining Differences between Samples.   Applied research in aging can also address problems that require determining whether two or more samples or subsamples are different with respect to some variable, often the case when experimental or quasi-experimental designs are used. Did the group receiving home-based services have higher rates of institutionalization than the control group? Was compliance with prescription drugs higher among those who received the special instructions than among those who received no instruction? Sometimes it is beneficial to compare two or more samples when a nonexperimental research design is employed. Does a sample of white caregivers differ from a sample of nonwhite caregivers with respect to perceived burden?

Frequency distributions are used to examine differences in nominal and ordinal variables across two or more samples. The researcher reviews the distributions along the categories of each variable to determine whether they are essentially similar or different. This procedure can be troublesome when there are a large number of categories. Differences in the mode (for nominal variables) and the median (for ordinal variables) might also be beneficial in determining whether the two samples differ with respect to the variable.

With interval or ratio levels of measurement the means are generally examined to determine whether variables differ from sample to sample. The mean is a very useful summary measure for these kinds of comparisons because it takes into account information from all of the cases. Because of its utility, a wide variety of inferential statistical procedures have been designed to determine whether differences in the means for two or more samples reflect actual differences in the populations from which they were drawn. These and other types of inferential statistics are described in the next section.

Inferential Statistics

Descriptive statistics use numbers to describe characteristics of samples, but we are usually interested in using our sample information to make inferences about the target populations from which they were drawn. We use inferential statistics, or significance tests, to make inferences about the population based upon the sample. Tests of significance indicate how likely it is that observed associations, distributions, or differences could occur in the samples, if they did not really exist in the populations. We do so by following rules and making decisions that allow us to test hypotheses regarding one or more population *parameters.* Population parameters are the quantities or measures that exist in the population. *Statistics,* on the other hand, are characteristics of the samples.

Just as there are many different types of descriptive statistics, there are also many kinds of inferential statistics. The choice of an appropriate inferential statistic depends chiefly upon whether you are interested in making inferences about individual variables, associations among variables, or differences between samples, and upon the level of measurement of the variables. In the following sections some of the more frequently used inferential statistics are described briefly to make you aware of the variety of available techniques. More complete descriptions of the statistics, including the assumptions behind them and methods of calculation, are available in the Suggested Readings section of this chapter.

Inferential Statistics for Individual Variables. Quite often, once you have described the sample variables, you would like to be able to draw inferences about the same attributes in the population. The statistical tests to make such inferences are relatively easy to calculate, and the rules and formulas to be applied are in most introductory statistics texts. The more commonly used approaches are described here.

A very frequently used test of significance for individual nominal and ordinal variables is the chi-square test. The chi-square test is based upon a comparison of the sample cell counts on some variable with the counts that would be expected based upon the assumption that all categories have an equal number of cases. Thus, chi-square helps us decide whether to reject an hypothesis that there are equal cell frequencies on the attribute of interest within the population.

It is also possible to calculate confidence intervals for nominal or ordinal variables. Confidence intervals can be useful because they give you a sense of the range within which the true population percentage might lie given some acceptable level of statistical confidence. Table 6-1 presented confidence intervals for various distributions of a binomial variable at the 95% confidence level.

Another test of statistical significance is available for variables that are at least ordinal in nature. The Kolmogorov-Smirnov one-sample test uses the additional information available in ordinal variables by comparing the cumulative relative frequency distribution for a sample variable with a hypothesized cumulative relative frequency distribution (equal numbers of cases in each category). The *cumulative relative frequency distribution* for some level of a variable is the number of cases at or below that level, divided by the total number of cases in the sample. Because this concept depends upon the ability to order categories, it has no interpretation for nominal variables.

When interval or ratio variables are being considered, researchers most frequently wish to draw inferences about the population mean of some attribute based upon the sample mean. The tests used to make such inferences are based upon hypothetical distributions of sample scores, called sampling distributions. The z test is used when the sample size is 30 or more, and the t test is the appropriate choice for smaller samples. These tests are used to accept or reject a hypothesis that the population mean is 0, given a mean equal to or greater than that found in the sample. The information about the sampling distributions can also be used to calculate confidence intervals for means.

Inferential Statistics for Associations between Variables.

When you find an association between variables in the sample, you might wish to determine whether there is an association between those variables in the population from which the sample was drawn. The statistical tests described in this section are meant to help draw inferences about whether two or more variables are associated in the population.

Tests of significance for associations between nominal and ordinal variables are based upon information that can be drawn from contingency tables. The most frequently used test of significance for associations among nominal and ordinal variables is the chi-square statistic. When used to test the significance of associations, chi-square compares an observed distribution of cell frequencies with the distribution that would be expected if there were no association between the variables. Chi-square is best used with larger samples or when the number of cells in the contingency tables is small. If the expected frequency in any cell of a table is 5 or less, standard correction procedures should be introduced, or another test of statistical significance should be utilized. When the number of cases in the sample is small, and the research problem is one that produces a 2x2 contingency table (e.g., comparing yes and no responses for men and women), Fisher's exact probability test would be an appropriate inferential statistic to employ.

Significance tests for associations among interval or ratio variables are generally based upon the Pearson product-moment correlation. Analysis of variance tests, sometimes called F tests, are used to draw inferences about whether the Pearson r in the population is equal to 0, given a Pearson r of equal or greater absolute value than that found in the sample (Blalock, 1960).

Inferential Statistics for Differences between Populations.

Suppose you have drawn samples from different populations and note differences between the two samples on some attribute of interest. It is reasonable to ask whether the differences reflect actual differences in the population or are due to sampling error. This section briefly describes statistical tests that may be used to draw inferences about whether there are differences between two populations on the attribute, based upon what we know about the sample data.

For nominal and ordinal variables, the most commonly used test for determining whether populations differ with respect to some attribute is, again, the chi-square test. As an example, suppose a researcher was interested in possible differences among impaired men and women in desire for the types of services offered by adult day care programs. Samples of impaired men and women were given a description of typical services offered by adult day care programs and were then asked whether they would like to receive this set of services. The chi-square test could be used to help us make inferences about actual differences between the populations of impaired men and women, given our sample statistics. A significant chi-square would lead us to reject the hypothesis that there is no difference between men and women on this issue. As described earlier, Fisher's exact probability test should be used with smaller samples when the problem produces a 2x2 contingency table.

A number of statistical tests may be used in addition to chi-square when the variables are at the ordinal level. When the researcher is interested chiefly in differences in dispersion rather than the central tendency of the attribute, the runs test is most appropriate. When the focus is on differences in central tendency, the Mann-Whitney or the Kolmogorov-Smirnov tests are most appropriate.

When the attributes were measured by means of interval or ratio variables, the most common statistics are the test for difference between two means (called the t test), and analysis of variance or F tests (also sometimes called ANOVA). Analysis of variance is a very flexible procedure that can be adapted to a variety of situations.

A Note about Significance in Inferential Statistics. It is now common practice to use tests of significance in applied research. The availability of computers and statistical software packages has played an important role in the increased use of statistical tests because they make it possible to quickly and inexpensively carry out complex, sophisticated statistical analyses. You should remember, however, that statistical tests are based upon many important assumptions regarding the sample, the variables, and the underlying sampling distributions. Rarely are all of these assumptions met (Blalock, 1960). Prudence therefore demands that statistical tests be used with caution. You should also be straightforward with the consumers of your research regarding how close the data come to meeting the assumptions behind the statistical tests that you use.

You must remember, particularly in applied research, that statistical significance and substantive or practical significance are separate concepts. Very small measures can be statistically significant if the number of cases in the sample is quite large. However, despite being statistically significant, the measure can be so small that it is of no practical consequence from a policy or programming perspective. Do not be too quick to place more credibility on the value of statistical tests than they deserve.

Multivariate Analysis

Research problems frequently require use of statistical procedures that take into account more than one or two variables at a time. A wide variety of multivariate statistical techniques for describing the sample and for drawing inferences about the population can be carried out at all levels of measurement. Many of these techniques are actually mathematical extensions of the analytical procedures that have just been described. Because a detailed description of multivariate analytical procedures is well beyond the scope of this text, you should consult a statistician or a statistics text for more information.

Analyzing Qualitative Information

Statistical procedures for describing samples and drawing inferences from samples to populations are very effective. But what if the information is in the form of field notes, in-depth interview tapes, or other qualitative forms? Qualitative records usually can be converted into quantatitive data through the application of procedures similar to content analysis (Clark and Anderson, 1967). Although, this conversion may open the data to statistical manipulation, it may also place severe constraints on an otherwise rich and diverse set of information. Therefore, employment of qualitative analytical procedures may be best.

Proper preparation is as crucial for qualitative analysis as it is for quantitative analysis. Poorly scribbled or tape-recorded information should be typed, preferably with sufficient margins and space between lines for notes and comments because you will definitely find occasion to write leads and ideas on the typed forms. Multiple copies of the notes can be used for setting up different kinds of files to facilitate the analysis.

Two types of files that should be established are chronological files, which organize all events and activities in order by date and time, and subject files, which group people, places, events, and organizations. Lofland and Lofland (1984) term these basic files "mundane files" because they are the practical, ordinary support files for the project. Later, as you begin a systematic review of notes, you will establish one or more analytical files, which group trends and patterns that emerge.

Analysis, according to Lofland and Lofland (1984), is a process that depends upon quiet contemplation and provisional writing. The analysis proceeds more smoothly if it is assisted by a general outline derived from the research problem. Analysis usually consists of moving from the files to interpretation and provisional writing back to the files again, and so forth.

What do you look for in qualitative analysis? Babbie (1979) suggests that you can begin by looking for normal things and for deviations from the norms. See if you can establish common events, typical occurrences, everyday ways of behaving, and things that everyone does in a very similar fashion—all indications of patterns, traits, or norms that exist in the environment you are studying. Finding that certain groups behave in similar ways while other groups have their own typical ways of dealing with situations is useful information because it helps you to discern patterns of behavior.

Considering whether some individuals do not follow the usual pattern of behavior is also useful. These individuals may be either outcasts or leaders, but examining their behavior should help you to more fully understand the expectations and constraints within the group.

Sometimes a part of the analysis process may entail returning to the site of data collection to pursue hunches or leads. Such an occasion may be appropriate for use of more structured data collection procedures. For example, forms might be devised that allow you to focus on actions that address a hunch or hypothesis that emerged during the initial analysis (Keith, 1980).

The importance of organizing and writing in qualitative analysis cannot be overemphasized. The general outline for the report should be continually refined during the analysis phase. The outline is a useful organizational tool that will help you to focus your thoughts and eliminate unimportant information. You may also find it helpful to establish new analytical files, organized to reflect the trends you have discovered. Writing about trends and patterns as they become evident is especially important because thought often seems to be triggered by the process of writing.

SUMMARY

Once you have the information in hand, a number of steps are involved in making sense of it. All of these steps will run more smoothly if the analysis is carefully planned before, rather than after, the information is gathered. The first steps after the information is collected consist of getting the data in shape. It should be edited, categorized, and coded in preparation for analysis. In cases where the data consist of many variables, a codebook should be developed to help you keep track of all the pertinent information. Part of the preparation for analysis also consists of reviewing what you have collected so that you are thoroughly familiar with the information in its raw form. This knowledge can help you deal with problems and issues that arise during the analysis phase.

When the research problem and the data are appropriate for quantitative analysis, two types of statistics might be used. Descriptive statistics are employed to describe characteristics of the sample. Inferential statistics are used to draw inferences from samples to the populations from which they are drawn. Examples and discussion of some frequently used descriptive and inferential statistics have been provided. However, many more statistical techniques than are disccused here are available and probably one can meet your specific research needs. Consulting a statistical text or an applied statistician as you plan your research project is a good idea so you can design an analytical approach that meets your needs.

Some research problems are handled best by qualitative analysis. As with quantitative information, preparation is an important precursor to qualitative analysis. Editing and reviewing the data as well as establishing basic files are valuable preparation activities. Analysis is a process of moving from the files to interpretation to preliminary writing and back again and is facilitated if there is a general outline to follow. This outline becomes more precise as the analysis proceeds. In carrying out the analysis, it is often useful to look for typical events as well as deviations from the norm.

SUGGESTED READINGS

Blalock, H. M. (1960). *Social statistics.* New York: McGraw-Hill. An introduction to statistical analysis, this book begins at a very basic level and progresses through most descriptive and inferential statistics.

Lofland, J., and Lofland, L. H. (1984). *Analyzing social settings: A guide to qualitative observation and analysis* (2nd ed.). Belmont, Calif.: Wadsworth. All the mechanics of field studies are described in this book, from planning the research through preparing and analyzing the data.

Mueller, J. H., Schuessler, K. F., and Costner, H. L. (1970). *Statistical reasoning in sociology* (2nd ed.). Boston: Houghton Mifflin. A very good introductory statistics text, this book does not cover the more sophisticated multivariate techniques, but it describes the simpler statistical analysis procedures in a very logical, easy-to-understand manner.

REFERENCES

Babbie, E. R. (1979). *The practice of social research* (2nd ed.) Belmont Calif.: Wadsworth.

Blalock, H. M. (1960). *Social statistics.* New York: McGraw-Hill.

Clark, M., and Anderson, B. G. (1967). *Culture and aging: An anthropological study of older Americans.* Springfield, Ill.: Charles C. Thomas.

Keith, J. (1980). Participant observation. In C. L. Fry and J. Keith (Eds.), *New methods for old age research: Anthropological alternatives.* Chicago: Loyola University Center for Urban Policy.

Liebetrau, A. M. (1983). *Measures of association.* Sage University Paper series on Quantitative Applications in the Social Sciences, No. 07-001. Beverly Hills: Sage.

Lofland, J., and Lofland, L. H. (1984). *Analyzing social settings: A guide to qualitative observation and analysis* (2nd ed.). Belmont, Calif.: Wadsworth.

Mueller, J. H., Schuessler, K. F., and Costner, H. L. (1970). *Statistical reasoning in sociology* (2nd ed.). Boston: Houghton Mifflin.

Ott, L., Mendenhall, W., and Larson, R. F. (1978). *Statistics: A tool for the social sciences.* North Scituate, Mass.: Duxbury.

Rosenberg, M. (1968). *The logic of survey analysis.* New York: Basic Books.

10

Presenting the Information to Others

Jay A. Mancini and Laurie Shea

PROBLEMS TO BE SOLVED

Has the goal of my research been met? Have I answered the question upon which the study was based?

What discoveries appear to be useful, interesting, or significant?

Who needs or wants to know about these research discoveries? Relatedly, who will benefit from or will implement my discoveries?

What can I do to facilitate the impact of the study results?

How are my findings effectively communicated? Can technical information be made interesting to varied groups of people? What are the keys to oral and written communication skills?

Congratulations! We now assume that you have successfully planned and executed an applied gerontology research project. Depending upon your research goals, you now may know more about the needs of particular groups of older citizens or may know something about the relationships between several variables and characteristics of being old. Or, you may have evaluated and determined whether an existing program for older people is effectively meeting its goals. You are in a position to disseminate information that may influence program and policy decisions that could benefit the aged or that, at the least, will enlighten others about the nature of age and aging. At this phase in the research enterprise the goal is to translate dry findings into meaningful conclusions via effective communication. Because applied research by definition seeks information for practical purposes, your task as a researcher is unfinished until facts, figures, and findings are told to others. The adequate presentation of information to others involves a series of questions and decisions.

ASSUMPTIONS ABOUT RESEARCH AND RESEARCHERS

A number of assumptions underlie the suggestions contained in this chapter. Because we believe that one factor in communicating is being clear about why you are saying what you are saying, we shall briefly note our assumptions about you and your research. First, applied researchers are continually expanding the knowledge of the gerontological community and their discoveries are of value to the larger scientific community. This applied information demands exposure equal to that whose relevance to everyday life is less clear. Second, sharing information avoids unnecessary duplication of effort and repetition of mistakes and can be instructive for others who desire to conduct applied research. Third, researchers skilled in generating and interpreting data are often not equally skilled in communicating with those who can implement it. How often have you commented that a particular person is knowledgeable but cannot seem to "get it across" to others? Fourth, unless findings generated by applied researchers are, in fact, *applied,* the research effort has lost some of its importance. We mean here that these findings must be considered and attended to rather than always used with the expectation of change in a policy or a program. A fact of applied research life is that there is no promise that results must be accepted by decision makers, program administrators, or others in positions of influence. However, the application potential is diminished if the researcher shrinks from presenting information to others. Fifth, interesting and significant research can be presented in a ponderous fashion that subsequently blunts its impact. How often have you resorted to counting ceiling tiles during someone else's speech and how much from that speech did you remember? Great ideas or earth-shaking research findings will not, on their own, insure that others understand or remember them. Sixth, researchers often give insufficient consideration to techniques of effective communication. "How to" considerations are perhaps seen as obvious common sense and practically beneath the level of skill of the researcher. But, if they are so obvious, why are so many reports poorly written and oral presentations dull? Seventh, techniques of effective communication can be learned. The purpose of this chapter is to sensitize you to the importance of presenting information to others and provide a few hints on how to do so.

FOCUS ON THE ORIGINAL PROBLEM

Things that are obvious and mundane at first glance may be critical and significant at a second or third glance. So it is with focusing on the original problem. Your research was conducted for a particular reason and a problem was identified using the Applied Problem Solving model (chap. 1 and 2). Those earlier chapters suggested that when a problem is clearly defined the solution is much clearer. We suggest that it is all too easy to lose sight of the original problem and, if that occurs it becomes difficult to know what to communicate to others.

Losing sight of the original problem occurs for numerous reasons, including waning interest in the problem and the deluge of data. Our advice regarding waning interest is brief: remind yourself of the context, situation, and conditions under which the research was undertaken. Somewhat less brief is a guideline concerning the deluge of data. Even a modest research project seems to produce a voluminous amount of information, especially when one analyzes means, computes correlations, and focuses on subgroups within a sample. Although the tools described in chapter 9 (on making sense of the information) are necessary, continuing analyses can move us further from what we wanted to know. This continued inquiry is problematic insofar as it may prevent one from clearly stating the original problem and its solution. You may wonder why the original problem is seemingly so important, but remember that applied research is undertaken for a particular reason that relates to everyday life (and usually to a quality-of-life domain, at that). And while ongong exploration of the data is interesting to you as the investigator, it is probably not nearly so interesting to others. These reminders are relevant to presenting information to others. Whether one is communicating in written or oral form, there must be a framework or method of organization. Focusing on the original problem is the overarching framework. This focus enables you to answer, "Has the goal of my research been met and have I answered the question upon which the study was based?" If you can answer these questions then you are well on the way to clearly telling your audience what has occurred.

In short, if the original problem was worth a research endeavor, then logically it ought to remain the focal point of what is communicated to others. If a problem statement is clear enough to research, then it likely is clear enough to state to an audience or a reader. Refer again to chapter 2 for guidance on developing a clear statement of the problem. Once you are convinced that you know all facets of the problem and how your research has addressed them, then you are ready to consider the nature of the audience to whom you will speak or the reader that will receive your report.

FOCUS ON THE AUDIENCE

Now that you know you have something significant to report, these questions must be asked: Who wants or needs to know about the information? Who can benefit? Who should be contacted to insure that the study findings are appropriately considered?

The outlets for imparting the results of applied gerontological research are many: from professional journals to popular magazines to agency news-letters; from international conferences of experts to agency administrators and staff; and from local gatherings of concerned citizens to radio or television shows. In each case the basic question of the listener or reader is the same: What does this information mean to me? However, the specific form of the question varies. Whereas the journal editor is concerned with the relevance of the theoretical contribution, the agency director wonders where the funds necessary to implement policy recommendations will come from, and the local chapter of the AARP is interested in how many more of their members can be served effectively if the changes you advocate are adopted. Your task is to understand the characteristics, goals, and interests of each potential audience and design your presentation accordingly.

That job becomes more complicated when the results of your study must be shared with varied audiences and for different reasons. For example, as a staff member of an agency on aging, you become aware of the disappoint-ment of many clients with the pension plans they had relied on for retirement income and the collapse of several local pension funds. With the coopera-tion of a university professor interested in finance, you design and execute an investigation of the impact of the growing population of retirees upon pension plans. Your findings indicate that, as administered, many current plans are in danger of collapse, but you also identify some promising strategies to prevent that from happening and some novel suggestions for retirees to protect themselves. You believe that your findings have relevance for indus-try, the government, for retirees, and for other researchers who may wish to duplicate or extend your effort.

At the least, these findings could be shared with administrators at your agency; the Social Security Administration; professional journals; local, state, and national advocacy groups; business and financial experts; fellow researchers gathered at professional meetings; lobbyists and legislators; and the news media (newspapers, radio, and television). In all of these instances the background, technical expertise, and interest of the audience will differ. Furthermore, in each case your reason for sharing your knowledge will differ. Among those reasons are thanking those who helped you and informing them about the results; showcasing your talents and advancing your career; drawing administrative attention to areas in which the agency might be more helpful to clients; publishing your research; informing your audience about steps they may wish to take to protect themselves; seeking critical feedback from colleagues; effecting legislative changes; and drawing public attention to the issue. It will be up to you to tailor your specific presentation to the needs, interests, and understanding of each audience while simultaneously accomplishing your purpose.

Most of the time a speaker or a writer can "gather intelligence" about the average listener or reader. Developing a sense of who will entertain your ideas is well worth the effort. It is our practice, in the case of a speech, to ask others about who the audience will be (unless it is a local group with which we are already familiar). We recently spoke before a group of social workers, volunteers in the aging network, teachers, and interested citizens. Because this meeting was not local we had to ask others about the audience and as a result tailored our remarks to be clear to a heterogeneous group by not dwelling on theoretical-academic issues, but briefly discussing the technicality of research, and spending considerable time focusing on the major, widely recognized issues that pertained to everyday quality of life.

A part of getting the message across is knowledge of the audience but many other guidelines also help us to communicate effectively.

COMMUNICATING EFFECTIVELY

You have drawn your conclusions, identified your audience, and have a specific purpose in addressing that forum. Achieving your purpose may require you to write a lengthy formal research report or to summarize your position in a 30-second interview. It may involve delivering a formal address before a group of professionals, speaking informally to an area agency on aging board, or entertaining questions from an audience of college students. It may very well require that you do all of those things. The challenge is to convince each audience that your findings are interesting, valuable, and relevant to *them*.

What is the most effective way for you to communicate with a specific audience? Which is preferable, a written report or an oral presentation? Careful consideration of both the characteristics of the target audience and your goals will help you determine the most effective and practical means of presentation (see Table 10-1).

The first step in the actual preparation of either the written or the oral report, and ultimately the most important step, is planning. Consider your project in its entirety—what you have done and what you are recommending— and develop a clear, concise thesis sentence (Weisman, 1975) that indicates your position and its underlying logic. If you cannot summarize what you want to report in one sentence, you are not ready to proceed to the communication stage.

WRITTEN COMMUNICATION

A report is "organized, factual, and objective information brought by a person who has experienced it or accumulated it to a person who needs it,

Table 10-1. Choosing an Effective Method of Communication

Audience	Goal	Method
Directors and agency staffs	Inform about evaluation Discuss policy implications	Written report and oral presentation
Professional journals and researchers	Disseminate technical information via publication	Written report (format specified by journal)
News media and general public	Publicity	Press release
	Raise public awareness and support	Interview
	Solicit volunteer help	
University students	Seek research assistance	Lecture
	Teach	Question and answer forum
Study participants	Thank for involvement	Brief summary report
	Inform on results	
Elected officials	Raise awareness of issues	Summary report
	Influence policy	Speech
Older adult groups (local AARP, for example)	Inform, increase awareness of issues	Speech

wants it, or is entitled to it" (Weisman, 1975, p. 31). Facts are its basic ingredients. Effective written communication does not just happen; writing is a craft that can be learned. Writing, as Eisenberg (1982) points out, though not a tidy process, is an orderly one that can be defined, outlined, and followed. Report writing can be divided into the following steps (Turner, 1971).

1. *Planning.* Organization is the key. Before you begin writing, spend some time thinking about your goals and strategy. Find out if a specific format is required by the publication outlet or the agency that is to receive your finished report. Determine whether there are page restrictions on your report. Develop a time schedule, planning backwards from known deadlines to insure that they are met. Be sure to allow time for the typing, collating, distributing, and mailing of your report (Bates, 1978).
2. *Collecting Materials.* Make sure you have gathered everything you need before you begin—your data, reference materials, and style guide, if required.
3. *Outline.* Organize your thoughts into a logical sequence that allows you to see the project both as a whole and as a collection of parts. You can see where you are going as well as how you are going to get there. You can see

the relationships between sections, and missing pieces should be obvious. You can then break your writing task into a series of more manageable steps that can be tackled in any order.

4. *Rough Draft.* The goal here, according to Hays (1965), is to write quickly, getting your main ideas down on paper in rough form so you have something to work with. Trying to write the perfect sentence or trying to make your first draft your final draft is inefficient.

5. *Illustrating.* Because research indicates that 85% of information is learned visually (Carnegie, 1977), you may wish to include visual aids in your report. Diagrams, tables, charts, data sheets, and graphs are useful when they can convey ideas more clearly than text (Hays, 1965). Turner (1971) adds that effective visuals can enhance your report by minimizing text requirements, documenting conclusions, presenting summaries, and providing a concise way to classify and arrange certain types of data to improve readability and clarity. When visuals are used, keep them to one page, do not pack too much information into any one, caption them so that they can be understood without reference to the text, and relate them to the report.

6. *Revising and Rewriting.* Turner (1971) suggests three separate revisions: the first to check technical accuracy; the second to check logic (it is important to read the entire report through at one time to make sure that the logic flows from section to section and the whole thing makes sense when put together); and the third to concentrate on language mechanics (grammar, spelling, punctuation, sentence structure, and paragraphing). Edit your work ruthlessly and then ask a colleague to edit it, preferably one who feels comfortable enough to point out its shortcomings.

Structure of a Report

Specific requirements regarding the structure of your report will vary. You must familiarize yourself thoroughly with the expectations of those for whom you are preparing the report or writing the article. Although, as was pointed out in chapter 2, little applied gerontological research appears in the literature, at times you will wish to publish your findings. A formal research report following a specific format will then be the method of choice. If publication is your goal, spend some time browsing through the journal(s) to which you plan to submit your work. By such perusal you will develop a flavor for the type of articles accepted, for editorial policy, suggested format, and submission procedures. This information is published in each journal issue. If a specific style manual (e.g., *Publication Manual of the American Psychological Association,* 1983) is recommended as a guide, get an up-to-date copy and follow it exactly.

Generally, when specific report guidelines are unavailable the following structure is acceptable (Turner, 1971): title page, abstract, table of contents, introduction, methods, results and discussion, conclusion, references, and appendices. Each section serves a separate purpose and provides a different piece of the overall report puzzle.

The title must contribute to the overall purpose of the report (Gray, 1970; Turner, 1971) and should be interesting, promising, and descriptive. It should inform readers about the subject of the report and also state, if possible, how this report differs from others on the same topic. Often the subtitle suggests the uniqueness. The abstract should present an overview of the entire report: objectives, results, conclusions, and implications (Eisenberg, 1982). Remember that the abstract often serves as the decision point at which readers judge whether the report is worth their time. Often, it will be all they read (Eisenberg, 1982). The introduction defines the scope and significance of the problem under consideration, reviews the relevant literature, and provides an overview of the goals of this reasearch. Again, capturing the reader's interest is essential if he or she is to continue through the report. In the methods section, complete technical descriptions of the processes by which you conducted your study are detailed: how you selected your sample and the characteristics of that sample, how you collected your data, how you measured your defined variables, and how you analyzed your data.

In the results and discussion section you say what you found, indicate if the finding is expected or not, and then explain the finding if it was not expected. In this section you indicate clearly what happened in the course of following the procedures outlined in the methods section. Define terms and statistics in order to support your statements, demonstrate points, and clarify results. If available to you, use quotes and anecdotes to illustrate, highlight, and personalize the data. The conclusions section tells the reader what it all means. Your conclusions are convictions arrived at on the basis of evidence, and they should seem sensible to the reader who has followed the logic of your report. In this section, you are probably also going to make some recommendations either for further study or for action based upon your findings. Recommendations follow logically from conclusions and should be well supported and documented by what has preceded them (Gray, 1970). The recommendations you make should not surprise or startle a reader who has understood your report to that point. A one-page summary of your results and conclusions is often helpful for readers with little time.

A list of all published and unpublished references consulted in the course of your project is included with your report. Although references are primarily listed alphabetically by last name of the senior author, it is also sometimes necessary to include a reference list with the works listed in the order in which they were cited in the report. If requirements are not specified, use a publication manual and follow it consistently. All important supplementary material that would be obstructive if presented in the main text of the report belongs in the appendix (Turner, 1971), including charts, tables, sample documents, interview questions, or questionnaires used in the research.

The Executive Summary

Another method of increasing the chances that your report will be read is the writing of an executive summary. This kind of summary focuses on major findings and recommendations, and is cautious about bogging the reader down in the intricacies of the research. Decision makers often do not have the time to read the "bottom line" of research. Sections of the summary are as follows: brief introduction to the problem and major findings of the study; more detailed background information on the problem or issue; sections on each major finding (e.g., if the study has examined the program and service needs of the aged who live alone and of those who live with others, then each would have a separate section); technical appendix (where you would overview the research methods). It is important to know that throughout the executive summary recommendations are presented, and each one follows a finding from the research.

A Comment on Moving from Analysis to Action

The writing of implications and recommendations is especially important in applied gerontology research. Rothman (1980) has noted the importance of making clear programmatic implications of findings from research. One respondent in a survey conducted by Rothman (1980, p. 133) remarked, "You need to know what to do about what you find out." How does the applied researcher know what to do? Rothman speaks of a group that he calls "operational people," that is, people who will use the research information. After the research report is written these operational people should be asked to respond to it regarding possible applications to programs, policies, and people. This task is not so difficult if operational people were consulted when the research was being planned. Remember that ideally and pragmatically the researcher ought to have the input of people in the field because they will ultimately decide if the research was worthwhile and use it (or decide that it is not useful). Their input should tell you about how to move from analysis to action. If your research was designed to address a specified applied issue, then the barriers to stating recommendations will be few.

A Note on Style

The teaching of literary style (mechanics of spelling, grammar, punctuation, sentence construction, paragraphing, and word choice) is beyond the scope of this chapter but we are not without a few opinions and suggestions about technical writing.

Less is generally better; both science and scientific writing ought to be parsimonious. Eisenberg (1982) tells us to attend to the ABCs of technical writing: accuracy, brevity, and clarity. According to Bates (1978), be concise; avoid long sentences, especially if you want to give emphasis to particular points; use concrete, generally understood words rather than jargon, slang, and gobbledygook; use words that say what they mean; repeat words and phrases only when that repetition enhances clarity; and, arrange the material logically in a step-by-step fashion. Our practice and advice to you is to keep several good reference books at hand and to consult them freely (see list at the end of this chapter). We also recommend liberal use of a dictionary and thesaurus.

ORAL COMMUNICATION

In addition to, or instead of, submitting a formal written report of your research project, you may be invited to present your findings, or portions of them, to various live audiences. The range of possibilities may include a board meeting at your agency, an international gathering of the foremost experts in the field, a class meeting of undergraduates at the local university, or a meeting of the AARP. Your audience may be primarily interested in the technical aspects of your research procedures, in the human interest stories encountered along the way, or in your recommendations. Your reasons for accepting invitations will also vary; you may wish to share information; to document policy and program recommendations that should be implemented; to demonstrate your abilities and accomplishments; to solicit funds, volunteers, or other types of support; to entertain; or to receive critical feedback from other professionals.

Again the crucial first step is planning, organizing, and thinking. Who is your audience? Consider age, sex, education, occupation, interests, organization membership, and level of knowledge and experience with regard to your subject (Abernathy, 1964). What do they want to know? How can you present that information to them in the most interesting, informative, and convincing way? How can your knowledge help them solve their problems and reach their goals? What is your goal in addressing them? If you are seeking support of some kind from them, can you find a way to couch your request in terms of their interests and potential gains (Turner, 1971; Carnegie, 1977)? Once these questions are answered and you have a clear sense of both your goals and the goals of the audience, you are ready to plan your presentation.

Visual Aids

Research indicates that we give 25 times as much attention to what we see compared to what we hear (Carnegie, 1977) and that 85% of what we learn comes through visual channels (*Communication Briefings,* 1984). Visual aids will attract attention as well as emphasize, clarify, and summarize your major points. When using charts, graphs, slides, chalkboards, and photos, be sure that they can be seen clearly by everyone in the room and keep them out of sight until needed lest they distract the audience.

When your presentation is complex, summary handout statements of significant points are often useful. Be careful they do not include too much detail and do not distribute them too soon lest they distract from, rather than clarify, your presentation.

Setting

Beyond preparing your presentation, one other detail to attend to before the day of your speech is becoming familiar with the actual room in which you will be speaking. Check the seating. Are there enough chairs? Are they arranged appropriately for the mode of audience participation you anticipate? Can the podium be seen from every seat? Check whatever equipment you will be using. Does the microphone work? Are electrical outlets where you need them? Are extension cords available? Do you know how to operate the projector and any other devices? Check the physical environment. Can you control the temperature? Are there any drafts? Will sun shining in the window blind your audience? Are there intrusive outside noises? Most interferences and equipment problems can be prevented.

Delivery

You have carefully prepared your speech; you have several charts and graphs illustrating your main points; you are thoroughly familiar with the room, and all equipment is functioning. You are fully prepared, but you are nervous. Expect to be nervous! A recent poll of people's fears revealed that the largest number of respondents (41%) named public speaking as the single thing they feared most (*Communication Briefings,* 1981). Therefore, if you are nervous, your audience understands. Remind yourself that you have been invited to speak because you are an expert on your topic. You will be sharing information that this audience is eager to hear. The following suggestions will help make your delivery effective.

Do not read or memorize your speech. Use an outline that organizes your thoughts but allows you to use a conversational tone and to respond to audience cues.

Attend to grooming and attire. Your appearance should not detract from your point either by being out of place or overdone.

Watch nonverbal communication, that is, your posture, gestures, and body language. People make judgments about others within the first four contact minutes, usually based upon appearance and nonverbal cues (Leonard, 1979).

Do not use the microphone unless necessary. Most audiences would rather you did not. However, if you choose to forego a microphone, be absolutely certain that you can be clearly heard from every location in the room.

Maintain eye contact with your audience as much as possible. Be aware of their reactions to what you are saying and match their responses with your own.

Use anecdotes and quotes whenever appropriate to attract attention. Painting word pictures helps the audience visualize what you are saying and lends concrete support to your points (Leonard, 1979). The audience will remember anecdotes and quotes long after they have forgotten everything else you said.

Project interest and enthusiasm for your subject. It is contagious (Leonard, 1979)!

Speak forcefully and loudly. This manner expresses and communicates confidence, enthusiasm, leadership. Speaking softly, on the other hand, may convey doubt and hesitation (*Communication Briefings,* 1983).

Use pauses judiciously (*Communication Briefings,* 1985). They can be powerful and purposeful and indicate that the speaker is in control. They command attention, yet help the audience catch up in thought. They punctuate and emphasize the previously made point. They allow the speaker to gauge audience reaction and provide a moment to think. Beware, though, of filling a well-timed pause with "er," "uh," or "ah."

Beginnings and endings carry the greatest impact in oral presentations. Plan to capture the attention of the audience quickly at the beginning, and be sure to summarize your main points and relate everything together in your closing remarks. Be sure you have an ending that effectively concludes your speech. If you are appealing for action as a result of your presentation, the conclusion is your opportunity to summarize your appeal (Abernathy, 1964). Remember that if in your first breath you promised your audience that certain points would be addressed, both you and they should be clear that has been accomplished by your final breath.

NEWS MEDIA

You may wish to draw public attention to your findings. When attempting to gain media attention, aim to relate your work to current topics of media interest. For instance, your pension fund research could become more interesting to the media if linked with a recent local pension fund collapse, accompanied by several human interest stories of hardships encountered by retirees you interviewed, or related to Congressional hearings on Social Security. You may have to discover and draw attention to such parallels on your own. Emphasize what is newsworthy about your story, how people are affected, and how it is linked to larger stories. News releases may be submitted to outlets ranging from agency newsletters to campus newspapers to national wire services. Gould (1978) suggests that when preparing a news release (1) you have something newsworthy to say, (2) you summarize in one paragraph, (3) you provide a short (2-3 word) title and 8-10 word caption, (4) you give the complete name, title, address, and phone number of a person to be contacted for confirmation or clarification, and (5) you mail it to the proper editor by name and title.

SUMMARY

Introspection and reflection are key preparatory elements to disseminating information. Certain of the decisions only you can make. For example, you know best whether the research goals were met and whether the question upon which the study was based was answered. By the time your study was concluded you knew which findings appeared useful, interesting, and significant, but other people may also have important perspectives on the findings. You will learn their opinions and views as you communicate about the study. The third area of decision concerned who needs to know about the research, and who will benefit. Even before conducting the research you had a vague idea about this prospective audience but as the study continued you probably became more aware of the consumers for your information. Moreover, this awareness will sharpen as you begin presenting the study findings; in our experience effective communication has created additional dissemination opportunities.

The decision regarding facilitating the impact of the study is closely related to applying the suggestions previously mentioned. It requires an awareness that even interesting information can seem dull, and therefore requires the writer to apply concrete methods of clear expression. A final and pivotal decision pertains to whether you will apply principles and strategies of presenting information so it is remembered. We have noted how findings are communicated, how pitfalls can be avoided, and how your preparation before presenting information can make or break that experience. Some hints for effective oral and written communication have been explicated. Our society relies on communication and dissemination of information and decisions are based on what people know. These facts would seem sufficiently motivating to encourage one to systematically apply techniques of communication. As we have already said, one distinction of applied gerontology research is its relevance for understanding everyday life. This distinctiveness in purpose presupposes that we present information to others.

SUGGESTED READINGS

Abernathy, E. (1964). *A manual of persuasion.* New York: David McKay. In one sense all communication is geared toward persuading one or more people to see your point of view or to have them understand what you are saying. This volume discusses the many facets of persuasion and provides a useful approach to knowing why what we say is either understood or misunderstood.

Carnegie, D. (1977). *The quick and easy way to effective speaking.* New York: Pocket Books. We suppose that this little book is one of the better-known statements on the "tricks" of the communication trade. It is easy to read and insightful, and the skills on presenting yourself and what you have to say are readily applied.

Communication Briefings. This newsletter offers valuable, useful, and concise ideas for people who need to communicate information to others. The ideas and techniques are down-to-earth and easily applied to diverse needs and situations. The newsletter can be obtained by writing to *Communication Briefings,* P.O. Box 587, Glassboro, NJ 08028.

Strunk, W., and White, E. B. (1979). *The elements of style* (3rd ed.). New York: Macmillan. This book may be the briefest one ever published on how to write effectively. In spite of (or perhaps because of) its brevity this volume is used by a variety of popular and scholarly writers. Rules of word usage and principles of composition are discussed, and the book concludes with twenty-one valuable reminders for those who desire to write clearly. We recommend it highly.

REFERENCES

Abernathy, E. (1964). *A manual of persuasion.* New York: David McKay.
Bates, J. D. (1978). *Writing with precision.* Washington, D.C.: Acropolis.

Carnegie, D. (1977). *The quick and easy way to effective speaking.* New York: Pocket Books.

Communication Briefings. (1981, December). What do people fear most. *Communication Briefings,* p. 3.

Communication Briefings. (1983, December). Speak louder. *Communication Briefings,* p. 4.

Communication Briefings. (1984, August). Communicating with visuals. *Communication Briefings,* p. 4.

Communication Briefings. (1985, February). Pauses put you in control. *Communication Briefings,* p. 4.

Eisenberg, A. (1982). *Effective technical communication.* New York: McGraw-Hill.

Gould, J. R. (1978). *Directions in technical writing and communication.* Farmingdale, N.Y.: Baywood.

Gray, D. E. (1970). *So you have to write a technical report.* Washington, D.C.: Information Resources Press.

Hays, R. W. (1965). *Principles of technical writing.* Reading, Mass.: Addison-Wesley.

Leonard, D. J. (1979). *Communication in business* (4th ed.). New York: McGraw-Hill.

Publication Manual of the American Psychological Association (1983). Washington, D.C.: American Psychological Association.

Rothman, J. (1980). *Using research in organizations: A guide to successful application.* Beverly Hills: Sage.

Turner, R. P. (1971). *Technical report writing.* San Francisco: Rinehart.

Weisman, H. M. (1975). *Technical report writing.* Columbus, Ohio: Charles E. Merrill.

Part III

CONCLUSIONS AND PERSPECTIVES

11

Putting It All Together

The preceding chapters have taken you through the major steps of research, offering examples along the way from real or hypothetical applied research projects. This final chapter serves two purposes, both related to putting these steps together in applied research. The first section represents a brief case study of a real-world applied gerontological research project. As you read through this case study you will learn about the decisions that were made as well as some of the problems that occurred and had to be resolved. The second section serves as both a conclusion to the text and an invitation to become involved (if you have not already) in applied gerontological research. Your initial attempt at putting it all together will be the real conclusion to this book. Each of you will write it differently based on your interests, the research problem you seek to address, and the context in which you carry out your study.

A REAL-WORLD EXAMPLE OF APPLIED GERONTOLOGICAL RESEARCH: THE STATEWIDE SURVEY OF OLDER VIRGINIANS

Background

The Statewide Survey of Older Virginians was initiated because the administrative staff of the Virginia Office on Aging,* the lead agency for Older Americans Act funds, wanted a better understanding of the characteristics

---

*Now the Department for the Aging.

and needs of its target group (Virginians 60 years of age or older). The information was to be used to plan and target services and to enhance the Office's role as advocate for Virginia's older citizens. The Office on Aging was able to obtain the financial support of the Virginia Department of Welfare.* The Department of Welfare was willing to fund the project because it is responsible for administering Title XX services in Virginia and wanted to know more about older individuals receiving this form of assistance. Another organization, the Virginia Center on Aging was interested in working on the project and had been recently named the state research and training center for gerontology by the Virginia Legislature, and one of its charges was to conduct applied gerontological research.

The research was organized as a contract project (see the Appendix for more on applied research contracts versus grants). The funding organization, the Department of Welfare, contracted with the Office on Aging for the overall administration of the project. The research was actually conducted by the Virginia Center on Aging through a subcontract with the Office on Aging.

An advisory committee was established to review and critique the research plans and to provide suggestions regarding specific procedures. The advisory committee consisted of eighteen planners and practitioners representing both local and state offices of the major agencies serving older people in Virginia. The committee did offer useful guidance. It also gave a certain level of legitimacy to the project, and it helped assure that those who were in a position to implement the findings would understand and feel comfortable with the project.

Research Problem

As with many large-scale applied research projects involving multiple agencies, there were several research problems, all related to the noninstitutionalized Virginia population 60 or more years old. The section "Selecting People to Study" gives a more complete description of the population. Some of the major research problems addressed by the study are as follows:

1. Measure perceived or felt need for basic health and social services
2. Measure the objective characteristics and conditions that are related to service need
3. Measure use of services provided by informal sources (family, friends, and neighbors)
4. Measure use of services provided by formal sources (public and private agencies and organizations)

---

*Now the Department of Social Services.

5. Determine the relative mix of formal and informal service use (i.e., the proportion of services supplied by formal and informal sources)
6. Determine the level of unmet need for various services by comparing both perceived need and objective characteristics with formal and informal service use

Research Design

The cross-sectional survey approach was selected as most appropriate for this research. The project was not established to determine the impact of one or more interventions, but to provide a reasonably comprehensive "snapshot" of a rather broad array of conditions and circumstances as they existed at one point in time.

Measurement Techniques

A number of existing research instruments were reviewed in hopes of finding one that would work well for the project. The Duke University Older Americans Resources and Services (OARS) instrument was selected because it met several important criteria. Some of the features that made it an appropriate choice for the survey follow.

1. It was designed to provide a comprehensive assessment, rather than focusing on only one or two issues.
2. It includes measures of objective characteristics of people that can be logically related to service use as well as measures of perceived need.
3. It measures service use and need in terms of generic service definitions based upon specific activities performed, rather than by means of service labels. This feature was important to us because more than one agency potentially could benefit from the results. Agencies use different labels for the same services. Thus, we needed a common language for measuring services.
4. It has been used and found to be a practical assessment instrument in many different applied settings.
5. Some information was available regarding the validity and reliability of major components of the instrument.
6. A reasonably complete manual was available, and the instrument itself was easy for interviewers to understand and use.
7. The OARS instrument was designed so that informants could be substituted for respondents who were unable to complete all or parts of it.

Based upon the advisory committee's recommendations, and our own research interests, a few additional items were incorporated into the instrument. An effort was made to add these items without harming the integrity of the OARS.

Method of Collecting Information

Face-to-face interviewing was the procedure employed to gather the information. The face-to-face interview approach was viewed as appropriate because we were interested in having a reasonably high level of coverage. For example, phone interviewers would miss a small but potentially important group of respondents. In addition, we knew that the interview would be longer than is usually acceptable for the telephone or mail formats.

Selecting People to Study

The target sample size (2250) was, in actuality, a "guesstimate." We estimated the cost per interview for field work and data preparation and the need for reasonable accuracy of the results. We chose the largest number of cases we felt was feasible without stretching our field work and data preparation funds to the point where major problems could arise.

The target population was all individuals 60 or more years old residing in noninstitutional settings in Virginia at the time of screening. Noninstitutional settings included houses, apartments, and mobile homes. Not included were hospitals, prisons, nursing homes, homes for adults, military barracks, hotel and motel rooms, mental health facilities, and so forth. Specific definitions and a decision tree were employed to determine which housing units should be defined as part of the population.

Sampling was based upon a multistage area probability design. At the initial stage minor civil divisions or parts of minor civil divisions were selected. Because service use could be related to socioeconomic status and level of urbanization, the minor civil divisions were stratified on these two characteristics. The second stage consisted of clusters of housing units. The third stage was formed by preparing complete listings of housing units in the clusters. Sample housing units were randomly selected from the listings. The sample housing units were then screened to locate age eligibles. Approximately 87% of the persons found to be eligible consented to be interviewed. This figure included 196 cases in which informants were used for some or all of the questions because eligible respondents were too physically or mentally handicapped to be interviewed. We did not want to lose information on these cases, because they tended to represent people with high levels of need and great service use.

Preparations for Data Collection

As was discussed in chapter 7, applied research must often be completed within a very tight timeframe, and the project has to be designed to operate within an established schedule. The total time alloted for the project by the sponsoring agencies was 18 months, a very brief schedule for a survey covering all areas of a large state and employing face-to-face interviews. Some early phases of the project had to be completed rapidly so as to allow sufficient time for field work, data preparation, analysis, and report writing.

Considerable time was saved by contracting with a large survey research firm for some aspects of sample selection. The firm had recently completed a statewide survey for the Virginia Department of Health, so it was able to quickly and efficiently select clusters of housing units and identify specific units to screen, using our sampling criteria. It also had already produced all the maps and other materials needed to locate and screen the selected housing units.

The OARS instrument, along with the added questions, were submitted to a pretest on a small sample of older noninstitutionalized people selected to represent the broad range of characteristics that could be expected during the actual survey. Based upon the pretest, the instrument and interview procedures were slightly revised and then pretested again. Due to time constraints, there was no effort to pretest all phases of the project.

We decided to use paid professionals rather than volunteers because we were working against a tight time schedule. We felt that volunteers would not be willing to work full time or nearly full time. Most of the methods described in chapter 7 were employed to locate approximately 40 interviewers as well as four field supervisors who were hired to ensure the quality of data and to keep the work flowing efficiently. Manuals were developed for supervisors and interviewers. The training took place in a central location and was conducted by the research staff.

Supervisors were paid by the hour; interviewers were paid by the interview. Interviews completed in rural areas were reimbursed at a rate 25% higher than ones completed in urban areas. In addition to their payments for completed interviews, interviewers were paid for screening, and were reimbursed for travel.

A number of steps were taken to improve the response rate. Identification cards were issued, law enforcement agents were contacted, a letter of introduction was composed and reproduced, news releases were distributed, and radio and television appearances were scheduled. In addition, a toll-free number was arranged so that potential respondents could call to ask questions.

Just before the field work was to begin, valuable time was lost because the questionnaires were not yet printed. Although they had been sent to the print shop in plenty of time to meet its normal schedule, a mechanical malfunction led to unanticipated delays. We were able to reproduce enough copies to get the field work started, but the experience taught us to have all the materials printed and on hand well before the field work begins.

Gathering the Information

Field work in large household studies is full of surprises. Some of the problems encountered by the interviewers (unfriendly dogs, unfriendly people, streams across country lanes, mapped roads that seemed not to exist, etc.) have been mentioned in earlier chapters. In addition, a few interviews had to be completed under less than ideal conditions. For example, interviewers had to ask questions while respondents finished farm chores or prepared meals or repaired their cars. In these cases, it was obvious that the interviewer had to either make the best of the situation or lose the interview.

Early in the data-gathering phase, we discovered that some staff members of the agency that volunteered use of its toll-free number had not been given adequate information about the study. Thus, they were unclear about how to handle questions. The problem was quickly resolved by developing a fact sheet about the survey and discussing the project with all the staff who might answer the toll-free phone. However, two or three potential respondents may have been lost, or at least made more apprehensive about the survey, before we discovered the problem. We also found it was necessary to add the principal investigator's home phone to the list of numbers prospective respondents could phone for assurance. In this case the call could be made collect. This adjustment was necessary because many of the interviews took place after normal working hours or on weekends.

We had anticipated that most of the interviewers would work full time or nearly full time. This assumption was built into our decisions about the correct number of interviewers to hire. During the job interviews, applicants were told of this expectation, and most agreed to it. We soon found, however, that a substantial proportion worked only part time while others worked on a variable schedule (e.g., full time one week and part time the next). Many professional interviewers select this type of work because of the flexibility it affords them. In order to compensate, we had to hire and train additional interviewers. This extra step was costly in terms of time, and it also stretched our supervisory/management resources to the limit, because field work had to continue while the new interviewers were being sought.

As forms and questionnaires were returned, we found we had not planned sufficient easily accessible storage space. We organized a shelved storage room in a lockable walkin broom closet that (though not perfect) met our basic needs.

One final problem was encountered near the end of the information-gathering phase. Some of the cleanup work in a few areas began to drag as interviewers found that trying to obtain the last one or two interviews was unproductive. To overcome this obstacle we hired some of the more efficient interviewers on an hourly basis to complete the task.

Making Sense of the Information

Data preparation went smoothly, although we found that categorizing and coding the few open-ended questions that we had added to the form was somewhat more time consuming than we had anticipated. The analysis for the final report consisted of producing contingency tables. Most of the results were also presented separately for key age, race, and residence subgroups. This initial analysis was all that was specifically requested by the funding agency and all that was feasible within the timeframe. However, as the final report was being produced, we were already beginning more in-depth analysis of the information.

Presenting the Results to Others

The major document of the project was a final report containing the results of the contingency analysis plus a brief executive summary. The results were also disseminated by means of scheduled briefings with the agencies involved. At the briefings, we summarized what had been learned, described how the information could be used for more thorough analysis to address specific issues, discussed the implications of the results, and answered questions about the methods used. After the project period, dissemination continued in several ways, including (1) testimony at legislative hearings, (2) the production and distribution of brief special reports, (3) a series of research and practice workshops, (4) publications in professional journals, and (5) book chapters. In addition to disseminating the results of the study, the data set was made available to other researchers for additional analysis. It is now a holding of the Duke University Data Archive for Aging and Adult Development.

Impact

The results of the Statewide Survey of Older Virginians have been success-fully incorporated into the planning and policy processes of a number of state and local agencies in Virginia as well as other states. In addition, the Virginia Legislature has used the results to help justify, design, and implement a state Long-Term Care Council and a network of local long-term care coordinating committees. Some of the information was also used by the Task

Force on the Future of Older Virginians in its effort to determine the major present and future issues facing older people in the state. The staffs of a health systems agency and an area agency on aging are currently incorporating the results into a model designed to estimate service use and service needs at the local level.

Discussion

As you can tell from the preceding description, the Statewide Survey of Older Virginians was not a letter-perfect applied research project. Many of the problems we encountered could have been prevented by (1) more thorough planning, (2) a full pretest of all aspects of the project, and (3) an extended timeframe. Frequently, however, applied research must be carried out when the circumstances and resources are not ideal. Although perfection may not be possible, the researcher must maintain a commitment to the eight characteristics of scientific research discussed in the Introduction. The goal is to do the best possible job in spite of the existing constraints.

As the project was being carried out, numerous unanticipated problems appeared. Efforts were made to resolve these problems in ways that did not jeopardize the collection of accurate information or the external validity of the results. We also learned from the mistakes made and problems encountered; they are less likely to occur in our future research projects. As was noted in chapter 1, monitoring the effectiveness of decisions leads to refinement in one's problem-solving skills. The objectives of the Statewide Survey of Older Virginians were met in spite of the problems that were encountered. From this perspective, it can be viewed as a success.

CONCLUSIONS

The Introduction emphasized the importance of becoming involved in an applied gerontological research project. As you read through this text, we hope you had an opportunity to participate in some real-world research. If you have, you undoubtedly learned much from this practical experience that will be of value as you begin your next research effort. If you have not had a chance to participate in applied gerontological research, we hope you will actively seek opportunities to become involved.

By now, your level of anxiety about research should be diminished. You have learned some of the logic, terminology, and procedures of research as well as a method for dealing with problems that develop as you carry out research projects. It is time to get started. Your confidence as well as your competence as a researcher will be strengthened by direct experience in putting all the steps together to address an applied research problem.

Although you should strive for perfection in your research plans, you will in all likelihood find that some compromises will be necessary. Additionally, unforeseen situations, such as those described in the preceding section, may arise as you carry out your work. You should always attempt to do as well as possible under the circumstances. Sloppy applied research has no place in gerontology. If you give careful thought to your design and plans and approach the problems you encounter as challenges that can be dealt with creatively, the project has a great chance of being a success. It should not only be a valuable learning experience, but ought also to have significant practical consequences.

Appendix
A Brief Guide to Proposals and Funding

When you become involved in applied gerontological research, you will almost certainly eventually write proposals. In applied research projects, proposals are a fact of life. They are necessary for obtaining funds from outside agencies, and they are also sometimes required within organizations for obtaining approval to undertake a project. This Appendix offers a brief guide to proposal writing and obtaining funds in applied gerontology. The Suggested Readings will provide more detail on these topics.

GRANTS VERSUS CONTRACTS

Applied research can be funded under two different mechanisms: grants and contracts. Most private foundations and some federal, state, and local funding agencies provide research assistance through *grants*. Grants are relatively flexible mechanisms for supporting research and are a very common way of funding basic research projects. Normally, the oversight and control of project activities by the funding agency are minimal with grants.

Applied research is frequently funded through *contracts*. Contracts are relatively structured funding mechanisms employed by agencies to procure research that meets fairly specific requirements. They give far more control to the funding agency (Baker, 1975). Normally, the project officer (the title differs from agency to agency) and contract officer of the funding agency can exercise considerable control over the research activities, even after the contract has been signed. The funding agency maintains fairly strong control because it is interested in purchasing the research to address a constricted research problem in which it has some stake. Thus, it is interested in ensuring that the project activities are all oriented toward meeting the research needs of the agency.

The process of writing proposals is similar for research grants and contracts. However, under contract funding, negotiation is far more likely to occur prior to final approval of the project. Negotiation of contracts usually includes both the budget and the technical components of the proposal.

Grant and contract research differ also with respect to publication rights. In most cases researchers are free to publish the results of their grant research. However, the contracting agency usually has the final word about the publications resulting from contract research. Although approval for publication is normally given, it must be formally requested from the contracting agency (Baker, 1975).

PURPOSES OF PROPOSALS

Proposals are written to convince others of (1) the importance and value of the research problem, (2) the appropriateness of the methods for addressing the problem, (3) the adequacy and reasonableness of the resources (funds, time, staff, etc.) to be used, and (4) the capacity of the research staff to successfully complete the project. The proposal is not likely to be approved unless it manages to thoroughly convince reviewers on all four counts.

DEVELOPMENT PROCESS OF PROPOSALS

Writing the proposal is only one aspect of the art of seeking and getting grants and contracts. It is an important step in the process but is not necessarily the most time consuming. Figure A-1 displays the principal steps involved in the preparation of an applied research proposal. It assumes that the idea is generated by an agency that requires outside funding. As the figure demonstrates, much of the time involved in getting a proposal ready to submit is spent in preparation for proposal writing (Bauer, 1984; Kennicott, 1983). Frequently the success or failure of a proposal can depend upon the adequacy of the developmental work, because it helps ensure a clear, logical proposal that addresses the interests of the potential funding agency and establishes a strong case for the project.

SEEKING SOURCES OF FUNDING

Many public and private agencies are interested in funding applied gerontological research. After you have a general idea about the topic you wish to research, a good idea is to go to one of the many directories of funding sources to identify organizations that might be appropriate to contact. The book by Cohen and her associates (Cohen, Oppedisano-Reich, and Gerardi,

1979), described in the Suggested Readings, lists public and private funding sources in gerontology.

If you are near a university you may have access to a computerized research-funding access system, such as the SPIN (Sponsored Programs Information Network) system. These systems operate in similar ways to computerized bibliographic search systems; key words are used to locate organizations that fund within certain priority areas. They are updated on a regular basis, so the information is current.

The *Federal Register,* a daily publication of the federal government, is an excellent resource for locating research-funding possibilities. It provides detailed information on specific grant and contract opportunities. The

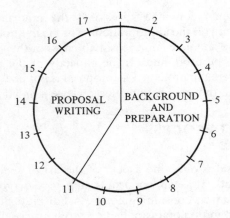

1. Identify research need
2. Search for possible sources of funding
3. Review agency priorities and proposal guidelines
4. Make personal contact with funding agency to clarify issues (if needed)
5. Contact other staff or outside agencies to obtain their ideas and cooperation
6. Review the literature
7. Refine and evaluate the research problem
8. Reach agreement among participants on the problem and methods
9. Write and submit a concept paper (if appropriate)
10. Review evaluations of concept paper
11. Make decision to write proposal
12. Assign responsibilities for writing proposal
13. Develop a rough draft
14. Revise and edit proposal
15. Complete all required forms
16. Review all materials in final form
17. Reproduce and submit

Figure A-1. Steps involved in the preparation of applied research proposals.

government occasionally sponsors workshops on how to read and use this valuable document. The *Catalog of Federal Domestic Assistance,* published annually, provides a comprehensive description of federal funding programs and contains a valuable guide to proposal writing.

CHARACTERISTICS OF SUCCESSFUL PROPOSALS

Successful proposals have certain distinguishing features (Davitz and Davitz, 1977; Leedy, 1980). The following descriptions of characteristics that differentiate successful proposals from those that fail ought to help you understand what the end product of the proposal writing process should be.

Straightforward Content

Successful proposals are straightforward documents that should contain all the necessary, but not any unnecessary, information about the research project. The proposal should also be planned so that a reviewer can follow a line of thought without being sidetracked by irrelevant details. Prudent use of appendices can help assure that important details are included in the proposal but do not clutter the main body of the document.

Clear Communication

Successful proposals communicate clearly. A good proposal is less a literary document than a carefully worded statement of the research problem, methods, and procedures. Precision, logic, and clarity are the principal goals of the proposal writer. The reviewer should understand precisely what you plan to accomplish, how you will accomplish it, and what implications the results will have. Your ability to carry reviewers through the project without losing them because of unclear or illogical passages will reflect well on your ability to accomplish the research. One way to ensure that the proposal communicates clearly is to have someone with little background in the area review and critique it for you.

Good Organization

Successful proposals are well organized. The better the organization of the proposal, the stronger will be the message that you have carefully thought out all the details and can carry the project to successful completion. Funding agencies frequently impose a degree of organization on the researcher by providing a format that establishes the order and content of each major section. If the agency does provide a format for organizing the proposal, it should be closely followed. If the agency does not, you may want to follow the format presented in Table A-1. You should also emphasize organization within major sections through appropriate use of headings and subheadings.

Adherence to Agency Guidelines

The guidelines that many funding agencies send to prospective applicants help to standardize submissions so they can be reviewed quickly and efficiently. The guidelines also help ensure that the major criteria for funding established by the agency are addressed. If you fail to follow the guidelines two results (both negative) are likely to obtain. First, the proposal may fail to meet an initial technical review designed to discover and exclude documents that do not follow guidelines. Second, the reviewers may give your proposal lower marks because it does not follow the established format.

Compatible Objectives

Successful proposals are in line with the objectives of the funding agency. You should learn what agencies are interested in funding and either revise your project so it meets agency objectives or seek another funding source. This step is part of the background work for proposal preparation described earlier. You can learn whether your topic is of interest to an agency by examining its published priorities, reviewing the topics of recently funded proposals, calling on agency staff, or submitting a brief concept paper or preproposal. Some agencies are very flexible with regard to the kinds of topics they will fund, while others fund only a fairly narrow range of topics. Agencies also shift their interests or develop special research initiatives. Therefore, you should always investigate agencies to discover whether your topic is in line with their current objectives.

Reasonable Budgets

The budget should reflect the actual total costs of the project, including the costs to be borne by the funding agency and the costs that will be covered by the research organization. Although the budget is an estimate, it should be carefully considered and it should be fully justified. If it is too high or too low, the reviewers will wonder whether you fully comprehend the nature and scope of the project. In either case, your ability to carry the project to successful completion may be questioned.

Thorough Information

Successful proposals are complete. When proposals do not contain all the required documentation or when all the necessary signatures are not included,

Table A-1. Format for Organizing a Research Proposal

Section	Questions to be Answered
ABSTRACT	What are the key elements of the research, including problem, objectives, design, sample, measurement, data collection, and analysis?
INTRODUCTION	
Statement of the problem	What needs to be done and why? What has already been done (by yourself and others) that is relevant to this project?
Objectives	What are the specific, testable goals?
METHODS	
Design	What is the design you will use? How will this address issues of internal and external validity?
Measurement and data collection	What concepts will be measured? How will they be operationalized? What method of data collection will be used? What will be required to prepare the data for analysis?
Sample	What is the target population? What will be the size of the sample and how will it be drawn?
Analysis	How will the results be analyzed? How does the analysis fit the research problems and data?
Schedule	How much time will be needed to complete each phase of the project? How do the phases fit together temporally?
SIGNIFICANCE	What contribution will the study make? How will you ensure that the results will be used?
PERSONNEL AND FACILITIES	Who will do the study? What is their experience and competence? What available resources will be used to complete the work?
BUDGET	What will be the cost of each component of the project (e.g., salaries and wages, fringe benefits, travel, computer, printing, supplies and materials, overhead)? What is the justification for the cost of each component?
APPENDIX	What are the supporting materials for the proposal (e.g., letters of support or agreement, research instruments, etc.)?
REFERENCES	What are the references for all the materials cited in the proposal?

they are not likely to be funded. Carefully review all the requirements and be sure they are fully met. Are all the necessary forms, including cover sheets, assurances, budget sheets, and so forth completely filled out, signed, and placed in the appropriate location with the document?

SUMMARY

Applied gerontological research typically involves writing proposals to obtain funding and/or approval for the research project. Two distinct mechanisms exist for financing research. Grants are more flexible, and contracts normally give greater control to the funding agency. Whether they are written for grant or contract research, proposals must convince others that the research problem is important and that the methods, resources, and staff are all appropriate. The success or failure of proposals often depends upon the adequacy of the developmental work. Good proposals are straightforward, communicate clearly, are well organized, follow agency guidelines, meet the objectives of the funding agency, have reasonable budgets, and are complete. Recognizing these characteristics of good proposals and refining your proposal so that it aproaches them will help assure the funding of your proposal.

SUGGESTED READINGS

Bauer, D. G. (1984). *The "how to" grants manual: Successful grantseeking techniques for obtaining public and private grants.* New York: Macmillan. This book is a thorough description of all phases of the art of getting grants.

Cohen, L., Oppedisano-Reich, M., and Gerardi, K. H. (1979). *Funding in aging* (2nd ed.). Garden City, N.Y.: Adelphi University Press. A useful guide to funding sources in gerontology, this book covers most of the large private and public resources that fund basic and applied gerontological research.

Lefferts, R. L. (1983). *The basic handbook of grants management.* New York: Basic Books. You will need a resource to tell you how to handle administrative and budgetary issues. This book will help you organize and manage the grant or contract so you can complete it on time and within budget.

REFERENCES

Baker, K. (1975). A new grantsmanship. *American Sociologist,* **10,** 206–219.

Bauer, D. G. (1984). *The "how to" grants manual: Successful grantseeking techniques for obtaining public and private grants.* New York: Macmillan.

Cohen, L., Oppedisano-Reich, M., and Gerardi, K. H. (1979). *Funding in aging* (2nd ed.), Garden City, N.Y.: Adelphi University Press.

Davitz, J. R., and Davitz, L. L. (1977). *Evaluating research proposals in the behavioral sciences: A guide* (2nd ed.) New York: Teachers College Press.

Kennicott, P. C. (1983). Developing a grant proposal: Some basic principles. *Grants Magazine,* **6,** 36-41.

Leedy, P. D. (1980). *Practical research: Planning and design* (2nd ed.). New York: Macmillan.

AUTHOR CITATION INDEX

Abernathy, E., 223, 227
American Psychological Association, 163, 167, 169
Anderson, B. G., 210, 212
Arling, G., 120
Atchley, R. C., 3, 5, 6, 12

Babbie, E. R., 9, 12, 96, 102, 119, 122, 129, 138, 144, 151, 153, 163, 165, 166, 169, 179, 184, 185, 187, 189, 211, 212
Bagnall, J., 15, 20, 30, 31
Baker, K., 240, 241, 246
Baltes, P. B., 64, 76
Banziger, G., 70, 76
Bates, J. D., 219, 223, 227
Bauer, D. G., 241, 246
Benjamin, A. E., 13
Biondi, A. M., 15, 30, 31
Blalock, H. M., 198, 208, 209, 212
Block, M. R., 119, 120
Bloom, M., 182, 183, 189
Borkan, G. A., 81, 102
Bounds, W. G., Jr., 75
Bowling, C., 120
Brenner, M. N., 40, 57, 58
Brody, E. M., 81, 103

Cadell, D. M., 169, 172, 174, 176, 178, 179, 180, 181, 186, 189
Campbell, D. T., 60, 72, 76, 120
Carkhuff, R. R., 30

Carnegie, D., 220, 224, 227, 228
Carner, E. A., 67, 76
Center for the Study of Aging and Human Development, 82, 102, 182, 190
Chappell, N. L., 163, 168, 169, 170
Chu, A. S., 170
Clark, C. H., 18, 19, 31
Clark, M., 210, 212
Cohen, L., 241, 246
Collesano, S., 119, 120
Committee on International Collaboration, 38, 58
Committee on Research and Development, 42, 58
Committee on Research and Development Goals in Social Gerontology, 12, 38, 58
Communication Briefings, 224, 225, 227, 228
Cormier, W. H., 75
Cornelius, S. W., 72, 76
Costner, H. L., 203, 204, 212, 213
Cozby, P. C., 36, 58
Cutler, S. J., 108, 119

Davis, G. H., 15, 31
Davitz, J. R., 243, 247
Davitz, L. L., 243, 247
Demos, V., 110, 119
Dillman, D. A., 114, 119, 158, 169, 187, 190

Duchon, E., 189
Duffy, M., 66, 76
Duncan, G. J., 66, 76

Eden, C., 15, 31
Eisenberg, A., 219, 221, 223, 228
Elwell, F., 106, 119
Estes, C. L., 3, 8, 13

Fillenbaum, G. G., 108, 119
Finney, J. M., 142, 144
Finsterbusch, K., 7, 13
Fowler, F. J., Jr., 141, 144
Freeman, H. E., 8, 13
Frires, G., 189
Fry, C. L., 117, 119

Gaitz, C. M., 111, 120
Gauvain, M., 103
George, L. K., 108, 120
Gerard, L., 13
Gerardi, K. H., 241, 246
Gibson, R. C., 142, 144
Goldfarb, A. I., 102
Gould, J. R., 226, 228
Goulet, L. R., 64, 76
Gray, D. E., 221, 228
Gubrium, J. F., 108, 116, 120

Hagen, E. P., 79, 103
Hand, J., 69, 76
Hanson, H., 189
Harrington, C., 13
Harris, C. S., 119, 120
Hauck, M., 158, 170
Hays, R. W., 220, 228
Heincke, S. G., 64, 76
Henretta, J. C., 108, 120
Herzog, A. R., 112, 120, 142, 144
Hochschild, A. R., 69, 76
Hoinville, G., 156, 160, 170, 177, 187, 190
Hopkins, K. D., 91, 92, 102, 103
Huck, S. W., 75
Hurd, G., 189

Institute for Program Evaluation, 54, 58

Jache, A., 110, 119
Jacobson, S. G., 119, 120

Joint Legislative Audit and Review Commission, 53, 58
Jones, S., 15, 31
Jowell, R., 156, 160, 170, 177, 187, 190

Kahn, R. L., 91, 102
Kane, R. A., 95, 102
Kane, R. L., 95, 102
Kastenbaum, R., 37, 58
Keith, J., 117, 119, 211, 213
Kennicott, P. C., 241, 247
Kish, L., 125, 126, 130, 137, 144
Kivnick, V., 69, 76
Koberg, D., 15, 20, 30, 31
Krug, D. N., 157, 158, 160, 162, 169, 170, 172, 174, 175, 176, 177, 178, 179, 180, 181, 184, 185, 186, 189, 190
Kulka, R. A., 112, 120

Larson, R. F., 200, 213
Lawton, M. P., 81, 84, 102, 103
Lebowitz, B. D., 8, 13
Lee, G. R., 142, 144
Lee, P. R., 3, 13
Leedy, P. D., 45, 50, 51, 53, 58, 243, 247
Lefferts, R. L., 246
Leinbach, R. M., 114, 120
Lemke, S., 103
Leonard, D. J., 225, 228
Liebetrau, A. M., 204, 213
Lindeman, D. A., 13
Lofland, J., 210, 211, 212, 213
Lofland, L. H., 210, 211, 212, 213

McAuley, W. J., 107, 112, 120
McCarthy, P. J., 140, 144
McDonald, R. D., 166, 170
Makarushka, J. L., 166, 170
Mangen, D. J., 95, 102, 103
Max, W., 103
Mehren, B., 103
Mendenhall, W., 200, 213
Moos, R. H., 81, 103
Morgan, J. N., 67, 76
Motz, A. B., 7, 13
Mueller, J. H., 203, 204, 212, 213

National Council on the Aging, 46, 66, 76
Newcomer, R. J., 13

Noller, R. B., 15, 30, 31
Norris, A. H., 81, 102
Nutty, C., 120

Oppendisano-Reich, M., 241, 246
Oppenheim, A. N., 102, 103
Osborn, A. F., 22, 31
Ott, L., 200, 213

Pardini, A., 13
Parnes, S. J., 15, 30, 31
Patton, M. Q., 50, 58
Peck, A., 102
Perkins, W. M., 157, 158, 160, 162, 169,
    170, 175, 177, 184, 185, 186, 190
Peterson, W. A., 95, 102, 103
Pfeiffer, E., 91, 103
Pollack, M., 102
Publication Manual of the American
    Psychological Association, 220,
    228

Reich, W. T., 163, 169, 170
Rodgers, W. L., 112, 120
Rosenberg, M., 202, 213
Ross, K. M., 170
Rothman, J., 37, 58, 222, 228
Roush, S., 70, 76
Rubin, A., 66, 76
Rubin, H. J., 119
Ryff, C. D., 64, 76

Schaie, K. W., 72, 76
Schmidt, M. G., 181, 190
Schuessler, K. F., 203, 240, 212, 213
Schwartz, R. D., 120
Scott, J., 111, 120
Sechrest, L., 120

Shuttlesworth, G. E., 66, 76
Siegel, S., 87, 103
Simon, J. L., 37, 58, 127, 144
Sims, D., 15, 31
Sinnott, J. D., 108, 119, 120
Slonim, M. J., 144
Smith, H. W., 75
Sohr, M. A., 169, 172, 174, 176, 178, 179,
    180, 181, 186, 189
Sommer, B. B., 75, 76
Sommer, R., 75, 76
South, V., 189
Special Committee on Aging, 3, 13
Spradley, J. P., 75
Stanley, J. C., 60, 76, 91, 92, 102, 103
Steinkamp, S., 158, 170
Stephan, F. F., 140, 144
Strain, L. A., 163, 168, 169, 170
Strunk, W., 227
Survey Research Center, 153, 170
Swan, J. H., 13

Taylor, C., 107, 120
Thorndike, R. L., 79, 103
Travis, S., 107, 120
Turner, R. P., 219, 220, 221, 222, 224, 228
Turner-Massey, P., 81, 103

Waxman, H. M., 67, 76
Webb, E. J., 117, 120
Weisman, H. M., 218, 219, 228
Weiss, C. H., 75
White, E. B., 227
Wolk, R. L., 117, 120
Wong, S. J., 170
Wood, J. B., 13

Yordi, C. L., 167, 168, 170

SUBJECT INDEX

Abilities as variables, 81–82
Accessions, 46
Activities of daily living (ADL), 82
Advance letter, 175
Ageline, 46
Alternatives
  evaluating, 26–27
  generating, 22–25
    analogies, 23–24
    brainstorming, 22–23
    checkerboard, 24–25
Analogies, drawing, 23–24
Analysis
  goals of, 196–197
  preparing for, 148–149, 191–196
  qualitative, 210–211
  secondary, 105
  time for, 149
Analysis of variance test, 208
ANOVA. *See* Analysis of variance test
Applied problem solving (APS) model
  describing populations and, 125
  ministeps, 17
  steps, 15–16, 19–30
    sequence of, 17
Applied research, 7
  vs. basic research, 7–9
Association, measures of, 201–206. *See also* Statistics, descriptive
Audience, focusing on, 216–218
Available subjects, 140

Basic features as variables, 80
Basic research, 7
  vs. applied research, 7–9
Biased questions. *See* Questions
Binomial, 128
Brainstorming, 22–23, 44

Callbacks, 174
  forms for, 186
Categorizing, 149, 193–196
Cause-and-effect determination, 62
Central tendency. *See* Mean; Median; Mode
Challenges, problems as, 17–18, 19
Checkerboard method, 24
Checklisting, 23
Chi-square, 207, 208, 209
Clearances, 174–176
Cluster sample, 136–138
  homogeneity of clusters, 137
  precision in, 137
  stratification of, 137
Codebook, 196
Coding, 149, 196
Communication
  effective, 218, 219
  oral, 223–226
    delivery, 224–226
    setting, 224
    visual aids, 224

written, 218-223
  analysis to action, 223
  executive summary, 222
  report structure, 220-222
  style, 223
Competence of respondents, 100
Confidence interval, 128-129, 207
Confidence level, 128
Consent
  form, 164 (fig.)
  informed, 163
  voluntary, 163
Construct validity, 93
Content validity, 91
Contingency questions, 100
Contingency tables, 201-203
Contracts, 240-241
Convenience sample. *See* Available
  subjects
Correlational studies. *See* Descriptive
  studies
Cost. *See also* Evaluation of
  alternatives
  of alternative approaches, 26
  of research problems, 47-48
Coverage
  of instruments, 96
  of sample, 141
Criterion validity, 92-93
  concurrent validity, 92
  predictive validity, 92
Cross-sectional designs, 63
  vs. longitudinal designs, 62-63
Cross tabulations. *See* Contingency tables
Cumulative relative frequency
  distribution, 207-208
Current Literature on Aging, 46

Daily progress reports, 186
Data Archive for Aging and Adult
  Development, 109
Decisions, making, 27, 29
Dependent variables, 202
Description vs. explanation, 61-62
Descriptive statistics. *See* Statistics
Descriptive studies, 62
Dispersion. *See* Range; Standard
  deviation; Variance

Dissemination. *See* Information,
  presenting
Distributions, joint. *See* Contingency
  tables
Double-barreled questions. *See* Questions

Editing, 192
Elderly. *See* Older people
Ethics, 162-168
Ethnographic interviews, 69
Evaluation
  of alternatives, 26-27
  of instruments, 95-96
  of research problems, 46-49
  suspending, 18
  as threats, 18-19
    apologetic phrases, 19
    killer phrases, 19
Evaluation research, 5, 42, 74
  formative, 74
  summative, 74
Executive summary, 222
Exhaustive values, 89, 195
Existing information, 105-111
  exclusive use of, 106
  new information and, 106
  sources of
    expressive materials, 110-111
    mass media reports, 110
    official records, 107-108
    previous studies, 108-110
  validation with, 106-107
Expense sheets, 186
Experimental designs. *See also*
    Quasi-experimental designs
  between-subjects, 70-71
  validity in, 71
  within-subjects, 71
Explanation vs. description, 61-62
Expressive material, 110-111
External validity, 24, 61

Face-to-face interviews, 111-113
Feasibility
  of alternative approaches, 26
  of research problems, 47
Field edits. *See* Editing

Files
  analytical, 210
  chronological, 210
  mundane, 210
Fisher's exact probability test, 208, 209
Fixed-choice questions. *See* Questions
Focusing
  on audience, 216-218
  on problem, 216-218
Formative evaluation, 74
Frequency distributions, 206
F test. *See* Analysis of variance test
Funding, sources of, 241-243

Gamma, 203-204
Goodman and Kruskal's lambda, 203
Goodman and Kruskal's tau, 203
Grants, 240-241

Harm, avoiding, 165-166
Heterogeneity, 5-6
Honesty, maintaining, 166-167

Identification. *See* Clearances
Impact
  of alternative approaches, 26
  of research problems, 48
Independent variables, 202-203
Informants, 182-184
Information
  existing, 105-111
  gathering, 171-188
  new, 111-117
  presenting, 214-227
Informed consent. *See* Consent
Instruments, constructing, 96-101
  vs. existing, 94-95
Instruments, existing
  vs. constructing, 94-95
  content, 96
  evaluating, 95-96
  format, 95-96
Internal estimates of reliability, 89-90
Internal operations, 41
Internal validity, 60-61
Interval variables, 85-88, 198, 199
Interviewers
  agency staff vs. others, 155-156
  clearances, 174-176

number of, 158-159 (fig.)
payment, 156-158
  hourly, 157
  per interview, 156-157
recruitment of, 160
screening, 160-161
selection, 158-161
training, 161
volunteer vs. paid, 156
Interviews
  beginning, 177-178
  closing, 180
  conducting, 177-181
  consistency of, 180
  ethnographic, 69
  face-to-face, 111-113
  monitoring, 184-185
  phone, 111-113
  probes in, 179-180
  problems, 181-184
  recordkeeping, 185-186
Issues, research and policy, 56-57
Items. *See* Questions

Kendall's Tau b, 204
Kendall's Tau c, 204
Kolmogorov-Smirnov test, 207-208
Kuder-Richardson Formula 20, 90-91
Kuder-Richardson Formula 21, 90-91

Lambda. *See* Goodman and Kruskal's
  lambda
Leading questions. *See* Questions
Levels of measurement, 85-89
Lists as sample frames, 126
Literature, review of, 45-56
Loaded questions. *See* Questions
Longitudinal designs, 64-65
  vs. cross-sectional designs, 62-63

Mail surveys, 113-114, 187-188
Mann-Whitney test, 209
Mass media reports, 110
Master log, 185
Mean, 199, 206
Meaningful values, 89, 195
Measurement
  definition of, 77-78
  importance, 78-79

levels of, 85-89
non-traditional, 116-117
as problem, 6
proxies in, 78
of variables, 84
Measures
of association, 201-206
desirable qualities in, 89-94
physical, 116
Median, 199, 206
Methodological problems in
gerontological research
defining older people, 5
heterogeneity of population, 5-6
measurement, 6
research design, 6
sampling, 6
Ministeps, in problem solving, 17
Mode, 198-199, 206
Monitoring, 184-185
Mutually exclusive values, 89, 195

National Archive of Computerized Data
on Aging, 109
National Data Base on Aging, 109
Needs, meeting, 167-168
Needs assessments, 5, 40, 73-74
Negative questions. *See* Questions
News media
advertising in, 160, 175
dissemination in, 226
Nominal variables, 85-88, 198
Nonexperimental designs, 66-70
vs. experimental designs, 65-66
Nonrandom sample, 130, 139-140

Observational method, 67-70, 114-116
disclosure, 115
observer involvement, 115
participant, 68
structured, 68-115
Observations, systematic, 78
Official records, 107-108
Older Americans Act, 3
Older Americans Resources and
Services (OARS), 82-83, 233-234
Older people
defining, 5
interviewing, 181-184

meeting needs of, 167, 168
sampling, 141-143
Older respondents. *See* Respondents,
older; Older people
Open-ended questions. *See* Questions
Operational definition, 84
clarity of, 96
Operationalization of variables, 83-85
Ordinal variables, 85-88, 198, 199
Organizational priorities, 40-41
Organizational support, 43
Outlets for results, 217-218

Parallel forms reliability, 89-90
Parameter, 207
Participant observations, 68-69
Participation, maximizing, 186-188
Pearson product-moment correlation,
204-206, 208
Pearson r. *See* Pearson product-moment
correlation
People
to contact for research problems
agency staff, 57
elected officials, 57
professional organizations, 57
special interest groups, 57
voluntary organizations, 57
as sources of additional information,
44-45
Permission, obtaining, 172-177
Phone interviews, 111-113, 186-187
Physical environment variables, 81
Physical measures, 116
Pilot testing. *See* Pretests
Population
defining, 123-125
heterogeneity, 5
selecting methods and, 118
Prediction in research, 62
Pretests
conducting, 153-154
reasons for, 151-153
Previous studies, 108-110
Privacy
anonymity, 165
confidentiality, 165
Probability sample, 130
Probes. *See* Interviews, probes in

Problem
  focusing on, 215
  perception of, 19-20
  sources. *See* Problems, sources of
  stating, 20
    restatement exercise, 20-21
    why exercise, 20-22
Problem-solving. *See also* Applied
      Problem Solving Model
  research as, 10-11
Problems, sources of
  general, 36-37
    common sense, 36
    observation, 36
    organization setting, 39-43
    past research, 37
    practical issues, 37
    theory, 37
    work-related, 14
  Gerontologist, The, 37-38
  organizations, 38-43
  requests for proposals, 38
Problem statements
  characteristics of, 50-51
  examples of, 53-55
  faulty, 51-52
  purposes of, 49-50
  refining, 52-53
  research and, 35-36
  as steps in solutions, 16, 20
Program efficiency, 42
Program evaluation. *See* Evaluation
      research
Projective techniques, 117
Proposals, research
  development of, 241, 242 (fig.)
  organized, 245 (fig.)
  purposes, 241
  successful, 243-245
Proxies, 78
Pure research. *See* Basic research
Purposive sample, 139

Qualitative analysis, 210-211
Qualitative designs, 67-70
  ethnographic interviews, 69
  participant observation, 68
  structured observation, 68
  validity of, 69-70

Quasi-experimental designs
  pretest-posttest nonequivalent control
      group, 72-73
  regression discontinuity, 72
  time series, 72
  validity of, 73
Questionnaires. *See* Research instruments
Questions
  applicability, 100
  appropriateness, 100
  asking, 178
  biased, 98-99
    leading, 99
    loaded, 99
  contingency, 100
  double-barreled, 98-99
  fixed-choice, 97
  negative, 99-100
  number of, 98
  open-ended, 97
  order of, 101
  respondents', 176-177
Quota sample, 139-140
  bias in, 140

Random sample, 130-131
Range, 200
Rare element telephone screening,
      142
Ratio variables, 85-88, 198
Recordkeeping, 185-186
Records, official
  agency documents, 107
  census, 107-108
  registration information, 107
Refusals
  accepting, 177
  converting, 177
Regression line, 206
Relevant values, 89
Reliability
  determining, 89-91
    internal estimates, 89-90
    parallel forms, 89-90
    test-retest, 89-90
  estimating, 90-91
  of existing instruments, 76
  minimum, 91
  vs. validity, 91

Reports
  mass media, 110
  structure of, 220-222
  style in, 223
  writing, 219-220
Research
  applied, 7-8
  basic, 7-8
  gerontological
    example of, 231-239
    problems, 5-7
    sources of problems, 36-44
  phases of, 146-150
  as problem solving, 10
Research designs
  cross-sectional, 63
  experimental, 65-66, 70-73
  longitudinal, 64-65
  nonexperimental, 66-70
  qualitative, 67-70
  quasi-experimental, 72-73
  selecting, 75 (table)
  sequential, 65
  survey, 66-67
Research instruments
  constructing, 96-101
  existing, 94-96
Research problems
  as challenges, 17
  evaluating, 46-49
  in gerontology, 5-7
  method selection and, 117-118
  sources of, 36-44, 56-57
Resources and method selection,
    119
Respondents
  competence of, 100
  health of, 182
  locating, 172-177
  older, 181-184
    interviewing, 183
Response rate, 171
Responses
  editing, 181
  recording, 180
Restatement exercise, 20-21, 52
Reviewing raw data, 192-193
Rho. See Spearman's rho
Runs test, 209

Sample. See also Sampling
  differences, 206
  drawing, 130-141
  efficiency, 128
  nonrandom
    available subjects, 140
    purposive, 139
    quota, 139-140
    snowball, 139
  probability, 130
  random
    cluster, 136-138
    simple random, 130-131
    stratified, 131-136
    systematic, 138-139
  size, 127-130
Sampling. See also Sample
  frame, 127
  in gerontology research, 6
  multistage, 136-137
  reasons for, 121-123
    accuracy, 122
    efficiency, 123
  steps in, 123-126, 143 (table)
Scaling of items, 96
Scattergram, 205-206
Science, characteristics of, 9-10
Secondary analysis. See Analysis
Selecting people, 121-144. See also
    Sample
Self-completed forms, 113-114
Sequential designs, 65
Service delivery and use, 41-42
Service effectiveness, 42
Significance, tests of, 206-211
Simple random sample, 130-131
Snowball sample, 139
Social environment variables, 81
Spearman-Brown formula, 90-91
Spearman's rho, 204
Staff, selection of, 147
Stage, in sampling, 127
Standard deviation, 200-201
Standardization, 95
Standards, codes of. See Ethics
Statewide Survey of Older Virginians,
    231-239
  background, 231-232
  gathering information, 236-237

impact, 237-238
making sense of data, 237
measurement, 233
preparations, 235-236
presenting the results, 237
problem, 232-233
research design, 233
selecting people to study, 234
Statistics, 207
  descriptive, 197-206
  inferential, 206-210
  measurement and, 88-89
  multivariate, 210
Stratification. *See* Stratified sample
Stratified sample, 131-136
  disproportionate, 135-136
  precision in, 132
  proportionate, 134-135
  purpose of, 132
  strata in, 132
Structured observations, 68
Studies, previous, 108-110
Summative evaluation, 74
Survey research designs
  panel, 67
  static group comparison, 67
  validity issues, 67
Systematic sample, 138-139
  bias in, 138
  sampling interval in, 138

Tau. *See* Goodman and Kruskal's tau
Tau b. *See* Kendall's Tau b
Tau c. *See* Kendall's Tau c
Telephone survey, 111-113, 186-187
Test-retest reliability, 89-90
Tests of significance. *See* Statistics,
  inferential
Time considerations
  available time, 146
  methods, 146
  resources, 146
Time sheets, 186
Timetable, 145-151
  format, 150 (fig.)
Time sheets, 186

True experiments. *See* Experimental
  designs
t test, 208

Utility
  of alternative approaches, 26
  of research problems, 48

Validity
  construct, 93
  content, 91
  criterion, 92-93
    concurrent, 92
    predictive, 92
  of existing instruments, 96
  external, 24, 61
  internal, 60-61
  of measures, 91
  threats, 60-61
  vs. reliability, 91
Values
  exhaustive, 89, 195
  meaningful, 89, 195
  mutually exclusive, 89, 195
Variables
  defined, 79
  dependent, 202
  guidelines for, 85, 89
  independent, 202-203
  joint distributions of, 202-203
  levels of, 85-89
    interval, 85-88, 198
    nominal, 85-88, 198
    ordinal, 85-86, 198, 199
    ratio, 85-88, 198
  operationalization of, 83-85
  selecting, 83
  types of, 80
Variance, 201
Voluntary consent. *See* Consent

Weighting samples, 136
Why exercise, 20-21, 22, 52

z test, 208